Aspects of Arnhem

Also available by Richard Doherty:

Wall of Steel: The History of 9th (Londonderry) HAA Regiment, RA (SR); North-West Books, Limavady, 1988

The Sons of Ulster: Ulstermen at war from the Somme to Korea; Appletree Press, Belfast, 1992

Clear the Way! A History of the 38th (Irish) Brigade, 1941–1947; Irish Academic Press, Dublin, 1993

Irish Generals: Irish Generals in the British Army in the Second World War; Appletree Press, Belfast, 1993

Only the Enemy in Front: The Recce Corps at War, 1940–46; Spellmount, Staplehurst, 1994

Key to Victory: The Maiden City in the Second World War; Greystone Books, Antrim, 1995

The Williamite War in Ireland, 1699–1691; Four Courts Press, Dublin, 1998

A Noble Crusade: The History of Eighth Army, 1941–1945; Spellmount, Staplehurst, 1999

Irish Men and Women in the Second World War; Four Courts Press, Dublin, 1999

Irish Winners of the Victoria Cross (with David Truesdale); Four Courts Press, Dublin, 2000 *Irish Volunteers in the Second World War*; Four Courts Press, Dublin, 2001

The Sound of History: El Alamein 1942; Spellmount, Staplehurst, 2002

The North Irish Horse: A Hundred Years of Service; Spellmount, Staplehurst, 2002

Normandy 1944: The Road to Victory; Spellmount, Staplehurst, 2004

Ireland's Generals in the Second World War; Four Courts Press, Dublin, 2004

The Thin Green Line: A History of the Royal Ulster Constabulary GC, 1922–2001; Pen & Sword, Barnsley, 2004

None Bolder: A History of 51st (Highland) Division, 1939–1945; Spellmount, Staplehurst, 2006

The British Reconnaissance Corps in World War II; Osprey Publishing, Oxford, 2007

Eighth Army in Italy 1943–45: The Long Hard Slog; Pen & Sword, Barnsley, 2007

The Siege of Derry 1689: The Military History; Spellmount, Stroud, 2008

Only the Enemy in Front: The Recce Corps at War, 1940–46 (revised p/bk edn); Spellmount, Stroud, 2008

Ubique: The Royal Artillery in the Second World War; Spellmount, Stroud, 2008

Helmand Mission: With the Royal Irish Battlegroup in Afghanistan 2008; Pen & Sword, Barnsley, 2009

In the Ranks of Death: The Irish in the Second World War; Pen & Sword, Barnsley, 2010

The Humber Light Reconnaissance Car 1941–45; Osprey Publishing, Oxford, 2011

Hobart's 79th Armoured Division at War: Invention, Innovation and Inspiration; Pen & Sword, Barnsley, 2011

British Armoured Divisions and Their Commanders 1939–1945; Pen & Sword, Barnsley, 2013

Victory in Italy: 15th Army Group's Final Campaign 1945; Pen & Sword, 2015

Churchill's Greatest Fear: The Battle of the Atlantic – 3 September 1939 to 7 May 1945; Pen & Sword, 2015

El Alamein 1942: Turning Point in the Desert; Pen & Sword, 2017

Monte Cassino: Opening the Road to Rome; Pen & Sword, 2018

Also available from David Truesdale:

Irish Winners of the Victoria Cross (with Richard Doherty); Four Courts Press, Dublin, 2000

Brotherhood of the Cauldron, Irishmen in the 1st Airborne Division from North Africa to Arnhem; Redcoat Publishing, Newtownards, 2002

Angels and Heroes: A Machine Gunner in the Great War (with Amanda Moreno); Royal Irish Fusiliers Museum, Silver Link Publishing, Horncastle, 2004

The Rifles Are There: 1st and 2nd Battalions, The Royal Ulster Rifles in the Second World War (with David R. Orr); Pen & Sword, Barnsley, 2005

Leading the Way to Arnhem (with Peter Gijbels), R.N. Sigmond Publishing, Renkum, 2008

A New Battlefield: The Royal Ulster Rifles in Korea 1950–51 (with David R. Orr); Helion & Co., Warwick, 2011

Arnhem Their Final Battle: The 11th Parachute Battalion 1943–1944 (with Gerrit Pijpers OBE); R.N. Sigmond Publishing, Renkum, 2012

'Young Citizen Old Soldier': From boyhood in Antrim to hell on the Somme; Helion & Co., Warwick, 2012

Arnhem Bridge Target Mike One: An Illustrated History of the 1st Airlanding Light Regiment RA 1942–1945 North Africa-Italy-Arnhem-Norway (with Bob Gerritsen and Martijn Cornelissen); R.N. Sigmond Publishing, Renkum, 2015

Ulster Will Fight (2 volume history of the 36th Ulster Division with David R. Orr); Helion & Co, Warwick, 2016

Steel Wall at Arnhem: The Destruction of 4 Parachute Brigade, 19 September 1944; Helion & Co., Warwick, 2016

Theirs is the Glory: Arnhem, Hurst and Conflict on Film (with Allan Esler Smith); Helion & Co., Warwick 2016

Victoria's Harvest: The Irish Soldier in the Zulu War of 1879 (with John Young); Helion & Co., Warwick, 2016

For Queen and Company, Vignettes of the Irish Soldier in the Indian Mutiny (with John Young); Helion & Co., Warwick, 2019

Aspects of Arnhem

The Battle Re-examined

Richard Doherty and David Truesdale

Foreword by
Allan Mallinson

Pen & Sword
MILITARY

First published in Great Britain in 2023 by
Pen & Sword Military
An imprint of Pen & Sword Books Limited
Yorkshire – Philadelphia

ISBN 978 1 39904 391 5

Typeset by Mac Style
Printed in the UK by CPI Group (UK) Ltd, Croydon, CR0 4YY.

Pen & Sword Books Limited incorporates the imprints of After
the Battle, Atlas, Archaeology, Aviation, Discovery, Family History,
Fiction, History, Maritime, Military, Military Classics, Politics,
Select, Transport, True Crime, Air World, Frontline Publishing, Leo
Cooper, Remember When, Seaforth Publishing, The Praetorian Press,
Wharncliffe Local History, Wharncliffe Transport, Wharncliffe True
Crime and White Owl.

For a complete list of Pen & Sword titles please contact

PEN & SWORD BOOKS LIMITED
47 Church Street, Barnsley, South Yorkshire, S70 2AS, England
E-mail: enquiries@pen-and-sword.co.uk
Website: www.pen-and-sword.co.uk
or
PEN AND SWORD BOOKS
1950 Lawrence Rd, Havertown, PA 19083, USA
E-mail: Uspen-and-sword@casematepublishers.com
Website: www.penandswordbooks.com

Contents

Maps

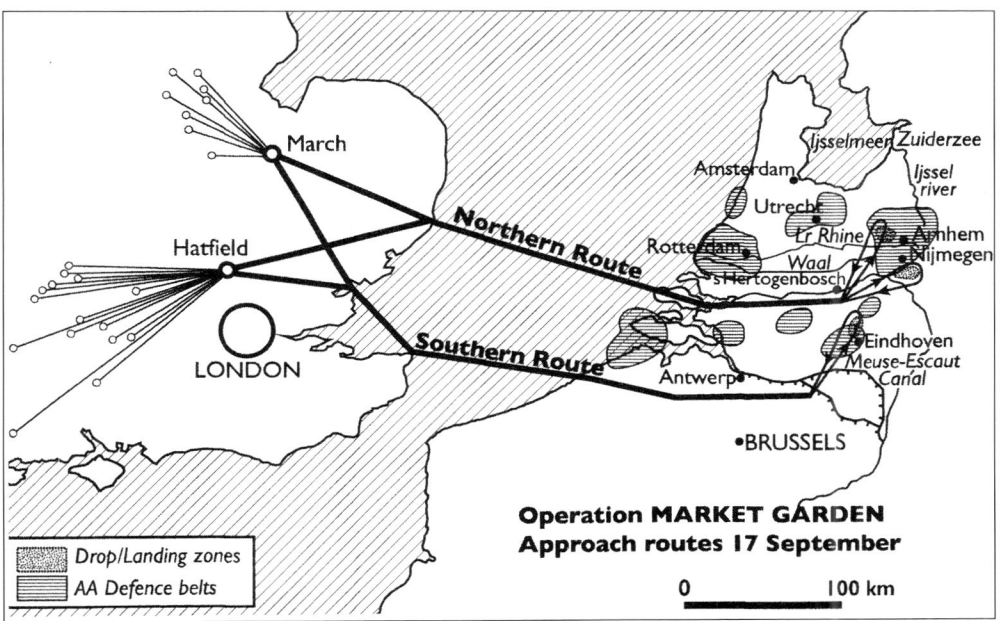

IJsselmeer

AMSTERDAM

Issel river

GDS | Adair | BR

Deventer

Apeldoorn

Thomas | BR

Zutphen

Utrecht

I Urquhart | BR

Oosterbeek
Wageningen

Neder Rijn

Arnhem

Driel

Elst

← Rotterdam 12 miles

Bemmel

Oosterhout

Nijmegen

Waal

Rhein

82 Gavin | US

Cleve

Maas

Oud Keent
Heesch

Grave

Mook

's Hertogenbosch

Willems Canal

Uden
Veghel

GERMANY

Tilburg

101 Taylor | US

Maas

HOLLAND

XXX Horrocks | BR

Helmond

Eindhoven

HOLLAND

Aalst

BELGIUM

Valkenswaard

Turnhout

Meuse-Escaut Canal

Weert

XII O'CONNOR | BR

Gheel
Bourg-Leopold

VIII RITCHIE | BR

Albert Canal

Hechtel

← Antwerp
22 miles

Helchteren

Beeringen

**Operation MARKET GARDEN
The Plan**

0   10   20   30 km

Louvain
9 miles

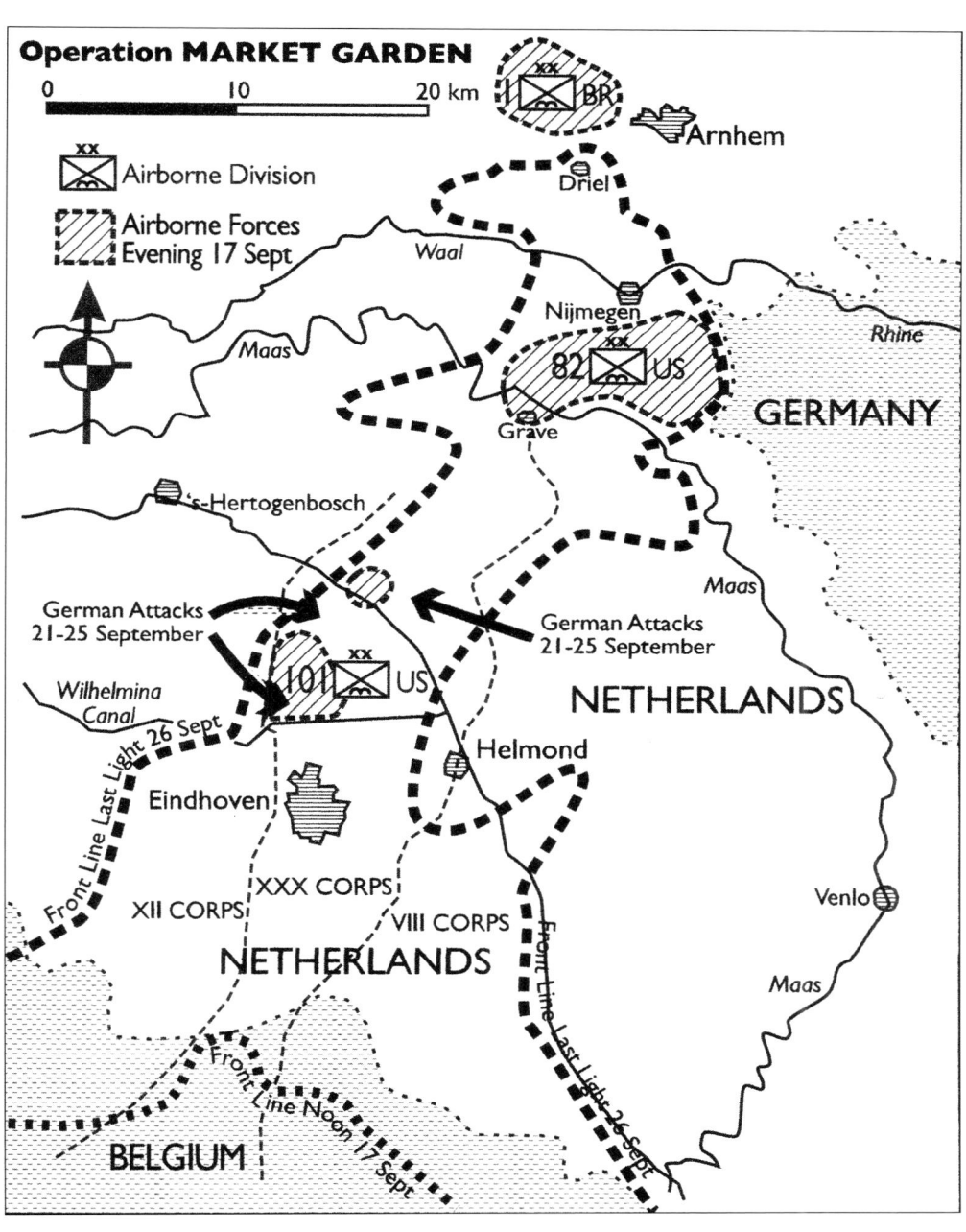

Operation MARKET GARDEN

0   10   20 km

Airborne Division

Airborne Forces
Evening 17 Sept

I BR

Arnhem

Driel

Waal

Nijmegen

Rhine

Maas

82 US

GERMANY

Grave

's-Hertogenbosch

Maas

German Attacks
21-25 September

German Attacks
21-25 September

NETHERLANDS

Wilhelmina
Canal

101 US

Helmond

Eindhoven

Front Line Last Light 26 Sept

XXX CORPS

XII CORPS

VIII CORPS

NETHERLANDS

Venlo

Front Line Last Light 26 Sept

Maas

Front Line Noon 17 Sept

BELGIUM

Arnhem Bridge and the Oosterbeek Perimeter

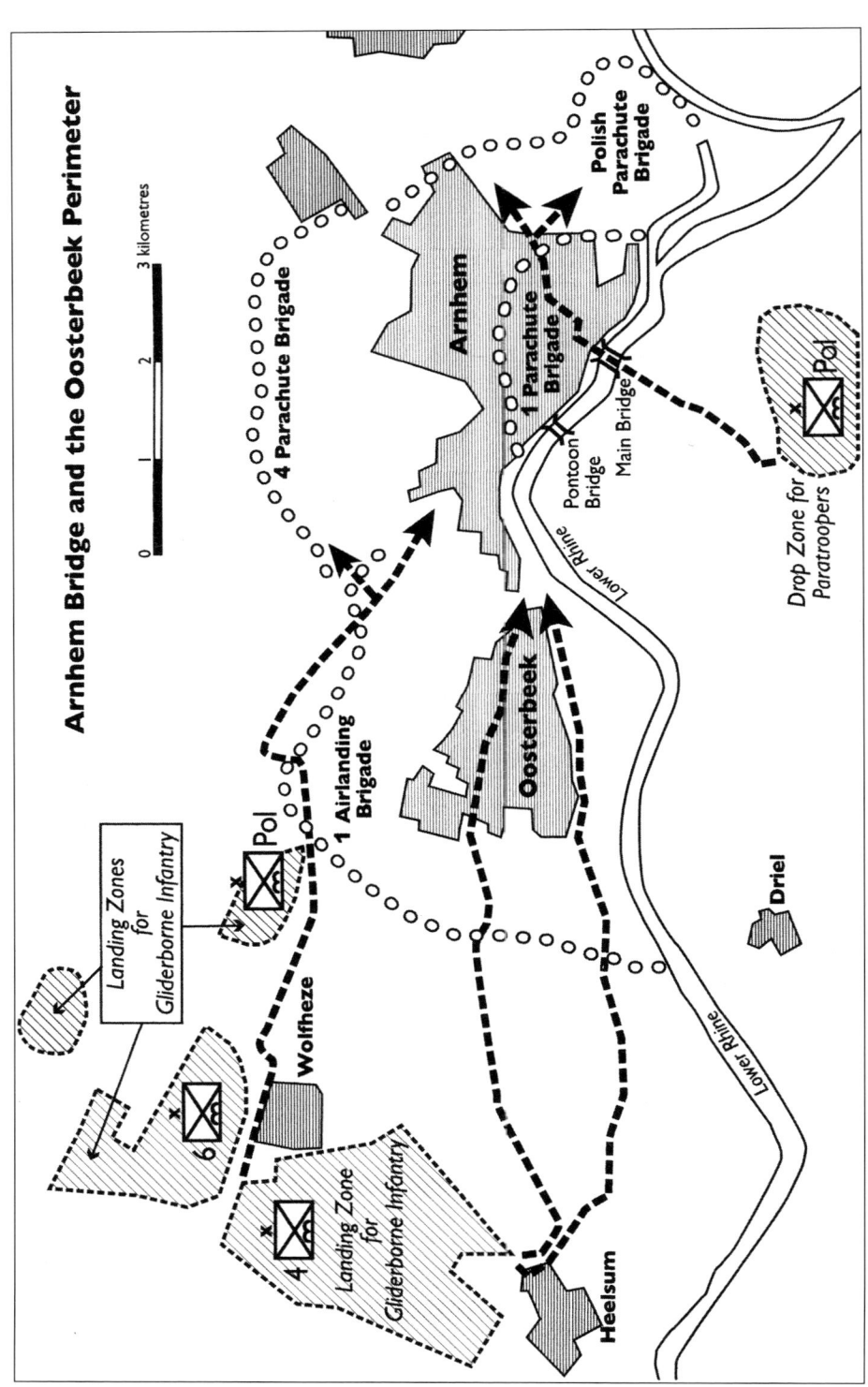

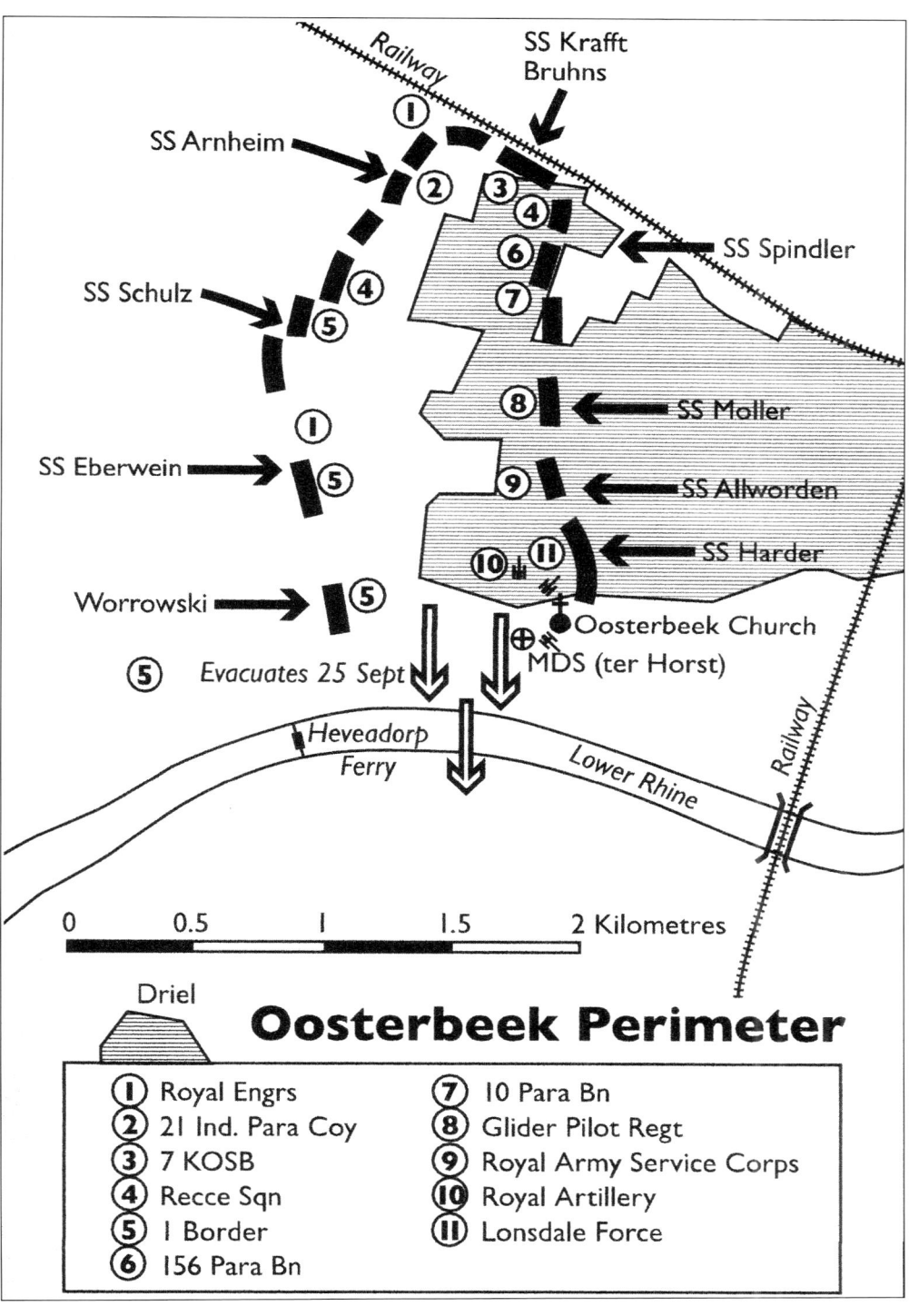

SS Krafft
Bruhns

Railway

SS Arnheim

SS Spindler

SS Schulz

SS Eberwein

SS Moller

SS Allworden

SS Harder

Worrowski

Oosterbeek Church

MDS (ter Horst)

⑤ *Evacuates 25 Sept*

Heveadorp
Ferry

Lower Rhine

Railway

0   0.5   1   1.5   2 Kilometres

Driel

Oosterbeek Perimeter

①	Royal Engrs	⑦	10 Para Bn
②	21 Ind. Para Coy	⑧	Glider Pilot Regt
③	7 KOSB	⑨	Royal Army Service Corps
④	Recce Sqn	⑩	Royal Artillery
⑤	1 Border	⑪	Lonsdale Force
⑥	156 Para Bn		

Glossary

AA	Anti-aircraft
AAC	Army Air Corps
AEAF	Allied Expeditionary Air Force
AFDAG	Airborne Forward Delivery Airfield Group
AFV	Armoured fighting vehicle (including tanks, armoured cars and SP guns)
Bn	Battalion
CAS	Close Air Support
CO	Commanding Officer
COMZ	Communications Zone: US Army term for lines of communication
Coup de main	(French) A sudden, surprise attack
D Day	the day on which an operation begins, e.g., 6 June 1944 was D Day for Operation OVERLORD.
DFC	Distinguished Flying Cross
DSO	Distinguished Service Order
DUKW	A US 6-wheeled amphibious lorry which could carry troops or equipment.
DZ	Drop Zone, for paratroopers
Flak	German anti-aircraft fire. Known as *Archie* during the First World War, several UK veterans used that phrase in interviews.
FOO	Forward Observation Officer (artillery)
GOC	General Officer Commanding (of a division)
HE	High Explosive
HQ	Headquarters
KOSB	King's Own Scottish Borderers
LZ	Landing Zone, for gliders
MC	Military Cross
MiD	Mentioned in Despatches
NCO	Non Commissioned Officer
O group	Orders group at which a commander outlines his plans and intentions for an operation

PIAT	Projector, Infantry, Anti-tank
PIR	Parachute Infantry Regiment (US)
POL	Petrol, oil and lubricants
PoW/PW	Prisoner of War
RAF	Royal Air Force
RAMC	Royal Army Medical Corps
RAOC	Royal Army Ordnance Corps
RASC	Royal Army Service Corps
RE	Corps of Royal Engineers
Recce	Reconnaissance/Reconnaissance Corps
REME	Royal Electrical and Mechanical Engineers
SHAEF	Supreme Headquarters Allied Expeditionary Force
SPG	self-propelled gun
StuG	*Sturmgeschütz*, or assault gun, usually mounted on a tank hull
TA	Territorial Army
TAF	Tactical Air Force
TCW	Troop Carrier Wing
USAAF	United States Army Air Forces

Acknowledgements

I am grateful to many individuals and organisations for assistance and support in researching and writing this book. Without such willing individuals and the staffs of museums, repositories and other establishments, the author of any history book would have a much more difficult task.

My first thanks go to my daughter, Catríona Anna Baillache. It was her decision to emigrate to Australia and subsequently marry there that took me to Western Australia in April 2019 and it was Catríona who took me to a Perth bookshop where I had a road-to-Damascus moment. I spotted Australian historian Phillip Bradley's book *D-Day New Guinea*; the blurb on the back proclaimed that the volume told the story of the first successful Allied large-scale airborne operation of the Second World War *and* one that could be described as a rehearsal for Operation OVERLORD in 1944. Intrigued, I bought the book, read it and realised that it provided answers to questions about the Arnhem operation that I have mulled over for many years.

David Truesdale had proposed a joint-author project on Arnhem and Phillip Bradley's book suggested the nature of such a work – an analysis of why the Arnhem element of Operation MARKET failed to achieve its objective. Many commentators, probably *most* of them, blame Field Marshal Montgomery; but did Monty really deserve all the blame? With David's wealth of knowledge on Arnhem and his range of Dutch contacts, we had a solid foundation on which to build. My thanks to David for the suggestion and for all his work, especially on photo research.

Pat Mooney, former US marine and a historian at the Marine Corps Museum at Quantico, Virginia, was able to provide guidance on some of the leads suggested by Phillip Bradley, which led to several US sources that proved invaluable in the research for this book. Sadly, Pat died unexpectedly in April 2022 and the world is poorer as a result. My thanks are due to Pat and to his dear wife, Robin, for all their help and friendship over many years. Semper Fi!

In spite of his very busy life, Andy Shepherd, another good friend but closer to home, agreed to read drafts of the book as they were prepared and made many useful comments, most of which have been incorporated in the final text. Hopefully, Andy will do some military history writing of his own in the near future.

Colonel Graham Shannon, late Royal Irish Regiment, a friend for many years, was kind enough to point me towards the archives of the US 101st Airborne Division, with which he served, when we were unable to find good-quality images of Private Joe Mann, who earned a posthumous Medal of Honor with the 'Screaming Eagles' during Operation MARKET. Thus I met, electronically, Lieutenant Colonel (Retd) John J. O'Brien PhD, of the Division's archives, who swiftly provided the images of Joe Mann that grace this book. Those images are from the US Army Don F. Pratt Memorial Museum and sincere thanks go to Graham, John and the Museum.

Tim Webster took some sketches and turned them into printable maps and thanks are due to him for his efforts, which help to clarify the complex story of the battle of Arnhem/Oosterbeek.

Other institutions that provided information and images include the Imperial War Museum Photographic Archives, the National Archives at Kew and the National Army Museum in Chelsea. All three are invaluable sources for information and even in the midst of the pandemic did their best to provide a service to researchers.

To the Pen and Sword team, especially Brigadier Henry Wilson, who commissioned the book, Matt Jones, the professional and imperturbable production manager, and Jon Wilkinson, who never fails to produce an eye-catching design for the cover, thanks for all your work and encouragement.

Allan Mallinson, columnist, historian and writer *par excellence*, took time to read the manuscript and to write the Foreword. Thank you, Allan, for doing so, and for your kind comments.

The support of my wife Carol, my children, Joanne, James and Catríona, sons in law, Steven McCurdy and Olivier Baillache, and grandchildren Cíaran, Katrina, Josh, Sophie, Hannah and Élias, has always been important to me; without it I could not have written any of my books.

Richard Doherty
Co. Londonderry
January 2023

When I wrote *Brotherhood of the Cauldron*, published in 2002, detailing the service of Irishmen in the 1st Airborne Division during the Second World War, little did I realise the road ahead. Since then, it has been my pleasure to work with two Dutch authors in producing histories of units involved. With Peter Gijbles in writing *Leading The Way To Arnhem* (2014), the story of 21st Independent Parachute Company, the Divisional Pathfinders. With Gerrit Pijpers OBE, recording the role of 11th Parachute Battalion, in *Arnhem Their Final Battle* (2012). Working with Bob Gerritsen and Martijn Cornelissen, we produced *Arnhem Bridge Target Mike One: An Illustrated History of the 1st Airlanding Light Regiment RA 1942–1945*. (2015 was a busy year.) In *Theirs is the Glory* (2016), co-authored with Allan Esler Smith, we detailed the making of the film of the same title, the first and in my opinion, best cinema representation of the battle. What I thought was my last book on the subject, *Steel Wall At Arnhem*, the story of 4 Parachute Brigade, was published in 2016. At the suggestion of my co-author, Richard Doherty, I have ventured into the much higher echelons of command in this study of the operation, detailing just what went askew in September 1944.

Despite a vast reference library and numerous files collected over the years, such a work is not produced without help and I am grateful to the following for their unstinting assistance. My son Nathan keeps my morale buoyed up with his phone calls and suggestions as to how I can improve my diet and urges me to 'get out more' and to finish 'that' other book. My health remains under the excellent care of Dr Kathy Neoh and her team, who have kept me going for another year. In the Netherlands Bob Gerritsen, Robert Sigmond and Martijn Cornelissen have been a continuing source of information; rarely is a query answered with 'I don't know'! In Belfast, David R. Orr, my co-author on both *Ulster Will Fight*, a history of 36th (Ulster) Division, *The Rifles Are There* and *A New Battlefield,* the Royal Ulster Rifles in the Second World War and later Korea, allows me to borrow books without hesitation. In Cumbria, Stuart Eastwood, former curator of the Border Regiment Museum in Carlisle Castle was ever generous, not only with information and research facilities, but also accommodation, wine and the best of company. In my various reference files, I have numerous notes from the late Adrian Groeneweg, formerly of the Airborne Museum, Oosterbeek. His kindness during my early years of research is beyond measure; he truly was an expert. A special thanks to Niall Cherry for his introduction to Helion, all those years ago, which has opened so many doors.

David Truesdale
Newtownards
Co. Down
January 2023

Foreword

I started reading about Arnhem even before I joined the Army – Roy Urquhart's book in the excellent Pan Battle Series. I have read since, I think – with varying degrees of attention and satisfaction – most books published in English about 1st Airborne Division's role in Market Garden, and a good many about the whole operation. There is first a thrill in reading about failure that comes so close to victory, and then inspiration in the defiant courage and bearing of the participants in defeat. In my first regiment we wore the glider badge on the arm, awarded for Sicily; but the regiment's 1st Battalion (1 Border) had been at Arnhem too, and so the battle was part of our operational heritage. Later came broader professional interest in the operation as such, and with it that feeling of 'If only …' and 'Why didn't …'

'Victory has a thousand fathers, but defeat is an orphan', said JFK famously after the Bay of Pigs fiasco (quoting Tacitus loosely, via Mussolini's son-in-law). Montgomery has been criticized for the concept of bouncing the Rhine rather than instead opening up Antwerp to relieve his 21st Army Group's logistic problems. I have always thought this to be dubious, if undoubtedly safer. (Brooke, the CIGS, certainly thought the concept a mistake, but only, as far as I can see, in retrospect.) And then everyone in the chain of command – down to Freddie Gough commanding the recce squadron – has attracted blame. And that's just in the British airborne element of Market Garden. What about 30 Corps, whose job was to race along the airborne carpet and reinforce the Arnhem bridgehead? General Sir David Fraser, who took part with the Guards Armoured Division, believed that had Patton been in charge, the outcome would have been different. Who knows, but it's one of the legitimate questions in searching for the reason why.

One man who has received much less attention is the US Army Air Forces' Lieutenant General Lewis Hyde Brereton, commanding the Allied Airborne Army. As indeed has the development of the concept of employment of airborne forces which led to the decision – Brereton's decision ultimately – as to how they should be used to achieve Montgomery's object of shortening the war by opening the way for a torrent of troops to flood onto the North German Plain before winter.

Richard Doherty corrects this deficit. Indeed, I would go as far as to say that it is both unfair and unsafe to come to any firm conclusion about Market Garden without reading his analysis. We have long been able to read of how, when and where the failures occurred, and therefore to draw certain conclusions, but to me it has never quite felt that we have got to the bottom of things. Richard Doherty tackles squarely not only the question 'How?', but 'Why?' His analysis, with the added research and advice of David Truesdale and Andy Shepherd, is forensic, formidable and scrupulously fair.

All this of course takes nothing away from the fighting achievement of those who took part, nor indeed – in my view – from the operational concept of bouncing the Rhine. It was a bold stratagem, a strategic *coup de main* whose prize was of capital value. Market Garden was indeed the only strategic use of airborne troops by the Allies. Could taking Antwerp instead have promised as much? I doubt it (but that's beside the point). In this respect, i.e. the strategic prize – and indeed in several tactical respects too – Market Garden had much in common with the attempt to force the Dardanelles in 1915. And of that failed naval and military stratagem, John Masefield wrote at the time, in his fine apologia *Gallipoli*, 'That the effort failed is not against it. Many great things and noble men have failed.'

The same is true of Arnhem, which ended in much the same way as Gallipoli – with successful withdrawal by night across water to the surprise of the enemy. And just as, failure though it was, Gallipoli powerfully forged Australia's and New Zealand's fighting reputation – the legend of Anzac – so Arnhem has inspired fighting spirit in the British army ever since, not least when disaster stares it in the face (and, lately, when disaster has overcome it).

That the effort failed is not against it.

But let us try fully to understand why indeed the effort failed.

Allan Mallinson, Salisbury Plain, January 2023.

Introduction

The battle of Arnhem, between 17 and 26 September 1944, was fought over ground that encompassed the city of Arnhem, the nearby town of Oosterbeek and the villages of Driel and Wolfheze. Protagonists were the British 1st Airborne Division, which included a Polish Parachute Brigade, and German *Heer* and SS units.

As part of Operation MARKET GARDEN, the British airborne soldiers, both paratroopers and glider-borne infantry, had attempted to seize the road bridge over the Lower Rhine in the city to facilitate an Allied punch into Germany spearheaded by Field Marshal Montgomery's 21 Army Group. The attempt failed, although a small mixed force of paratroopers, reconnoitrers, sappers, military police and others took one end of the bridge and held it for several days against determined German efforts to remove them.

The battle has become the stuff of legend since the war and, like all legends, is surrounded by mythology. Some of that myth-making was encapsulated in the 1970s film *A Bridge Too Far* and in books, articles and documentaries about the battle.

Part of the myth is that Montgomery was responsible for the plan that launched First Allied Airborne Army into Operation MARKET, the seizure by Allied airborne forces of bridges from the Meuse-Escaut canal to Nunspeet on the IJsselmeer (Zuider Zee) so that Second Army could advance over the river obstacles and then swing east into Germany. However, while Montgomery was overall commander, the airborne plans were made by the airborne army commander Lewis Hyde Brereton who proved inflexible when asked by Montgomery to change his plans.

The aim of this book is to examine various aspects of the battle for Arnhem, within the framework of the overall operation, and assess the responsibility of a range of individuals, from General George C. Marshall, overall commander of the US Army, down through Eisenhower, the theatre commander, Montgomery, Dempsey, Brereton and others involved in the planning and execution.

We believe that the analysis in this book is accurate and that it will persuade readers to re-consider their thinking on the battle and especially on who was responsible for 1st Airborne Division failing to achieve its objective at Arnhem.

Prologue

Nadzab in New Guinea is far distant from Arnhem in the Netherlands. Yet there is a real connection between the two. Arnhem, a name hard-wired into the British national psyche, is an icon of the courage, resolve and tenacity of the British soldier in the face of overwhelming odds. However, the Battle of Arnhem/Oosterbeek in September 1944 would never have happened had it not been for an antipodean airborne landing by the US Army's 503rd Parachute Infantry Regiment (503 PIR) almost exactly a year before. Flown into action by 54th Troop Carrier Wing (54 TCW) of the US Army Air Forces, 503 PIR seized Nadzab airfield in support of the Australian Operation POSTERN, the amphibious landings at Lae on the New Guinea coast.[1] How did that operation have an effect on what would happen in the Netherlands a year later?

To find the answer to that question, we need to go back a little further in time – to July 1943 and Operation HUSKY, the Allied invasion of Sicily which included the largest amphibious landing force of the war – bigger even than that at Normandy – and an airborne operation, LADBROKE. The airborne element was disastrous. US paratroopers of 505th Parachute Regimental Combat Team were making their first combat jump on the night of 9/10 July, but winds of up to 45mph blew the troop-carrying C-47 Skytrains off course. The paratroopers were scattered widely, disrupting their plans entirely. The British 1st Airborne Division's 1 Airlanding Brigade was to seize landing zones, but its towing aircraft and gliders were also blown awry, only twelve of 147 landing on target. Worse, sixty-nine crashed into the sea and over 200 men drowned. Both the brigade commander, Brigadier Philip Hugh Whitby Hicks, and divisional commander, Major General George Frederick Hopkinson OBE MC, found themselves in the water. Nonetheless, those who landed went on to carry out their missions despite the circumstances.

Airborne operations over the next few days were also plagued by problems. The British Operation FUSTIAN, in which 1 Parachute Brigade, supported by 1 Airlanding Brigade, was to capture the Primosole bridge, met with a series of difficulties, not least the inexperience of the American C-47 pilots carrying the paratroopers. Anti-aircraft fire from Allied ships, which were anticipating a

German air raid, caused casualties amongst aircraft that had strayed off course. The gliders carrying anti-tank guns to support the paratroopers lost two of their number in a collision while taking off; another, cast off early, crashed into the sea; yet more were shot down by enemy anti-aircraft fire.

In the post-operation examination, the performance of the airborne element was prominent. General Dwight D. Eisenhower, Supreme Allied Commander in the Mediterranean, concerned about the casualty levels, questioned whether using airborne troops in such large numbers was viable, concerns shared by Lieutenant General Lesley McNair, the US Army ground forces commander. Even before Sicily, the US Army had had a disastrous airborne operation as part of Operation TORCH, the Allied invasion of French North-West Africa. The airborne force, 509th Parachute Infantry Battalion in thirty-nine aircraft, failed to maintain contact during the long flight from Britain due to weather conditions and poor navigation, and sustained considerable losses of soldiers and aircraft for nothing. Eisenhower, aware of the heavy German losses in the airborne assault on Crete, had major doubts about deploying divisional-sized airborne formations. McNair considered airborne operations feasible only on a smaller scale. As a result, Eisenhower recommended to General George C. Marshall, head of the US Army, that the future of large-scale airborne operations should be examined. At that time, two US airborne divisions (82nd and 101st) were already operational, and both 11th and 17th Airborne Divisions were training in the United States; a fifth formation, 13th Airborne, was also training but, although deployed to Europe in 1945, would see no action. Eisenhower and McNair believed those divisions should be re-roled as infantry. In addition, their existence required a large airlifting capacity involving considerable numbers of troop-carrying and glider-towing aircraft.

Marshall was aware of the US Army's huge investment in creating the airborne formations and their troop-carrying air

General George Catlett Marshall became acting Chief of Staff of the US Army in July 1939 being confirmed in the post on 1 September, the day Germany invaded Poland. His re-organisation of the Army was critical to its effective wartime functioning. He was a supporter of airborne forces. Promoted to the new rank of General of the Army (five-star), he became President Truman's Secretary of State after the war. Responsible for the Marshall Plan for the rebuilding of Europe, he received the Nobel Peace Prize in 1953. (*NARA*)

wings, the air forces then being part of the Army. His reaction to Eisenhower's comments was to call for a close examination of the training and role of airborne forces and their transport counterparts. The task of carrying out that examination was given to Major General Joseph May Swing, whose 11th Airborne Division would serve in the Pacific.[2] Although Swing had been sent to the Mediterranean to advise Eisenhower on airborne operations, he had been unable to influence effectively the deployment for Operation HUSKY.

Since Swing had begun his work when 503 PIR dropped on Nadzab, his board was able to examine after-action reports from both the regiment and 54 TCW. What was most clear when comparing the Nadzab drop against those in North Africa and Sicily was the level of co-operation between the troop-carrying wing and airborne troops. Preparation and training had been exacting

Major General Joseph May Swing was charged with investigating the viability of the airborne divisions following the invasion of Sicily. The Swing Board recommended their retention. Swing subsequently commanded 11th Airborne Division in the Pacific. His final rank was lieutenant general. (*NARA*)

with airmen and paratroopers training thoroughly for the first combat airborne operation in the Pacific. In contrast, training for operations in North Africa and Sicily had been haphazard and perfunctory. Swing recognised this; his training of 11th Airborne Division emphasised the need for co-operation and understanding between airmen and paratroopers.

Swing remained committed to the airborne concept and the successful drop at Nadzab was proof of its value. When the Swing Board completed its study at the end of September 1943 its unsurprising principal recommendation was the need for closer co-ordination between airborne units and troop carrier commands, especially in training and preparation. However, reservations still remained at the highest level: Marshall and McNair continued to entertain doubts about the effectiveness of divisional-scale deployments. McNair then ordered Swing to plan and organise manoeuvres by 11th Airborne Division to prove that such formations could be effective operationally. With those manoeuvres due to take place in December, it was clear that the future of US airborne divisions depended on the outcome.

Doubts about the effectiveness of large airborne formations went even higher in the US hierarchy. Harry L. Stimson, Roosevelt's Secretary of War,

Roosevelt's Secretary of War, Henry L. 'Harry' Stimson en route to watch the 'Pea Patch Show' in November 1943. Although a leading Republican politician, he was an important member of a Democrat administration. (*NARA*)

also had reservations. In late November Stimson visited Camp Mackall, North Carolina,[3] to watch an airborne demonstration in what was called the 'Pea Patch Show', so called because the area had been used to grow peas. Stimson was suitably impressed and wrote to Swing on the 27th, commenting that 'The Airborne Division will play a great part in our future successes, and I know that the 11th Airborne Division will render outstanding service to our country on some not too far distant D Day.'

However, McNair still wanted further proof of the viability of airborne operations to ensure the reprieve of the divisions; the demonstration attended by Stimson had not been on a sufficient scale. Therefore, Swing's planned exercise, the Knollwood Manoeuvre, in North Carolina in December, would be the critical test: it pitted Swing's 11th Airborne Division, as 'Blue Force', against elements of 17th Airborne Division as 'Red Force'. Each was reinforced; 501 PIR was attached to the 11th and a battalion of 541 to the 17th.[4]

Without 503 PIR's successful drop at Nadzab, all seven US and British airborne divisions might have been re-roled as line infantry and Operation MARKET GARDEN would not have happened. The role of airborne troops could simply have been consigned to the scrapyard of impracticable and

Lieutenant General Lesley J. McNair, commander Army Ground Forces. After the Allied invasion of Sicily, he shared Eisenhower's doubts about large-scale airborne operations. He was killed by US bombs in Normandy in July 1944, one of the highest-ranking US casualties of the war. He was posthumously promoted to General. (*NARA*)

expensive military ideas, and the titles of the British 1st and 6th Airborne Divisions, the US 11th, 13th, 17th, 82nd and 101st Airborne Divisions, as well as 44th Indian, might be but brief footnotes in the history of the Second World War.

The Knollwood Manoeuvre proved the efficacy of airborne operations on a large scale. Thus, three Allied airborne divisions deployed as part of the landings in Normandy. Their role, however, was to secure the flanks of the seaborne assault formations. In spite of heavy casualties, in part due to dropping at night, 6th British and 82nd and 101st US Airborne Divisions succeeded in their task. However, airborne divisions had yet to be used in the strategic role – and that was the role assigned to them, as part of First Allied Airborne Army, in Operation MARKET GARDEN.

In that operation the airborne formations were to seize major water crossings to clear the way for an advance by ground forces into Germany. Co-operating with them were the British VIII, XII and XXX Corps of Second Army, with XXX Corps in the van. The successful execution of the strategic plan demanded good intelligence on the German forces, detailed planning, the availability of quick re-supply of all elements of the operation, an element of surprise, and highly competent commanders, able to think and react quickly, at all levels.

That those criteria were not all met is well known, which has fuelled much debate for decades. However, there has been a notable lacuna in that debate. Blame has been assigned in many directions, not least in that of Field Marshal Montgomery, with little directed at the commander of First Allied Airborne Army, Lieutenant General Lewis Hyde Brereton. Battles and the campaigns of which they form part are shaped by commanders and it is fair to say that Brereton misshaped the battle of Arnhem/Oosterbeek. He did so because he lacked the tactical and operational *nous* to recognise how the battle would develop. It may be said that he also failed in this respect in the other battles along the 'path' that the airborne were trying to create.

As one example of Brereton's failings, let us look briefly at the deployment of a British sub-unit at Arnhem and how it was affected by Brereton's decision to seize and hold drop/landing zones well removed from the actual objectives: those DZs and LZs were between four and nine miles from the objectives. The sub-unit in question is 1 Airborne Reconnaissance Squadron, the 'eyes' of 1st Airborne Division, whose OC was 'Freddie' Gough – Major Charles Frederick Howard Gough MC.

A descendant of a famous County Tipperary family with three Victoria Cross recipients, at Arnhem Bridge Freddie would have the chance of earning not only further glory for his family, but also their fourth Victoria Cross.[5] Had such an award been made, it would inevitably have been posthumous and a further memento of failures in the planning and execution of the operation at Arnhem.

Gough, a Royal Navy midshipman in the First World War, had commanded a provost section with the British Expeditionary Force in France in 1940 and was evacuated from the beaches of Dunkirk. His command at Arnhem had been formed from 31 Independent Brigade Anti-Tank Company. Renamed 31 Independent Reconnaissance Company in January 1941, when the Reconnaissance Corps was formed, in November that year it was assigned a glider-borne role as 1 Airlanding Reconnaissance Squadron.[6]

Field Marshal Sir Bernard Montgomery, commander of 21 Army Group, had proposed Operation MARKET GARDEN to Eisenhower who supported the plan since it involved using his sole reserve, First Allied Airborne Army. However, planning for the airborne element was not carried out by Montgomery's staff but by the Airborne Army staff, although Montgomery accepted responsibility in his *Memoirs*. (*Public domain*)

Squadron soldiers wore the distinctive Reconnaissance Corps badge and were equally distinctive in their role – enterprising, brave, enduring and highly skilled – although in some circles they were accused of 'bashing on too much'. (The Corps' unofficial motto was 'Bash on, Recce!') The squadron, equipped with jeeps and motorcycles, landed in Italy by ship at Taranto in September 1943. Advancing immediately after disembarkation, it was considered prudent to carry an Italian officer on the leading jeep's bonnet to deter interference from any Italian troops who did not realise that they were now on the side of the Allies.[7]

For Operation MARKET the jeeps and their drivers would travel by glider; the remainder would parachute in. Each unarmoured jeep was fitted with a

A 3-inch mortar in action with paratroopers in Greece. Adopted by the Army in the early 1930s to replace the Stokes mortar, it had become a more effective weapon with greater range – about 2,800 yards – by 1944. It remained in service until the 1960s. (*Taylor Library*)

single machine gun, the Vickers K. Apart from two 3-inch mortars, the only heavy weapons available to the squadron were two 20mm Polsten cannon, a version of the Swiss-manufactured Oerlikon anti-aircraft gun. With a rate of fire of 450 rounds per minute, these had been adapted for ground use on a very complicated light two-wheeled carriage towed by Support Troop jeeps. Gough had tried to obtain twin machine-gun mountings for his jeeps without success. He had also tried vainly to 'borrow' some Tetrarch light tanks from 6th Airborne Division. He later blamed a dearth of interest in the higher command of 1st Airborne Division.[8]

Gough had planned to send his three troops, each of eight vehicles, to scout ahead of the three parachute battalions of 1 Parachute Brigade, stressing that 'information not assault' was the squadron's role. Both Urquhart, the divisional commander, and Lathbury, the brigade commander, thought otherwise. Because of Brereton's insistence on landing a significant distance from the objectives, they wanted Gough to launch a *coup de main* against Arnhem bridge, holding it until the parachute battalions arrived. It was a role to which the Reconnaissance Squadron was unsuited, but orders were orders.[9]

Thanks to Brereton's decision to drop the assaulting troops some distance from their objectives, the element of surprise was lost completely. Urquhart accepted Brereton's plan, thus denying his division the opportunity of seizing Arnhem bridge. Instead of 'crashing' on the objective, Gough's squadron, having landed some miles away from the bridge, was 'to travel in … jeeps at top speed to the road bridge … at Arnhem, avoiding if possible any contact with the enemy and hold the bridge until the arrival of the parachute force'.[10]

At Wolfheze railway crossing the leading section was ambushed and several men were killed, wounded or captured. There were further encounters with the enemy as the squadron continued towards the bridge. As a result, there was no *coup de main* although some of the squadron reached the northern end of the bridge where they joined elements of 2nd Parachute Battalion, a number of sappers and others to hold the position against German efforts to overcome them.

That 1st Airborne Division failed to seize and hold the entire bridge cannot be blamed on the soldiers who fought there and who endured a brutal siege on the north end, suffering through determined enemy attempts to evict them. It can, however, be blamed on senior commanders, including Urquhart but, more especially, Brereton, whose abundance of caution stole the opportunity for success from the men who fought at Arnhem. More than any other man, Lewis Hyde Brereton 'shaped' Arnhem into the 'heroic defeat' immortalised in story and film.

Chapter One

When war broke out in September 1939, the Germans already had airborne troops, under command of the Luftwaffe. German military observers had been present at a Red Army parachute demonstration at corps scale in Ukraine in 1935; the following year the first German parachute course was held. Although the British military attaché attended the Ukraine demonstration, this was not followed by the formation of parachute units in the UK. However, the first nation to create airborne units was Italy, where the first true paratrooper drop was made in 1927, leading to the creation of two airborne divisions, 184th *Nembo* and 185th *Folgore* Divisions. Interestingly, during the First World War the Italian Eighth Army used RAF aircraft of No. 139 Squadron to drop individual soldiers on reconnaissance or sabotage missions behind Austrian lines. Their first mission was carried out on 9 August 1918; the aircraft, a Savoia-Pomilio SP.4 was flown by Major Barker with Captain Wedgwood Benn as navigator/observer.

Before the Italians had carried out that first true paratrooper drop, the US Army Air Service had conducted trials using soldiers, carried on the wings of aircraft, being pulled off by the opening of their parachutes into the slipstream. It is also worth noting that the US Army had considered deploying an infantry division by air had the Great War continued into 1919. The proposal had come from Brigadier General Billy Mitchell, better known for his advocacy of strategic bombing, as head of US Army Air Service in 1918. He had discussed the concept

Lieutenant General Lewis Hyde Brereton, commander of First Allied Airborne Army. His appointment as army commander was a major error and his insistence that there be no deviation from his original plans for MARKET led to the failure to seize objectives on D Day, in particular Arnhem bridge. (*NARA*)

with General John Pershing, commanding the American Expeditionary Force, who shelved it. Mitchell's chief of staff, Lieutenant Colonel Lewis Hyde Brereton, later claimed to have initiated the idea. Brereton subsequently commanded First Allied Airborne Army and is a major, if little-recognised, character in the Arnhem story.[1]

In April 1940, during the invasions of Denmark and Norway, General Kurt Student's *Fallschirmjäger* seized a bridge and an airfield in Denmark and the airfield at Oslo in Norway. A month later glider-borne troops landed on the Belgian fortress of Eben-Emael and disabled its artillery while in France Fieseler Storch light aircraft flew Brandenburgers in to seize bridges close to the invasion route through the Ardennes. This was part of the first major airborne assault when all the assets of the airborne corps were deployed. The operation was successful to a point, but one of the Dutch airfields seized by the attackers was re-captured after the Junkers 52s bringing in the first reinforcements were destroyed by anti-aircraft fire.[2] Over 1,000 men of the *Luftlandekorps* were captured and shipped to Britain before the Dutch surrender.

Winston Churchill, who had become prime minister on 10 May 1940, was impressed by the effect of this new type of unit and, on 6 June, called for the raising of a similar British force of 5,000 men.[3] The first British paratroopers began training at RAF Ringway, near Manchester, just over two weeks later. The US Army had also noted the effectiveness of the Fallschirmjäger, and a test platoon was formed at much the same time as their British counterparts, followed by a decision to form a battalion.

In 1941 Germany used paratroopers in the capture of the Corinth canal in Greece and in the assault on the island of Crete. Although there was intelligence about the deployment of Fallschirmjäger, and seaborne reinforcements were routed by the Royal Navy, the airborne assault prevailed, and British forces were compelled to evacuate Crete. However, it had been a pyrrhic victory for Germany. Of the 22,000 airborne or airlanding troops deployed, 4,000 died, the majority of them paratroopers. The casualty rate prompted Hitler to proclaim that the day of paratroopers had passed, and there were no further large-scale German airborne operations. However, both the British and US armies continued with the concept of airborne forces, increasing the numbers under training and creating glider-borne units as well; in the British case, line infantry battalions were converted to glider units and the Glider Pilot Regiment was formed as part of the Army Air Corps (AAC).[4]

The first British operation employing paratroopers was in Italy in February 1941 when a small force of thirty-eight men was dropped in the area of the Tragino aqueduct to sabotage the structure. Powell suggests that the 'aim was a trifle specious, the operation being, in effect, a field trial of equipment and techniques for the new arm'.[5] He opines that the operation was also intended to boost morale in 11th Special Air Service Battalion (formerly 2 Commando, the '11' being a none-too-subtle reference to the roman II) which later became 1st Parachute Battalion. This was a problem that would be recurrent in airborne forces: 'after six months of training, with no prospect of action and with their friends fighting in the Western Desert, men were applying to return to their parent units, or taking the law into their own hands and deserting.' Although the Tragino operation had little effect in Italy – the damage caused was repaired speedily – it had a morale effect at home where it was used to promote the image of the airborne forces, and it also influenced the next such operation. All the paratroopers were captured. One man, an Italian who had been posing as Free French, was executed.[6]

That next operation was a company-sized raid by 2nd Parachute Battalion on the Bruneval radar station in France. It was successful, thereby convincing the military authorities that there was a future for airborne forces. As the numbers of airborne soldiers increased, it was possible to deploy units and formations on airborne operations. Both the British and US Armies were building up their airborne strength. The operations in French North-West Africa provided an opportunity to deploy on a larger scale. This, however, was also the occasion when the deployment of 509th Parachute Infantry Battalion by air from Britain to Africa went awry with the carrier aircraft failing to maintain formation due to strong winds, cloud that caused navigational problems and a breakdown in communications. It was described by one US historian as 'A rather disappointing and greatly confused entry into parachute history … by the Americans.'[7]

British airborne operations in Tunisia were carried out by the units of 1 Parachute Brigade, including a drop by 3rd Parachute Battalion on the airfield at Bone, between Algiers and Tunis, another by 1st Battalion on a road junction at Beja and a third by 2nd Battalion, under John Frost, at Oudna. Intended to destroy enemy aircraft, the 2nd Battalion found the airfield abandoned. The battalion had to withdraw, a difficult manoeuvre as First Army's leading troops were being held up by adverse weather and fierce enemy opposition, although elements of the battalion were rescued by patrols of 56th Reconnaissance Regiment (a unit that would later rescue a complete Commando from behind enemy lines).[8] Inexplicably, 'Oudna' was awarded as a battle honour to the Parachute Regiment. British airborne forces created their reputation in Tunisia, but fought mostly as line infantry with the brigade for a time subsumed into the ad hoc Y Division, commanded by Brigadier Nelson Russell of the Irish Brigade.[9] During the Tunisian fighting the Germans described the brigade as *rote Teufel* – 'red devils' – not, as is popularly believed, from the colour of their berets, but from the colour of their uniforms when stained by the ubiquitous red Tunisian mud and by the fact that the crotch straps of their Denison smocks hung down like tails.

Powell reflected on the experience of the brigade in Tunisia:

It was as ordinary infantry, but infantry short of heavy weapons and transport, that [it] fought through the mud and rain of those bitter winter months against some of Germany's finest troops. It was, therefore, something of a paradox that, by the end of the campaign, the value of airborne troops *seemed* [authors' emphasis] to have been established.[10]

However, it was not long before that 'value' was being questioned at the highest levels. In July 1943 the Allies launched Operation HUSKY, the invasion of Sicily. That operation included a large amphibious landing force and an airborne assault, codenamed LADBROKE. The airborne element proved to be an example of how not to carry out such an operation. US paratroopers of 505th Parachute Regimental Combat Team were making their first combat jump on the night of 9/10 July, but winds of up to 45mph blew the troop-carrying C-47 Skytrains[11] off course, resulting in the paratroopers being scattered over a wide area, disrupting their plans entirely. The British 1st Airborne Division's 1 Airlanding Brigade was to seize landing zones, but its towing aircraft and gliders were also blown off course. Only twelve of their 147 gliders landed on target. Worse, sixty-nine crashed into the sea and over 200 men drowned. Both Brigadier Philip Hugh Whitby Hicks, commanding the brigade, and Major General George Frederick Hopkinson OBE MC, the divisional commander, found themselves in the water. However, those who did land went on to try to carry out their missions despite the circumstances.

Subsequent airborne operations over following days were also plagued by problems. The British Operation FUSTIAN, in which 1 Parachute Brigade was to capture the Primosole bridge with support from 1 Airlanding Brigade, met with a series of difficulties, not least the inexperience of the American C-47 pilots conveying the paratroopers and towing the gliders. Anti-aircraft fire from Allied ships, which were expecting German air attacks, caused casualties amongst aircraft which had strayed off course. The gliders carrying anti-tank guns to support the paratroopers lost two of their number while taking off due to a collision while another, cast off early, crashed into the sea and yet more were shot down by enemy anti-aircraft fire.

In the post-mortem, the performance of the airborne element was prominent. General Dwight D. Eisenhower, Supreme Allied Commander in the Mediterranean, concerned about the casualty levels, questioned whether it was viable to use airborne troops in such large numbers. He considered an airborne division too difficult to control in combat and, in his after-action report, wrote to Marshall:

> I do not believe in the airborne division. I believe that airborne troops should be reorganised in self-contained units, comprising infantry, artillery, and special services, all of about the strength of a regimental combat team. Even if one had all the air transport he could possibly use, the fact is at any given time and in any given spot only a reasonable number of air transports can be operated because of technical difficulties. To employ at any time and place a whole division would require a dropping over such an extended area that I seriously doubt that a division commander could regain control and operate the scattered forces as one unit.[12]

Instead, he felt that his favoured re-organisation could be co-ordinated by dropping a senior commander 'with a small staff and radio communications' in the operational area.[13]

Eisenhower was not alone in his doubts. Lieutenant General Lesley McNair, the US Army Ground Forces commander, felt likewise – and he had earlier been an enthusiastic proponent of the airborne concept. As we have seen above, the deployment in Operation TORCH of 509th Parachute Infantry Battalion, in thirty-nine C-47 aircraft, had led to serious losses of men and machines for no gain. Eisenhower was also aware of the great losses suffered by the Germans in the airborne assault on Crete. Like him, McNair thought that airborne operations were feasible only on a smaller scale. As a result, Eisenhower recommended to the US Army Chief of Staff, General George C. Marshall, that the future of large-scale airborne operations should be examined. At that time, two US airborne divisions (82nd and 101st) were already operational, and both 11th and 17th Airborne Divisions were training in the United States; a fifth formation, 13th Airborne, was also training but, although deployed to Europe in 1945, would see no action. Eisenhower and McNair considered that the divisions should be re-roled as infantry. Moreover, the existence of such airborne formations required a large airlifting capacity involving considerable numbers of troop-carrying and glider-towing aircraft.[14]

Marshall was aware of the huge investment made by the US Army in creating the airborne formations under Airborne Command and their troop-carrying air wings, the air forces then being part of the Army. The air wings, originally designated Air Transport Command, later became Troop Carrier Command. Marshall's reaction to Eisenhower's comments was to call for a close examination of the training and role of both airborne forces and their transport counterparts. The task of carrying out that examination was given to Major General Joseph May Swing, whose 11th Airborne Division would serve in the Pacific. At Eisenhower's request, Swing had been sent to the Mediterranean to advise him on airborne operations; the two had been classmates at West Point. However, Swing had been unable to influence effectively the airborne deployment for Operation HUSKY.

Born in February 1894, Joseph May Swing graduated from West Point in 1915. He then served in France with 1st Infantry Division (which might have become the world's first airborne division) and, after the war, became an aide to General Peyton March, whose daughter he married. Specialising in artillery, Swing attended the Field Artillery School, graduated from the Command and General Staff School at Fort Leavenworth, and from the Army War College in Washington DC, before serving as 2nd Infantry Division's chief of staff and, later, artillery commander of 1st Cavalry Division.

In 1941 he was promoted to brigadier general and organised 82nd Infantry Division's artillery just before that formation converted to the airborne role. A promotion to major general in February 1943 was accompanied by his appointment to command the new 11th Airborne Division before being sent to the Mediterranean to help plan the airborne elements of Operation HUSKY as Eisenhower's airborne advisor. Returning to the USA, he continued in command of 11th Airborne with the additional task of chairing the Swing Board, Marshall's investigation into the efficacy of large-scale airborne operations.

The board met at Camp Mackall to review both Allied and Axis airborne operations to that time. Membership included 'experienced paratrooper and glider officers, artillerymen, and Air Corps troop carrier and glider unit commanders and staff officers'.[15] Airborne divisional organisation was studied, as were the problems encountered by the troop carrier units in North Africa and Sicily. Over the following weeks they considered factors such as navigational and communication problems, frictions between airmen and airborne soldiers – all those difficulties peculiar to command and control of airborne forces both before and after deployment.[16]

It was while Swing's board was in session that 503rd Parachute Infantry Regiment dropped on Nadzab, and the board was able to examine the after-action reports of both the regiment and 54th Troop Carrier Wing. In comparing the Nadzab drop with those in North Africa and Sicily it was clear that preparation and planning had been much better in New Guinea with 54 TCW carrying out a practice formation drop in columns, using dummy paratroopers, while Colonel Ken Kinser had worked his paratroopers hard. Flown into action by 54 TCW, 503 PIR seized Nadzab airfield in support of the Australian Operation POSTERN, the amphibious landings at Lae on the New Guinea coast. Nadzab was then used for the fly-in of 7th Australian Division, which joined with 9th Division in seizing Lae and clearing the Huon peninsula. Overall preparation and training had been thorough for the first airborne combat operation in the Pacific. In contrast, training for operations in North Africa and Sicily had been haphazard and perfunctory. Swing recognised this, and his training of 11th Airborne Division emphasised the need for co-operation and understanding between airmen and the paratroopers and glidermen. The greater problem lay with the airmen.

As the commander of 11th Airborne Division, Swing was committed fully to the airborne concept and the successful drop at Nadzab was proof of its value. His board completed its study at the end of September and its unsurprising principal recommendation was that there was a need for closer co-ordination between airborne units and troop carrier commands, especially in training and preparation. The board's findings led to the War Department issue of *Training Circular 113* which quickly became holy writ for US airborne operations. The circular prescribed 'the relationships between the airborne and troop carrier commands, their several responsibilities, and the details of airborne operations from takeoff to drop and assembly'.[17]

US paratroopers of 503 PIR drop at Nadzab airstrip on 5 September 1943, securing it for the fly-in of 7th Australian Division as part of Operation POSTERN. This was the first successful major Allied airborne operation. (*NARA*)

However, reservations remained at the highest level: Marshall and McNair still had doubts about the effectiveness of divisional-scale airborne deployments. By then, however, 82nd Airborne Division had dropped two regiments into the Salerno beachhead, and 101st was in the United Kingdom training and preparing for operations in mainland Europe. In spite of 82nd's highly successful operation, remaining doubts prompted Marshall and McNair to seek 'proof beyond a shadow of a doubt' that an airborne division could truly be an effective combat formation. As a result, McNair ordered Swing to plan and organise manoeuvres by 11th Airborne Division to prove that such formations could operate effectively. With those manoeuvres due to take place in December, it was clear to all involved that the future of the US airborne divisions depended on the outcome.

Doubts about the effectiveness of large airborne formations went even higher in the US hierarchy with Harry L. Stimson, Roosevelt's Secretary of War, also having reservations about the concept, as we have seen. (Stimson, a Republican member of Roosevelt's administration, had served in the same post under President Taft from 1911 to 1913; he had been an artillery officer in the US Army in France in the First World War.) In late November Stimson visited Camp Mackall to watch the demonstration of airborne troops in the 'Pea Patch Show'. Stimson was suitably impressed, writing to Swing on the 27th with the comment that we have already noted 'The Airborne Division will play a great part in our future successes …'.

Since McNair wanted further and more comprehensive proof of the viability of airborne operations to ensure the reprieve of the airborne divisions, Swing's planned exercise, the Knollwood Manoeuvre, in North Carolina in December would be the decisive factor. The manoeuvre pitted Swing's 11th Airborne Division, as 'Blue Force', against 17th Airborne Division as 'Red Force'. Each division was reinforced – by an additional parachute infantry regiment, 501 PIR for the 11th, and a battalion of 541 PIR for the 17th.

HQ Army Ground Forces ordered that the exercise be executed within the parameters of *Training Circular 113* 'to provide practical and straightforward answers' to four questions:

Could an airborne division fly a three-to-four-hour instrument course, at night, across a large body of water and arrive on schedule at specially selected drop and landing zones?

Could such a force land by parachute and glider without sustaining excessive landing casualties?

Could the division then wage extended ground combat?

Could the division so landed be re-supplied by parachute and plane and glider landings?

The Knollwood Manoeuvre was held from 4 to 12 December 1943 and took its name from its main 'objective', the capture of Knollwood Airport. The principal 'examiner' was McNair himself, described by Devlin as 'the hard-nosed commander of Army Ground Forces' who had 'originally been a friend of airborne troops, calling them "high-spirited like the Rangers, but very fine soldiers".' However, he had changed his mind following what he described as 'unsatisfactory performances' in their operations in Tunisia and Sicily. His enthusiasm for the concept had cooled significantly. McNair would not be the sole observer of the manoeuvre: also present were Robert P. Patterson, Stimson's deputy at the War Department (he, too, had served in France in the First World War, as an infantry officer, earning the Distinguished Service Cross and Silver Star), Brigadier General Leo Donovan, who had just been appointed as commander of Airborne Command (another veteran of the First World War with service in France) and Major General Matt Ridgway, commander of 82nd Airborne Division, which he had led in Sicily and Salerno. (He would later succeed Eisenhower as SACEUR before becoming Chief of Staff of the US Army.) Teams of observers from the War Department, Army Ground Forces and Army Air Forces were also present.

The attacking force was Swing's 11th Airborne Division, with 501 PIR attached, and the exercise would also test whether that formation was fit for operational service. Defending Knollwood Airport was a composite regimental combat team drawn from 17th Airborne Division reinforced by a battalion of 541 PIR. Considerable planning and preparation went into the manoeuvre since it had been designed by McNair's HQ to

> test the feasibility of loading an airborne division in its jump transports and gliders, flying a four-hour triangular course – for the most part over water – hitting the drop and landing zones at night under blacked-out conditions, assembling the units into combat formations speedily, and then attacking the defending forces aggressively.[18]

On 4 December Swing's soldiers boarded lorries at Camp Mackall to carry them in convoys to five airfields in North Carolina and South Carolina. Next day the defenders deployed around Knollwood Airport and other key points.

Although weather conditions began deteriorating, the exercise went ahead, albeit delayed by twenty-four hours. Paratroopers and glidermen boarded their transports at the five airfields and awaited the signal for take-off. Departures from the airfields were timed to allow each group to join the aerial column in its assigned place in the line. With the aircraft and gliders in a V of Vs, nine aeroplanes wide, 'the long column headed east across the North Carolina

Paratroopers drop from C-47s over Knollwood in the Knollwood Manoeuvre which proved to Marshall and Arnold the viability of divisional-size airborne operations. (*NARA*)

shoreline out over the Atlantic, turned north, and finally headed back west toward the designated DZs and landing zones (LZs) located … to the west of the Fort Bragg reservation'.[19]

The first paratroopers made their jumps at 2300 with the gliders following not long after. Pathfinders who had landed earlier had marked the DZs and LZs and before long most of the division was on the ground. Only a single glider had gone astray: the divisional chief of staff's glider landed on Fort Bragg's artillery range. Paratroopers released their chutes and gathered themselves into their sub-units for the planned attacks while the glidermen unloaded their gliders. Artillery men assembled their weapons, and the advance to contact began. As the winter sun rose, Knollwood Airport was firmly in the hands of 11th Airborne Division. Then came the next phase of the exercise as aircraft carrying soldiers and others laden with supplies began landing, enabling the division to establish an airhead. (At Nadzab, once the airfield had been cleared of obstructions and US and Australian engineers had ensured its safety, including adequate drainage, US aircraft had begun flying in the men of Major General Vasey's Australian 7th Division. Vasey, a veteran of Greece and Crete, had argued against the original plan to deploy one parachute battalion, insisting that a regiment was necessary.[20] Seventh Australian Division thus became the first Allied airportable division of the war.)

For almost a week, 11th Airborne 'waged war' with 17th Airborne until Army Ground Forces HQ declared an end to the exercise. Weary and cold airborne soldiers boarded their vehicles for the return to Camp Mackall on a cold wet night.

Once at Mackall, the divisional staff and unit commanders drew up a post-operational report for Major General Swing. In turn, Swing submitted his report to McNair on the 16th. McNair responded:

I congratulate you on the splendid performance of your division in the Knollwood [manoeuvre]. After the airborne operations in Africa and Sicily, my staff and I had become convinced of the impracticability of handling large airborne units. I was prepared to recommend to the War Department that airborne operations be abandoned in our scheme of organisation and that the airborne effort be restricted to parachute units of battalion size or smaller. The successful performance of your division has convinced me that we were wrong, and I shall now recommend that we continue our present schedule of activating, training, and committing airborne divisions.[21]

As Flanagan wrote, 'The airborne division concept had been tried and tested, and found credible, workable, and functional. The five US airborne divisions were safe from further cuts, doubts, and controversies.'[22] Practical and straightforward answers had been provided to the four critical questions and the concept had been proved: a divisional-sized airborne force could undertake a journey of up to four hours, on instruments, across a large body of water to arrive over closely-defined drop zones on schedule; it could land airborne troops by parachute and glider without excessive casualties; it could then fight for a sustained period; it had delivered proof that an airborne division could be re-supplied by air drops and glider landings only. Of course, the operation at Nadzab had already demonstrated the feasibility of re-supply by air, as well as reinforcement by air.

Nadzab therefore played a significant but almost forgotten part in the history of airborne forces. The seizure of the abandoned airfield and the flying in of a full infantry division had played an important part in the liberation of New Guinea. It had also helped ensure the survival of the airborne divisions and, thus, the availability to Eisenhower of such formations in Europe, which allowed him to launch Operation MARKET GARDEN. The Nadzab operation had taken place just over a year before 1st Airborne Division dropped/flew into Arnhem/Oosterbeek to hardwire its place in history and the British national consciousness.

Without 503 PIR's drop at Nadzab all US and British airborne divisions might have been re-roled as line infantry with Operation MARKET GARDEN never happening. As already noted, the airborne division could simply have been scrapped.

Chapter Two

Following their breakout from Normandy, Allied armies had made a rapid advance and by 31 August were poised to strike into the Low Countries and across the border into Germany. Such had been the pace of the advance that senior commanders were beginning to believe that the war would soon be over. Montgomery predicted its conclusion by 1 November, while American generals were confident that the Rhine would be crossed at the beginning of the winter with the war ending soon after. Relying on information from US generals, Marshall was under the impression that the war in Europe was nearing its end and, on 13 September, wrote to senior commanders, including Eisenhower:

> While cessation of hostilities in the war against Germany may occur at any time, it is assumed that in fact it will extend over a period commencing any time between September 1 and November 1.[1]

However, the Allied ground forces, while surging forward, were outstripping their supply lines while the damage done to the French railway system by Allied bombing before Operation OVERLORD was increasing supply difficulties. Eisenhower had wanted to advance on a 'broad front', but the decreasing impetus of the armies was causing a rethink as far away as Washington. There was also an element of confusion created by Eisenhower at a conference on 20 August when he directed Omar Bradley's 12 Army Group to advance on the Saar and link up with 6 Army Group, a Franco-American force advancing from the south, while Montgomery's 21 Army Group was to advance north-east 'on the Channel ports, Antwerp *and* the Ruhr'. Since this was 'a mismatch of force and objectives', Montgomery's chief of staff, Major General de Guingand, asked Eisenhower not to issue a directive until he, Ike, had conferred with Montgomery. Although a meeting was arranged at the latter's HQ (it took place on the 23rd), Eisenhower had already reported his plan to the Combined Chiefs of Staff, but it was not exactly as outlined on the 20th, nor was his intention expressed as clearly. This was to lead to increased friction between Bradley and Montgomery, between the latter and Eisenhower and, more generally, between Montgomery and the American generals.

Eisenhower told the Combined Chiefs that 21 Army Group would advance on the Channel ports and Antwerp while, 'if the German forces "were no greater" than he thought, 21 Army Group's advance would pass Paris to the north-east before moving eastward to thrust south of the Ardennes. He reported that Bradley's rate of advance would be related to the clearing of the ports in Brittany and the improvement in the provision of supplies. A link with 6 Army group would be dictated by logistical considerations; if favourable, a column might be sent to help 6 Army Group's advance. 'This was a compromise, and not a good one.' The strength of opposition to 21 Army Group was not known with any accuracy while an advance to the Ruhr would need First US Army, but Ike had directed that formation to the Saar.[2]

The Ruhr region, which takes its name from the eponymous river, is Germany's industrial heartland. (Today it is part of North Rhine-Westphalia, created in 1946.) Geographically, it extends from the Rhine's left bank east to Hamm and from the Ruhr river north to the Lippe. It is also understood to include Krefeld and Düsseldorf on the Rhine and the urban belt connecting the latter city to Hagen through Wuppertal. It became heavily industrialised from the early part of the nineteenth century when the Krupp and Thyssen companies began large-scale mining of coal from one of the world's largest coalfields. Coal was being mined in the area before the Middle Ages and it was the availability of bituminous coal in such quantities that allowed the development of major iron and steel industries in the nineteenth century, leading to greater urbanisation. An extensive canal system was developed, followed by Germany's densest railway network. In all, the area covers almost 5,000 square miles, measuring some sixty miles (about 100 kilometres) from north to south and eighty (about 113 kilometres) from west to east. Essen became the centre of the Krupps' steel empire while other major industrial centres included Dortmund, Duisburg, Düsseldorf and Solingen. Naturally, the Ruhr became a major target for RAF Bomber Command and, later, the US Army Air Forces and was defended heavily. Its iron and steel meant that it could supply those essential materials to factories across Germany that built aircraft, artillery, armoured vehicles, ships, submarines and tanks, as well as everyday products such as household goods and bicycles.

In the meantime, the supply problem had to be dealt with. 'Red Ball Express', a standard American description of any emergency lift, whether on land, at sea or in the air, is believed to date from the latter part of the nineteenth century when the Santa Fe railway began using it for express materials, marking both trains and lines with the 'red ball' priority system. However, since the

Second World War it has tended to be associated with the road convoy system that began operating from Normandy from 25 August 1944 to supply the advancing Allied armies.

That road convoy system is seen generally as an excellent example of American improvisation, which it certainly was, but that hides the reality that it was the direct result of weaknesses in the organisation headed by Eisenhower. US Army logistics were in the hands of an organisation known as COMZ, or Communications Zone. However, COMZ also controlled 'common-user' essentials for all Allied ground forces, the most vital being petrol, oil and lubricants (POL) and the transport to deliver them.

Rather than being fully integrated, as in the British system,[3] COMZ, commanded by Lieutenant General John C.H. Lee, was not answerable to Eisenhower since it was outside SHAEF's control. Bedell Smith, Eisenhower's chief of staff, described Lee as a man who 'didn't know much about supply organisation' and tried to have him removed but without success since he enjoyed Marshall's favour: 'he was one of the crosses we had to bear.' (Lieutenant General Frank M. Andrews, Eisenhower's successor as commander of ETOUSA, was determined to ask Marshall to remove Lee but died in a plane crash in Iceland on his way to do so. Andrews is remembered today as one of the founders of the US Air Force and is commemorated in the name of Joint Base Andrews in Maryland.)

Lee chose to move his HQ to Paris after the liberation of the French capital, a move that meant he lost touch with his supplies and put himself out of contact at a crucial time. With the two army groups surging across France, the supply chain was being outstripped, but the man in charge was not to be found. Moreover, Eisenhower was committing similar errors, trying to conduct operational matters by telegrams, brief visits and conferences that inconvenienced his commanders. He was 'repeating the error that had cost French commanders the battle in 1940. Like them he was out of touch, not just physically with his commanders, but with the "feel" of operations.'[4]

Eisenhower's strategy for a broad-front advance depended on a logistical system that could cope. Lee's system seemed unable to do so. Montgomery brought the impending problem of petrol shortages to Eisenhower's attention on 9 September. Yet, as Graham and Bidwell point out, Eisenhower still continued to give Lee the impression in October and November that the war was close to an end and that logistical re-organisation was not an immediate necessity.

When Patton detached VIII Corps under Lieutenant General Troy Middleton to turn west into Brittany while the remainder of Third Army raced beyond Paris, Middleton soon ran out of ammunition and Bedell Smith had to issue a direct order to Lee to supply VIII Corps with ammunition.

A GMC 2.5-ton 6x6 cargo truck stuck in mud, one of many problems faced by drivers in the 'Red Ball Express', which continued into November 1944. Although less reliable than the Dodge 1.5-ton truck, the GMC was available in greater numbers and so bore the main burden. (*NARA*)

It is not surprising, therefore, that the Red Ball Express had to be organised. In its first twelve days of operation its vehicles carried more than 74,000 tons of supplies to Bradley's 12 Army Group. By mid-September railway trains were also operating as far as the Soissons area, but the combined total of road and rail supply was insufficient to keep both of Bradley's armies moving and divisions had to be grounded. In spite of the legend, the Red Ball Express had one great weakness: the US Army's GMC 2.5-ton trucks, the 'dooce an' a haff'. Other vehicles were used, both Dodge and Mack 1.5-tonners, but the GMCs provided the bulk of the lorries. However, the vehicle was not as robust as its appearance suggested and regular maintenance was a priority. Such maintenance was not provided, and vehicles had to be taken off the road for repairs, stretching workshops beyond their capacity: for every GMC on the road, four were awaiting repair.

The scheme itself worked and allowed African American soldiers, who were not then permitted in anything other than service roles, to feel that they were making a positive contribution to the war. Given priority on the roads chosen for the operation, they ran on a one-way loop and moved at the best speeds they could maintain. The operational scheme was attributed to Eisenhower himself, who already had a reputation as a logistician. Based on a French model, it later influenced President Eisenhower's oversight of the US Interstate Highway network.[5]

The US Chief of Staff, General George C. Marshall, aware that First Allied Airborne Army was sitting in England, prompted Eisenhower to use that army's divisions. (It had four available for active deployment – 1st British, 52nd (Lowland) Airportable, 82nd and 101st US, plus a Polish parachute brigade; 17th US Airborne Division had arrived in the UK but was not ready for action, while 6th British was still resting and re-organising after Normandy.)

Not everyone agreed with Eisenhower's broad-front policy. Among those who believed that he should instead make a well-supported narrow thrust into Germany were Field Marshal Sir Bernard Montgomery, commanding the British/Canadian 21 Army Group, and General George Patton, commanding US Third Army. Both argued that a concentrated thrust by a large Allied force would take the Allies through the Siegfried Line and into Germany itself. Although SHAEF staff had considered the point that a few divisions, with proper logistical support, could maintain momentum and the initiative much more effectively than a force of twice its size with uncertain logistics (as then being provided by COMZ), Eisenhower, intent on pursuing compromise, failed to consider it. A very clear demonstration of that truth was shortly to be given by the British XXX Corps (with fewer than four divisions, including two and a half armoured) as it raced into Belgium, liberated Brussels and pushed to the Albert canal, beyond Diest. (XXX Corps had made a faster advance over a greater distance than Patton en route to Metz; Lieutenant General Courtney Hodges' First Army diary noted the 'British … astoundingly rapid drive into Belgium completing the occupation (sic) of Brussels'.)

Montgomery and Patton considered that, since 6 June, the retreating German armies' casualties had been so heavy that the Siegfried Line defences

Sherman Hughes, one of three drivers of 666th Quartermaster Truck Company, 82nd Airborne Division, who each chalked up 20,000 collision-free miles since their arrival in the European Theatre. (*NARA*)

Lieutenant General George S. Patton, commander US Third Army, who was determined to fight the campaign in his own way and was probably equally determined to thwart Montgomery. He had been promoted to General when this photograph was taken (*NARA*)

would be weak and that a quick thrust would deny the enemy the opportunity of rushing reinforcements to meet the offensive. However, Eisenhower's prevarication was aiding the enemy.

The prize for an attack such as those envisaged by Montgomery and Patton would be the capture of either the Ruhr or the Saar areas, Germany's main industrial zones. Losing either would reduce greatly Germany's capacity to continue the war, with the Ruhr the greater loss. Moreover, the gains in ground thus made would provide a valuable jumping-off position for a rapid advance to Berlin, and an end to the war in the west by Christmas.

Eisenhower and Montgomery had an acrimonious discussion about strategy during a meeting onboard the former's aircraft at Brussels airport on 10 September. In the light of Eisenhower's disagreement with Montgomery, and the latter's outspoken comments, it would seem more likely that Ike would have accepted Patton's plan for Third Army to take the lead in the advance into Germany. However, Patton's force was short of fuel and ammunition although not, it seems, of rations, and so Eisenhower gave Montgomery the go-ahead for his plan. Why?

Eisenhower's doubts about the concept of large-scale airborne operations have already been noted, but the outcome of the Swing Board, the Knollwood Manoeuvre and Marshall's support for airborne forces had prompted a volte-face, although D'Este doubted if Eisenhower was 'ever completely sold on the worth of the airborne'.[6] D'Este's comment followed his reporting Ike's 10 August speech to 101st Airborne Division in which he asserted that 'one of the great futures of our success' lay in airborne operations. The creation of First Allied Airborne Army left Eisenhower little choice but to embrace the airborne concept. Thus, when Montgomery laid out a plan on 10 September to use First Allied Airborne Army in a thrust across the Rhine, Eisenhower gave it his approval. With Marshall looking over his shoulder, and the 'paratroopers and glidermen resting and training in England … coins burning holes in

The Siegfried Line included many 'Tobruk' defences, often including a tank turret set into concrete, an improvisation originally used by the Italian defenders of the eponymous Libyan port. This Tobruk was encountered on Omaha Beach. (*NARA*)

[Eisenhower's] pocket',[7] Montgomery received the Supreme Commander's *imprimatur*.

There would be no thrust by Patton's army. Airborne forces, co-ordinated with powerful ground forces, would make the thrust. And yet, there were other options – involving other US ground troops – that might have delivered a much better result.

On 24 August, as Allied armies surged through France, Hitler ordered new construction work on the Siegfried Line, or Westwall. Some 20,000 forced labourers, plus *Reichsarbeitdienst* (Reich Labour Service) personnel, the majority only boys, tried adapting the line for defensive purposes. Although it was obvious that the existing bunkers would not provide protection against contemporary armour-piercing weaponry, additional fortifications were built, including many 'Tobruk' one-man positions.

The first encounters with the Allies on the line took place in August. In early September V US Corps, under Major General Leonard T. Gerow, reached the Siegfried Line on a thirty-three-mile-long front. In the middle of that front was Wallendorf, a village on the banks of the Sauer river, the Luxembourg-Germany border. On the German side rises the Schnee Eifel, an area of farmland and woods that is a continuation of the Belgian Ardennes through which Guderian had launched his attacks on France and the Low Countries in 1940.

Gerow's V Corps, part of Hodges' First Army, included three divisions, 5th Armored and 4th and 28th Infantry. Hodges' command was on the left flank of Patton's Third Army and both army and corps were short of fuel and ammunition, while 5th Armored Division's tanks needed maintenance following the speedy advance from Normandy. Nonetheless, Hodges ordered Gerow to reconnoitre along his front to establish the German dispositions. Intelligence indicated that the Germans could assemble no more than 6,000 troops along Gerow's front while his Intelligence chief, Colonel Thomas J. Ford, assessed that an advance onto the Schnee Eifel would be countered only by the remnants of three divisions, Panzer Lehr, 2nd Panzer and 5th Panzer, formations that V Corps had pursued across France.

Lieutenant General Courtney Hodges, commander US First Army. A capable general who had risen from the rank of private, his army had advanced quickly across Europe. Soldiers of Hodges's formation were the first Allied troops to enter Germany. (*NARA*)

Hodges, hoping to use the advantages of the Allied momentum and the disintegration of the enemy, instructed his reconnaissance patrols to continue their advance unless resistance became strong. On 11 September Gerow ordered 5th Armored Division to reconnoitre into Germany across the Our river, a task led by Second Platoon, Troop B of 85th Cavalry Squadron, under Sergeant Warner W. Holzinger. That afternoon the German-born Holzinger and his platoon waded across the river beside a partly-demolished bridge and into the German town of Stalzemburg, becoming the first foreign troops to invade Germany since Napoleon. Speaking to local people, Holzinger learned that no German soldiers were in the area. Probing forward a mile and a half, the platoon found the first line of pillboxes. They had reached the Siegfried Line. The pillboxes were unoccupied. Elsewhere, a reinforced company from 109th Infantry Regiment (28th Division) crossed a bridge over the Our into the German village of Severnig, while a further patrol from 22nd Infantry of 4th Division also crossed near the German village of Hemmeres. Men of 22nd Infantry not only spoke to civilians, but also brought back a German cap, some money and a packet of soil.[8]

Further recces at Stalzemburg over the next two days reported some German troops moving forward to man pillboxes, but their numbers were nowhere near enough to stop an American advance. Two German armoured divisions were identified facing V Corps: 2nd SS Panzer *Das Reich* and 2nd Panzer, with three tanks each and a paucity of artillery, estimated at three 150mm guns, twenty-six 105mm howitzers and seventeen assault guns. As the US official historian noted, 'In the feeble hands of units like these had rested German hopes of holding the Allies beyond the Siegfried Line long enough for the fortifications to be put into shape.'[9] Moreover, divisions were such in name only, with some no more than regiments or even battalions in terms of manpower. MacDonald comments that some divisions 'had little left except a name'.[10]

There was another factor favouring the Americans, but one of which they were then unaware. Gerow's front faced a demarcation line not only between two German corps – I SS Panzer and LXXX – but also between two armies – First and Seventh – *and* two army groups – B and G. The intelligence over the previous days led to Gerow planning an attack into the Eifel. All three divisions made simultaneous advances, but it was 5th Armored's 'secondary' attack, centred around Wallendorf, that provided a 'genuine opportunity for a breakthrough which showed promise of welding the three separate division actions into a cohesive corps manoeuvre'.[11]

Major General Oliver of 5th Armored had a regiment of 28th Division attached to his command. His Combat Commands R (CCR) and B (CCB) deployed to patrol the front, ready to conduct a reconnaissance in force should the opportunity arise. On 13 September CCR made a reconnaissance by fire near Wallendorf that produced no response, there being virtually no Germans in the area. Once he received that information, Gerow ordered Oliver to advance through Wallendorf, move onto the high ground beyond the village and across the plateau to seize Mettendorf, five miles inside Germany, from whence the division would strike towards Bitburg; 1st/112th Infantry would support the operation.

Gerow had chosen well. The Wallendorf sector was on LXXX Corps' extreme right, the enemy's weakest point, into which no organised unit would move until the morning of the 14th. As indicated earlier, V Corps was also pushing at the boundaries of three levels of German command while the Siegfried Line was 'markedly thin because German engineers had leaned heavily upon the rugged nature of the terrain'. That bridges near Wallendorf had been demolished was not a problem since the river was narrow – about 40 metres in width – and fordable in several places.[12]

CCR began its advance after noon on the 14th and almost immediately encountered resistance from an 'alarm battalion' that was just arriving. With no anti-tank weapons, the resistance was unable to stop the Americans' progress which continued next day into the little hamlet of Niedersgegen where an understrength panzer company, possibly from Panzer Lehr, was encountered and driven out, although the Americans suffered some losses. With his armour rolling unopposed behind the enemy lines, Gerow ordered Oliver to move on and take Bitburg.

Resistance began stiffening with reinforcements being ordered in by Field Marshal von Rundstedt. Nonetheless, the advance continued and 5th Armored HQ was optimistic that, although German resistance would continue, the enemy could accomplish nothing more than to slow the advance. At this point, however, an apparent blindness, deafness or indifference appears to have beset the higher commands. The opportunity to exploit what V Corps had achieved at Wallendorf, 'a potential breakthrough delivered on a platter',[13] was ignored by First Army, 12 US Army Group and Eisenhower's HQ and no additional support was provided to exploit the situation. Colley argues that neither Eisenhower nor Bradley may have been aware of the situation, although First Army's war diary indicates that V Corps' advance and penetration of the Siegfried Line was known about.[14]

It is certainly the case that, on the evening of 16 September, German defences were no more than 'a papier-mâché cordon about the penetration with every available soldier from LXXX Corps as well as every man who could be spared from the neighbouring I SS Panzer Corps'.[15]

Yet that was when Gerow ordered Oliver to suspend his advance, consolidate his command and 'mop up' around Wallendorf. While he could continue patrolling towards Bitburg to assess enemy forces, he was to move to the defensive. MacDonald commented that this decision 'must have come as a shock to both troops and commanders'.[16]

Gerow's two infantry divisions had also been pushing into Germany, to the north of 5th Armored in the Schnee Eifel. Two regiments of 28th Division (112th was operating with Oliver's division) were advancing towards high ground about Uettfeld and Grosskampenberg, the first of the two villages being the objective of 109th Regiment and the other that of 110th Regiment which was to punch into Germany before joining 109th close to Uettfeld. That attack began on the 13th although, initially, only one battalion of each regiment could be deployed.

German opposition, although not strong, proved a real problem for the attackers since both regiments were moving from the line of march that had been the race across France and lacked equipment necessary to assault fixed defences, such as flame-throwers and explosive charges. Their attached tanks and SP tank-destroyers were also being repaired and their supporting artillery amounted only to 57mm anti-tank guns and towed tank-destroyers. However, partially due to the efforts of one tank commander who blew his way through the dragons' teeth with his Sherman's 75mm gun, some progress was made and Gerow was encouraged. Believing a breakthrough possible, he ordered Oliver to send an experienced tank commander to advise the infantry on tank/infantry co-operation.

On the 15th the arrival of an engineer team enabled the attackers to move forward as they destroyed a roadblock that had been hindering forward movement. That led to the seizure of Hill 553 overlooking the road to Uettfeld, the capture of almost sixty prisoners and the destruction of seventeen pillboxes. Against determined opposition, and the loss of almost an entire company, progress was made. By the end of the day on the 16th the attackers had advanced more than a mile and a half and had taken high ground that overlooked the sector for miles around. 'Beyond them lay only scattered Siegfried Line fortifications. Though the penetration was narrow and pencil-like, 28th Division had for all practical purposes broken through the Siegfried Line.'[17] Then came Gerow's order to hold fast. Once again, the men on the ground were surprised.

Equally surprised were the men of 4th Division, two regiments of which had also made a very speedy penetration of the Siegfried Line. The divisional commander, Major General Raymond Barton, had ordered 12th and 22nd Regiments to attack in line to seize 'commanding ground on the crest of the central plateau beyond the Prüm river, more than 10 miles away'. It was an ambitious objective. The GIs proved themselves capable of achieving it with 12th Regiment encountering light opposition and digging in for the night 'on Bogeyman Hill, all the way through the fabled West Wall'. Only once had they called for artillery support.[18]

Meanwhile, 22nd Regiment had encountered some sterner opposition, which it had overcome, to hold a breach in the Siegfried Line about two miles wide at the end of the day. One battalion was positioned on the eastern slopes of the Schnee Eifel, overlooking Hontheim, a mile and a quarter beyond the forward pillboxes. Barton went on to widen his position on the 15th as well as continuing with a motorised advance through the Losheim Gap. Bad weather prevented air support and mist slowed the advance while determined opposition was encountered at Losheim. More ground was taken on the 16th, but opposition was getting stronger although 1st/22nd took the high ground dominating the village of Sellerich, where casualties were sustained, including the commanding officer, who was one of eight killed.

Although 4th Division's advance continued on the 17th, as MARKET GARDEN began, with fighting also continuing, the ground gained was unsuitable for further exploitation. In any event, Eisenhower's new plan was already in operation.

It seemed that Allied commanders from Eisenhower down were in thrall to the concept of the MARKET GARDEN operation. Colley suggests that:

All eyes, however, were on Arnhem [sic] and MARKET GARDEN where thousands of paratroopers and ground troops from XXX Corps were about to descend on Holland to open the way around the Siegfried Line to the Ruhr. The Allied High Command believed the alliance needed a spectacular show at Arnhem.[19]

Chapter Three

Sixth British Airborne Division was deployed in Normandy in June 1944, and it was appreciated that there was a likely requirement for further airborne operations as operations on the mainland progressed; all would have to be planned and launched at short notice. As a result, Lieutenant General Frederick A.M. 'Boy' Browning, regarded as the father of British airborne forces, having commanded 1st Airborne Division, was attached to headquarters Second Army, commanded by his old friend Lieutenant General Miles Dempsey, with which he sailed to France on 5 June 1944.

Lieutenant General Sir Miles Dempsey, commander British Second Army, was responsible for Operation GARDEN and deployed VIII, XII and XXX Corps. By 17 September German forces were recovering their equilibrium after Normandy and provided tougher opposition than anticipated. (*IWM TR 1654*)

With the breakout from the Normandy beachhead in August 1944 it was decided to combine British and American airborne forces into an army to be styled First Allied Airborne Army. Command went to Lieutenant General Lewis Brereton, an American, with Browning appointed as deputy commander. Browning was unhappy with this appointment since his commission was marginally senior to Brereton's and, more importantly, he had a wealth of airborne experience to draw upon, whereas Brereton had none whatsoever since he was from an air force background, with some major mistakes in his record. This was not a wholly improper decision, however. The dependency of airborne forces on aircraft to deliver them into battle made it desirable to have a senior member of the airborne establishment who was familiar with the needs of the air forces, but it could certainly be argued that it would have been more sensible to have an airborne commander with an air force deputy rather than the reverse.

Lieutenant General Sir Frederick 'Boy' Browning, deputy commander First Allied Airborne Army and commander I British Airborne Corps. Browning was the father of the British airborne forces and there was friction between him and Brereton, who lacked airborne experience. (*IWM CL120*)

While the order to create First Allied Airborne Army was delivered by Eisenhower on 2 August 1944, the force behind its creation was General Marshall, whose advocacy of airborne forces was well known, and shared by General 'Hap' Arnold, commanding the US Army Air Forces. Although Eisenhower was to deliver a powerful speech to paratroopers and airmen eight days after the new army was formed, he probably felt that he had little choice other than to accept the concept. Such was the power of Marshall and Arnold, who may be described as the midwives of First Allied Airborne Army.

At the time of its formation, First Allied Airborne Army constituted Eisenhower's strategic reserve, 'a versatile force to be employed when and where [he] and SHAEF decided'.[1] The man appointed to command the new army was Lieutenant General Lewis Hyde Brereton, then commander of Ninth US Air Force, the US counterpart of the British Second Tactical Air Force. Brereton's departure from Ninth Air Force was welcomed by Omar Bradley, commander of 12 US Army Group, who had little time for him, describing him as 'marginally competent' and fond of high living. One British veteran of Arnhem wrote of him that he was 'a general whose fellow countrymen had even less to say in his favour than had his allies'.[2] Brereton became army commander on 17 July, ready for the army to be established formally on 2 August.

The name of Lieutenant General Lewis Hyde Brereton is not well-known, even to many familiar with the war in north-west Europe in 1944-45. He is certainly rarely associated with Arnhem and MARKET GARDEN, even though he was First Allied Airborne Army's commander. In fact, Graham and Bidwell comment that 'It is significant that in the many post-mortems on "Arnhem" his name is never mentioned' while summarising him as 'a feeble, dismal little man, by all accounts'.[3]

Brereton, born into a family of Irish-American descent in Pennsylvania in 1890, had planned to be a naval officer. He attended the Naval Academy at Annapolis, from which he was commissioned but almost immediately resigned his commission on the grounds of seasickness. Subsequently commissioned in the Army (he had earlier failed to secure admission to West Point) in the Coast Artillery

General Henry H. 'Hap' Arnold, commander of the US Army Air Forces. A pioneer of military aviation, he became commander of the US Army Air Corps in September 1938 and played a pivotal role in shaping the air arm during the war. Arnold was a firm advocate of airborne forces. (*NARA*)

Corps, he volunteered for the Aeronautical Section of the Signal Corps and became only the tenth pilot to qualify as a 'military aviator' on 27 March in 1913. As an instructor on floatplanes, he was involved in two crashes, one of them fatal, and asked to be relieved of aviation duties.

While war raged in Europe, Brereton was in the Philippines as a gunner but returned to aviation and an appointment in the Signal Corps aviation HQ office. Posted to France when the US entered the war in 1917, he became the commander of 12th Aero Squadron before being promoted to major as Air Service Officer to I US Corps. Brigadier General Billy Mitchell was impressed by him and gave him command of the Corps Observation Wing in August 1918. Less than three weeks later, Brereton earned the Distinguished Service Cross in an air combat clash. He continued to impress Mitchell who made him his assistant and promoted him to temporary lieutenant colonel.

Less than a month before the war ended, Brereton proposed an operation to transport 1st Infantry Division behind enemy lines. What would have been the first airborne assault was shelved by General John Pershing although it had Mitchell's support.

Between the wars Brereton continued to rise in the ranks, but his progress was affected by emotional problems; at one stage he asked for medical leave due to a fear of flying. At the time his marriage was collapsing, and the 'fear of flying' may have been, like his earlier seasickness, a subterfuge. Nonetheless, by the time the Second World War began in Europe, he was a brigadier general and highly regarded. Promoted to major general in July 1941, he was appointed by Arnold, Chief of the Army Air Forces, to command the Far East Air Force in the Philippines.

His preparations in the Philippines were disrupted when General MacArthur sent him to Australia to plan the use of bases there in the event of war. However, the Japanese attack on Pearl Harbor was followed by another on Clark Field, Manila, home of the Far East Air Force. Although Brereton had ordered his bombers and fighters into the air so that they would not be caught on the ground, the aircraft had to land to refuel and re-arm and, whilst on the ground, were attacked by Japanese planes from Formosa, now Taiwan. Surviving B-17 bombers were sent to Australia and the FEAF was broken up.

Brereton continued to serve, as deputy commander of ABDAIR, part of the American-British-Dutch-Australian Command (ABDACOM) but did not impress the air commander, Air Marshal Sir Richard Peirse, or the overall ABDA commander, General Sir Archibald Wavell. He then assumed command of a revived FEAF before moving to India to organise Tenth Air Force and set up an air supply route to sustain China. He was awarded the Distinguished Service Medal for his command of FEAF and the Distinguished Flying Cross for taking part in an operation against Japanese warships in the Andaman Islands.

In June 1942, with the threat of a German attack on the Middle East through the Caucasus, Brereton was posted to Egypt and began setting up the US Army Middle East Air Forces (USAMEAF), a command that included B-24 and B-17 four-engine heavy bombers, supported by a fighter group and a group of B-25 Mitchell twin-engine medium bombers. While the fighters and B-25s operated as tactical aircraft alongside the RAF's Desert Air Force, the heavy bombers continued operating from Palestine. The heavies refined operational procedures and tactics and later took part in bombing the oilfields at Ploesti in Romania. By then USAMEAF had been superseded by Ninth Air Force, with Brereton still in command.

With his reputation still high, Brereton was offered a choice of three commands, one in the USA, another in Cairo, or command of a new tactical air force being formed in the UK as part of the Allied Expeditionary Air Force. Brereton opted for the last named, which was to assume the title Ninth Air Force.

In April 1944 Brereton was promoted to lieutenant general as elements of his command began their campaign against transport targets in France in preparation for the landings in Normandy. However, he objected to a proposal to create an Allied Tactical Air Force by combining both British and US formations. His objection was based on the proposal that the combined force would be commanded by Coningham, commander of the British Second Tactical Air Force. A compromise was reached with Coningham in charge of an Advanced HQ of the Allied Expeditionary Air Force and Brereton beside him in the command team.

By August, all Ninth Air Force's fighter units were based in the Allied bridgehead in Normandy. The force continued providing effective support to the ground troops, but Brereton was about to lay down his command since Eisenhower had already told him that he was to command the airborne army. Although Lieutenant General Browning was four months senior to Brereton, the commander was to be an American. However, Browning was appointed as Brereton's deputy, as well as commanding the British I Airborne Corps. Inevitably, there was friction between them. Rostron refers to Brereton as 'an outstanding airman with no experience whatever of either land or airborne operations', and notes that Browning considered him 'confused, weak-willed and overcautious'.[4]

As the army commander, responsibility for planning operations fell to Brereton. When Eisenhower decided to implement Montgomery's proposal for a combined airborne/ground forces strike across the Rhine, it was Brereton who was given the task of planning it, not Montgomery although the Airborne Army came under 21 Army Group command. Brereton took the plans for the abandoned Operation LINNET – intended to use airborne forces to seize and hold Tournai on the Escaut river, in western Belgium – and adapt them for what became Operation MARKET GARDEN. LINNET was to have been executed by 1st British Airborne Division, 101st US Airborne Division, 1 Polish Parachute Brigade and the airportable 52nd (Lowland) Division.

The rapid advance of XXX Corps had rendered the LINNET plan redundant, but it formed the basis for the MARKET element of MARKET GARDEN with the addition of 82nd US Airborne Division. However, Brereton introduced changes, principally a major change in the use of gliders. Whereas LINNET was to have been conducted using double-tows, MARKET would be restricted to single tows. His rationale was based on a combination of factors: there had been poor weather; aircraft had been deployed for re-supply missions to the ground forces and standing by for dropping paratroopers all meant that IX Troop Carrier Command had had almost no opportunities for training.

Brereton considered that lack of training meant that double-towing would be too dangerous.[5]

That decision seems rational, as did his decision that MARKET would be a daylight operation, based on the experience of British and American airborne operations on D Day in Normandy which, undertaken under cover of darkness, had suffered high dispersion of both paratroopers and glider infantry. He was confirmed in his decision when D Day for MARKET GARDEN had to be delayed until 17 September, the dark moon. Since it was almost the autumnal equinox, Brereton decided to restrict the number of 'lifts' carried out by the transport aircraft and glider tugs. That final decision meant that it would take three days to complete 'lifting' the airborne force.

Deteriorating weather conditions over England, the flight paths to the Netherlands and the drop and landing zones led to further delays, including cancelling the scheduled drop of Sosabowski's Polish brigade and the lift of a US glider-infantry regiment. Those factors meant that the operation could not achieve all its objectives.

However, there can be no rational explanation for Brereton's refusal to allow the RAF's No. 83 Group, part of Second Tactical Air Force, to operate in the Arnhem area, nor for the failure to consult Montgomery's HQ over the choice of drop/landing zones. Graham and Bidwell comment that the lack of co-ordination began with the American failure to appoint a ground force commander, subordinate to Eisenhower, and in the latter's failure to recognise the problems of a divided command. They also note that Brereton later refused Montgomery's request for an airborne operation to support 21 Army Group's seizure of Walcheren Island. In their words, 'The commander of the Airborne Army, Major General (sic) Lewis H. Brereton lacked grip'.[6]

The respected USAF historian, Dr Roger G. Miller, in a major essay, summarised Brereton as 'a capable commander and effective leader, but not a great general. He was a solid product of the U.S. military system prior to World War II, and as such was neither a star performer nor mediocre failure. He fits into that large middle ground of competent but unspectacular American officers who brought victory in World War II.'[7] Thus Brereton is damned with faint praise.

'Capable commander' he may well have been, although there are solid grounds for doubting that. However, he was not the right man to command First Allied Airborne Army, in which role he showed more of the 'feeble, dismal little man'. Those who fought in MARKET and GARDEN deserved better. At no time did Montgomery criticise Brereton; he did not mention him in his *Memoirs* and Hamilton's biography of Monty has only brief references to him. It would have been quite easy for Montgomery to point out that the planning and execution of MARKET was not his responsibility, but that of Brereton who was almost the invisible man of the operation. Interestingly, in the film *A Bridge Too Far*, Brereton does not feature at all.

As noted earlier, Brereton's rival for command was Lieutenant General 'Boy' Browning, commander of the British airborne forces, who was senior to Brereton in terms of time in rank. D'Este notes that Browning had better credentials as a pioneer of airborne operations, the first commander of 1st Airborne Division and a qualified glider pilot, but that 'he lacked battle experience',[8] which is untrue and a surprising error on D'Este's part. Browning had served in the Grenadier Guards during the First World War in several major battles and had earned the DSO, as well as an excellent reputation for organisation and planning. However, he had not had battle experience in the Second World War, although he had commanded two infantry brigades.[9]

On 29 October 1941 Browning, on promotion to major general, was appointed Commander Parachute Troops and Airborne Troops, subsequently forming and taking command of 1st Airborne Division. Browning is frequently cited as the father of the British airborne movement; this is not inaccurate despite the fact that it had been founded more than a year previously. Some excellent men had played a part in improvising Britain's first airborne capability from nothing, developing training techniques and deployment theories which were to endure throughout the war, yet the force was still only a battalion and Browning faced the challenge of expanding this nucleus into a much larger and capable branch of the Army. It was a challenging time to be raising such a formation; the airborne movement was unproven in battle and struggled to survive amidst the continual demands for men from existing battalions, and for equipment, aircraft and aircrew from the Royal Air Force. Browning was the ideal choice to overcome such obstacles, having both the energy and organisational skill required, and he could call on an extensive list of influential friends made throughout his career, being unafraid to use them to obtain whatever his division required.[10]

A headquarters was essential. Browning began by staffing it with men whom he had selected personally and others who came with strong recommendations. Those appointments were not made on a whim; Browning required an efficient administrative staff, but he also needed extremely capable officers to serve as heads of services such as artillery, engineering, medical and ordnance branches Such men would be responsible for pioneering techniques and practices in their specialist areas in what was alien territory for the Army.

Browning found the efficiency of 1st Airborne Division to be an immediate problem. Although 1 Airlanding Brigade was in good shape, it included a large number of conscripts who were not yet up to standard, whilst the larger part of 1 Parachute Brigade had only just been formed by men from all corners of the Army, and its experienced nucleus, the 1st Battalion, had become somewhat relaxed through inaction. The answer to the problem was training and discipline and, to assist with the latter, he deliberately inserted a particularly high number of Guards sergeants to the staff, as he felt that only

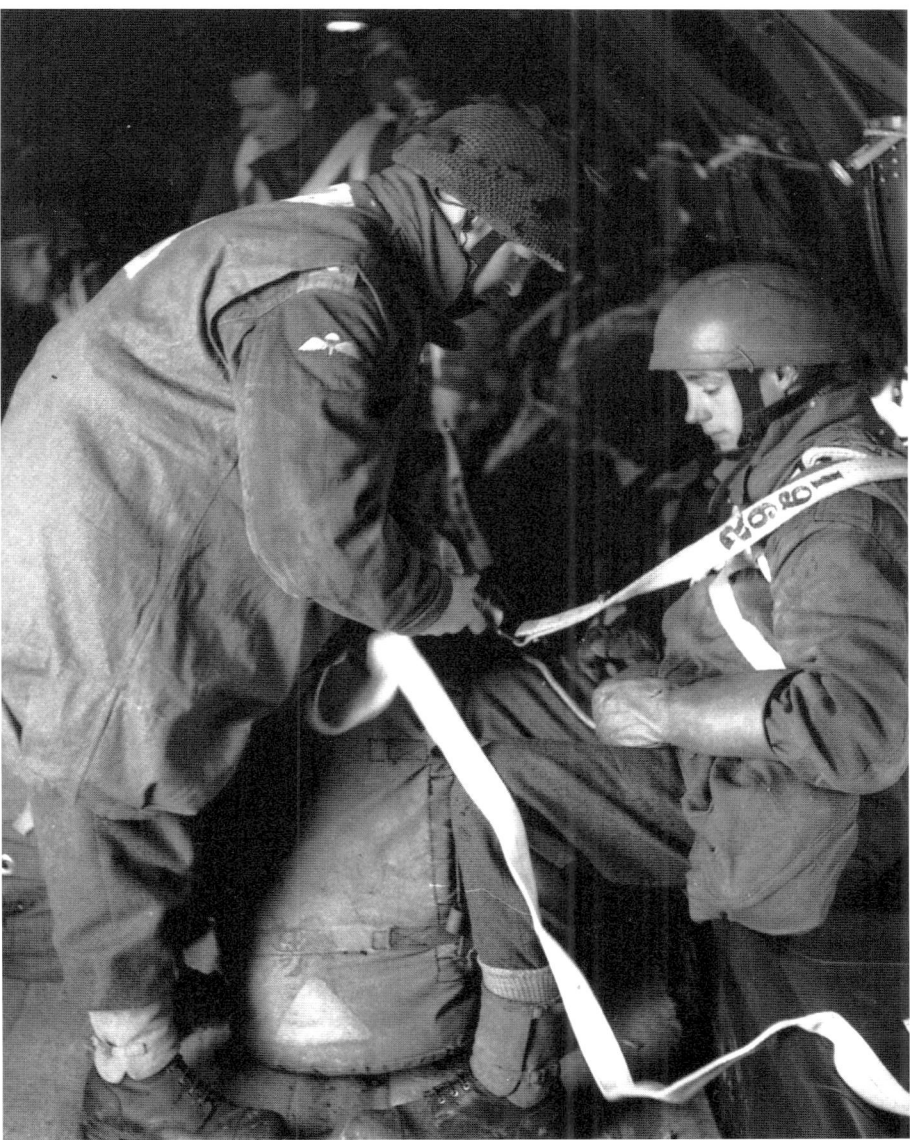

Paratroopers of 6th Airborne Division preparing for a jump. This image, taken on Exercise MUSH in April 1944, where the opposition was 1st Airborne Division, captures the scene in a C-47 Dakota. (*IWM H 377717*)

they could achieve the exacting standards required. His methods were not always appreciated, however, and the constant drilling led to him being known in some quarters as 'Bullshit' Browning. Nevertheless, morale improved under his regime, discipline became absolute, and a tremendous esprit de corps began to emerge.

This was the man who was appointed as deputy commander to Brereton, in addition to commanding I British Airborne Corps, one of the two major fighting components of First Allied Airborne Army, the other being Ridgway's US XVIII Airborne Corps. Brereton's command also included the USAAF IX Troop Carrier Command (50th, 52nd and 53rd Troop Carrier Wings) and would take Nos 38 and 46 Groups of the RAF under command operationally.

I British Airborne Corps included the British 1st and 6th Airborne Divisions, 52nd (Lowland) (Mountain) Airportable Division, 1 Polish Independent Parachute Brigade and the Special Air Service Brigade of 1st and 2nd British, 3rd and 4th French and 5th Belgian SAS Regiments. Of these, 6th Airborne had dropped in Normandy and fought on the left flank until August. Two of the US airborne divisions, 82nd (All American) and 101st (Screaming Eagles), in Ridgway's XVIII US Airborne Corps, had also dropped in Normandy, while 17th had arrived in the UK later, but was not ready for Operation MARKET GARDEN since many of its stores were still in transit. In 1945 a further division, 13th, joined the order of battle but never saw action.

Brereton did not have a high regard for Eisenhower who had demanded 'imagination and daring' from the new army. Although promising results, Brereton noted his feelings about Eisenhower in his diary: 'He does not leave anything to the imagination. He never does. I told [him] if he wanted plans with daring and imagination he would get them, but that I did not think his staff or the ground commanders would like it.' Brereton told his staff that the supreme commander 'wants the airborne army used in mass. He believes that if it is used that way the effect on the morale of the Germans would be devastating'.[12] Irrespective of these comments, Brereton was keen to see the airborne army deploy on 'a major operation of genuine consequence'.[13]

Thus, there were tensions between Eisenhower and Brereton and between Brereton and Browning, none of which bode well for the airborne army. Add to that the tensions with ground commanders and a recipe for serious problems seemed to be in the making.

There had been opposition to the creation of First Allied Airborne Army, some of it based on the use of the title 'army' since the formation was perceived as a reservoir of manpower to be deployed in support of the ground armies. That was overcome, as were arguments against including the US troop-carrier aircraft formations. However, the RAF held out: British transport aircraft were to be assigned to the army for operations but would not be placed under its command.

Elements of the future First Allied Airborne Army had fought in Normandy, but its first commitment as a discrete formation was to be Operation MARKET GARDEN, previous planned operations having been cancelled. Those were Operations TRANSFIGURE, cancelled when the dropping area was captured by advancing ground troops; AXEHEAD, intended to seize bridges over the Seine in support of 21 Army Group; BOXER, to capture Boulogne port; LINNET, the seizure of crossings around Tournai to create a bridgehead over the Escaut, cutting off retreating German formations; LINNET II, to cut off German forces in the Aachen-Maastricht area; INFATUATE, to seize Walcheren Island, cut off a German retreat across the Scheldt estuary and help open Antwerp; and COMET, dropping 1st British Airborne Division and 1 Polish Parachute Brigade to seize bridges across the Rhine, thus aiding the advance into north Germany.

Most proposed operations were overtaken by events, with ground forces advancing so quickly that the airborne plans were rendered redundant, even when First Airborne Army HQ had enough time to make plans, although Operation COMET was cancelled on 10 September following some days of adverse weather allied with concerns about strengthening German resistance. Nonetheless, COMET would form the model for MARKET GARDEN.

Operation MARKET GARDEN marked the Allied Airborne Army's first battle, and its sole deployment in a strategic role. It would also see action, in a ground role, in the Ardennes during the German offensive popularly known as the Battle of the Bulge, and in Operation VARSITY, supporting 21 Army Group's Rhine crossing, Operation PLUNDER, after which elements of the army continued to fight as ground forces. The army was disbanded in May 1945.

Chapter Four

Among the principles of war is 'Simplicity' which, in modern NATO parlance, means preparing plans that are clear and uncomplicated with clear and concise orders to ensure thorough understanding. The commander's intent should be clear, without the need for prescriptive detail, so that those executing the orders know exactly what is to be achieved; the way in which it is achieved is left to those in immediate command on the ground. Such plans and orders reduce considerably the opportunities for misunderstanding and confusion. When operations involve forces from more than one nation, simplicity becomes even more critical, since differences in culture, doctrine and language (even the difference in English and its American version) create complications.

Other principles include a clearly defined 'objective' that should be decisive and attainable, and ultimately an end state; 'economy of force' with commanders assigning the appropriate manpower for an operation, which involves the acceptance of some risk; 'manoeuvre' to place the enemy at a disadvantage; 'unity of command' with a single commander directing and co-ordinating the actions of all forces towards a common objective; and 'surprise' by taking actions that the enemy has not anticipated and for which he has not prepared.

While there are other principles, which have long been held, it is worth examining the planning for Operation MARKET GARDEN in the light of the following six. Were the plans simple? Was the objective clear? Was economy of force achieved? Did manoeuvre work? Was there unity of command? Was surprise achieved?

Simplicity is hardly a word that may be used accurately to describe Operation MARKET GARDEN. The first airborne operation with a strategic purpose, it was complicated in concept and involved two armies, First Allied Airborne and Lieutenant General Miles Dempsey's British Second Army. It involved laying what Field Marshal Montgomery described as a 'carpet' of airborne forces across five major waterways on the 'general axis of the main road through Eindhoven to Uden, Grave, Nijmegen, and thence to Arnhem'. XXX Corps, commanded by Lieutenant General Brian Horrocks, was to advance along that axis to link up with 1st British Airborne Division 'in the

Arnhem area' and create a bridgehead over the Neder Rijn north of Arnhem. As XXX Corps advanced, the axis of the advance was to be widened by VIII Corps, under Lieutenant General Sir Richard O'Connor, on the right flank and XII Corps, under Lieutenant General Sir Neil Ritchie, on the left.[1]

Once XXX Corps had effected its junction with 1st Airborne, Second Army was to establish itself 'in the general area between Arnhem and the Zuider Zee, facing east, so as to be able to develop operations against the northern flank of the Ruhr'. (The Zuider Zee in the north-west of the Netherlands was a shallow bay of the North Sea which had been closed off from the latter by the construction of a major dyke. The reduced body of inland water became a freshwater lake, the IJssel lake or IJsseelmeer.)

Of this plan, Omar Bradley wrote:

Had the pious teetotalling Montgomery wobbled into SHAEF with a hangover, I could not have been more astonished than I was by the daring adventure he proposed. For in contrast to the conservative tactics Montgomery ordinarily chose, the Arnhem attack was to be made over a 60-mile carpet of airborne troops. Although I never reconciled myself to the venture, I nevertheless freely concede that Monty's plan for Arnhem was one of the most imaginative of the war.[2]

Montgomery was happy to quote the comment about 'one of the most imaginative' plans of the war in his *Memoirs*.[3] However, 'imaginative' and 'simple' are not synonymous, and Monty goes on to mention that Bradley tried to have the operation cancelled, 'lest it should open up possibilities on the northern flank and I might then ask for American troops to be placed under my command to exploit them'.[4]

Eisenhower's support, thanks to Marshall's pressure to deploy First Allied Airborne Army, meant that MARKET GARDEN would go ahead. But Eisenhower believed that the successful conclusion of the 'bridgehead operation' would allow Montgomery to 'turn instantly and with his whole force to the capture of Walcheren Island and the other areas from which the Germans were defending the approaches to Antwerp'.[5] According to Montgomery, this had not been mentioned when he and Eisenhower met in the latter's aeroplane on 10 September.

This apparent confusion between Eisenhower and Montgomery leads us to consider if the objective of Operation MARKET GARDEN was clear at all levels, and if it was decisive and attainable. It does not appear to have been clear, especially since Bradley claims that he 'had not been brought into the plan' and considered that it would cripple the joint offensive 'we had agreed upon a few days before'.[6] Perhaps that also explains why Bradley did not halt Patton's Third Army immediately. As mentioned earlier, any plan must have a clear objective and end state. This confusion suggests that unity of command was lacking.

Was the principle of economy of force applied? For MARKET, the airborne operation, it could be argued that it was, but the provision of appropriate manpower was diminished by the decision to undertake only one drop on D Day. That, of course, could be described as acceptance of some risk, but it was a decision that was to prove fateful. Air commanders were prepared to make the extra drops on D Day, but the Airborne Army Commander, Brereton, demurred.

'Manoeuvre' and 'surprise' may be considered together since they are related closely: the first, intended to disadvantage the foe, assists the second, which is the effect of taking actions that the opposition has not anticipated and thus has not prepared to meet. Dropping three airborne divisions certainly was a manoeuvre that would take the Germans off balance, especially as they were expecting the Allied airborne forces to be used elsewhere. However, the manoeuvre would lose most of its surprise if the appropriate manpower was not deployed and there Brereton again let down his command by his arrangement of the lifts for his paratroopers and glidermen.

Was unity of command applied? No single commander directed and co-ordinated the actions of *all* the forces involved. Montgomery bluntly accepted responsibility for some of the more grievous errors: he accepted the blame for the airborne troops at Arnhem being dropped 'too far away from the vital objective – the bridge' and noted that:

> I should have ordered Second Army and I Airborne Corps to arrange that at least one complete Parachute Brigade was dropped quite close to the bridge, so that it could have been captured in a matter of minutes and its defence soundly organised with time to spare. I did not do so.[7]

However, planning was conducted in several HQs, with that for the airborne forces being the responsibility of Brereton's, and, to an extent, Browning's. Another factor was the speed with which the operation was planned, although an earlier plan, Operation COMET, formed the basis for MARKET GARDEN. But there were real tensions between Brereton and Browning which had become more acute following earlier planned operations.

The pair's relationship had begun unfavourably and deteriorated quickly. On 2 September, after several cancelled plans, Operation LINNET was proposed to insert Browning's HQ, the Polish Brigade, 1st British and 82nd US Airborne

Divisions, near Lille and Courtrai. To accommodate LINNET, Second Army halted its advance to function as the relieving force, but the operation was cancelled at the last moment when First US Army altered its course to take the area from under the noses of the British. Brereton immediately proposed LINNET II, using the same force to cut off the enemy's line of retreat around Aachen and Maastricht. However, such was the haste that there was no time to distribute adequate maps or hold briefings. Browning protested strongly at such reckless use of his force. Brereton ignored him and Browning offered his resignation. Differences in military culture meant that the Americans were appalled by Browning's stance; they regarded it as tantamount to disobeying an order. Browning quickly withdrew his threat when it became clear that Brereton would be happy to accept it and replace him with Lieutenant General Ridgway. It is questionable whether a complete American command structure would have been politically acceptable since most of the airborne army at the time was British. There were two British airborne divisions, plus the airportable 52nd (Lowland) Division, the Polish Brigade and SAS, whereas the Americans had only two airborne divisions, although a third, 17th, was assembling in England. It is more probable, as happened a few months later, that Browning would have been replaced by Major General Gale.

Brereton may have congratulated himself on winning this power struggle, yet there remained an inherent weakness in his command structure which he discovered several days later. I British Airborne Corps was part of Brereton's Army, but retained a certain independence, largely because the staff at Montgomery's 21 Army Group had not lost the habit of contacting them directly when they wanted an airborne plan. Brereton was furious, therefore, when another operation based around Browning's corps was proposed, only to discover that Browning had gone behind his back to commit it to Operation COMET in conjunction with Second Army. There is little doubt, therefore, that, by September, relations between Brereton and Browning, and Brereton and Second Army, were exceptionally poor.

Operation COMET envisaged 1st Airborne Division and 1 Polish Brigade dropping across Holland to secure a series of bridges at Eindhoven, Nijmegen and Arnhem, with each bridge the objective of a brigade group. Objections were based on such forces being insufficient to defend their objectives against counter-attacks. Chief among the critics was Major General Sosabowski, whose sound judgement played a part in Operation COMET being cancelled. However, his relations with Browning were not improved when he insisted on receiving his orders in writing.

The basic plan was not dead, however. On 10 September, Montgomery personally briefed Browning for MARKET GARDEN. The objectives remained the same, but the American airborne divisions entered the equation, and the areas around Eindhoven, Nijmegen and Arnhem respectively became the responsibilities of 101st, 82nd and 1st Airborne Divisions with the Polish Brigade under command of the last named.

It was agreed that Browning would participate in the battle alongside his previously untried tactical headquarters. This prompted some resentment with the Americans; Lieutenant General Ridgway was much more experienced and was bitterly disappointed at being overlooked, not least because he considered that the majority of airborne troops involved in MARKET GARDEN were American. His point was debatable: the Polish Brigade and the expected reinforcement of 52nd (Lowland) Division more than balanced numbers.

Browning naturally had close connections amongst the British ground commanders who would be coming to his relief, and, although his tactical headquarters was no older than Ridgway's – it had been in existence for just a month – it had planned Operation COMET, making his staff intimately familiar with the area, no small point since MARKET GARDEN was to be planned and launched in just seven days.

Haste was added to the problems facing the planners, and those taking part in the operation. A certain confusion is also suggested by the fact that Montgomery seems to have been under the impression that he had been 'allotted the First Allied Airborne Corps under Browning' which he placed under command of Second Army. In reality, Brereton's First Allied Airborne Army had been allotted to 21 Army Group. In practice, I Airborne Corps remained under Brereton's command, and it was Brereton who decreed that the 'primary responsibility of any air operation was that the first troops on the ground must secure landing zones for re-supply'. In contrast, Browning favoured seizing tactical objectives immediately by using the element of surprise and speed of manoeuvre. Since it was Brereton's doctrine that was used, it is clear that his headquarters made the final plan. In a post-mortem in his *Memoirs* Montgomery comments that the airborne forces at Arnhem 'were dropped too far away from the final objective – the bridge. … I take the blame for this mistake'. As noted on p. 36, he further comments that he should have ordered that a parachute brigade dropped 'quite close to the bridge'.[8]

Chapter Five

Arnhem bridge was the objective assigned to the British 1st Airborne Division, commanded since February 1944 by Major General Robert Elliott 'Roy' Urquhart, a Scot and Highland Light Infantry officer with previous service in North Africa, Sicily and Italy. He had commanded 231 Infantry Brigade, but Arnhem was to be his first experience of commanding airborne troops in action. There was resentment within the division from some who felt that a divisional officer should have been promoted to the post. Among those favoured was Ernest Edward (Eric) 'Dracula' Down, an 'original' in airborne terms who had commanded 2 Parachute Brigade. In fact, Down had taken command when Major General George Frederick Hopkinson, the previous GOC, was wounded fatally in Italy.[1] Although a superb soldier, Down treated his officers badly and was feared by his men. However, many officers felt that he would never have accepted drop and landing zones so far from the objective.

Down was due to take command of 9th Indian Airborne Division (subsequently 44th Indian Airborne Division) and thus Brigadier Bernard Howlett, commander of 36 Brigade in 78th Division, was selected to be the new GOC of 1st Airborne. Howlett, described as 'cheerful, friendly, hearteningly confident', was killed by German shellfire on 29 November whilst visiting units of his brigade in their front-line positions north of the Sangro river which 78th Division had just crossed. Howlett, known as 'Swifty' as a result of his bowling prowess, had commanded 36 Brigade since December 1942 and had been appointed DSO for his leadership in the battle for Longstop Hill in Tunisia. He received a Bar to the DSO for the Sicilian campaign and was posthumously Mentioned in Despatches; he had received a Mention in Despatches in 1940 as brigade major of 231 Brigade in the Dunkirk campaign. With Howlett's death, the mantle fell on Urquhart, previously commander of 231 Brigade.[2]

Since Howlett had much more experience in action and in command, this poses the inevitable question: might he have been a better commander than Urquhart? It is reasonable to suggest that he would have been, since he had seen much more active service in the war than Urquhart, who had been in

India for the first two years of war and, although he had commanded a brigade, much of his experience had been in staff posts. Although described by David Niven as 'a serious soldier of great charm and warmth', he was not in the same league as Howlett. Interestingly, Howlett's son Geoffrey followed his father into the Royal West Kent Regiment and earned the Military Cross in Malaya in 1952, but later transferred to the Parachute Regiment, commanding the 2nd Battalion and going on to command 16 Parachute Brigade. He was later colonel commandant of the Parachute Regiment.[3]

Down had returned to the UK with the division before he was sent to India and his record also suggests that he would have made a better commander than Urquhart. Although lacking Howlett's combat experience, he was an excellent trainer of airborne soldiers. Commissioned in the Dorsetshire Regiment in 1923, he was stationed in Jamaica when war broke out and came home to serve in staff appointments and to attend a Staff College course. However, in mid-1941 he was promoted to lieutenant colonel and given the role of converting '11th' SAS Battalion into a parachute battalion. The battalion had originally been 2 Commando and adopted the style II SAS Battalion, retaining the commando ethos. The SAS of its title had no connection with David Stirling's creation. (At the time the commando forces – all Army – were known as special service and II Battalion simply slotted 'Air' into the definition to indicate its operating element.)

Down was not a trained parachutist but arranged a brief training course before taking up his command. A hard taskmaster, he earned the soubriquet 'Dracula' from his soldiers whom he trained to be an effective battalion, ensuring his reputation as an outstanding trainer. He went on to command 2 Parachute Brigade in 1st Airborne Division but saw no fighting since the operation in Sicily to which the brigade was assigned was cancelled. Following Hopkinson's death, he commanded the division for the remainder of its brief time in Italy.[4] By the time it had advanced to the Foggia plain its task was complete, and it was withdrawn to return to the UK, although Down's previous command, 2 Parachute Brigade, stayed in Italy as an independent formation.

Another possible commander to succeed Hopkinson was suggested by Ronald Lewin in his biography of Montgomery: switch Gale from 6th Airborne to 1st. Lewin noted that Dempsey had told him that 'he would have preferred to have had Gale in Urquhart's place'. Why? The answer was simple since Gale believed 'that one should aim for a *coup de main* on the objective'. Whereas Urquhart deferred to Brereton, and to the RAF who advised him that anti-aircraft fire around Arnhem bridge ruled out a landing there, Gale would have ignored such advice. 'So the landing grounds selected were too many miles away from where 1st Airborne must arrive – *at the bridge*.'[5]

Dempsey's biographer, Peter Rostron, makes the point that Browning favoured 'the immediate capture of tactical objectives while the element of surprise was still in favour of the attacker'.[6] In contrast, Brereton asserted that the first troops on the ground in any airborne operation should have as their immediate priority the securing of landing zones for re-supply. Not surprisingly, Dempsey fully supported Browning's view; in Rostron's words, he 'had planned and launched more airborne operations than either of them'.[7]

First Airborne Division included three infantry brigades, plus supporting elements. Brigadier Gerald Lathbury's 1 Parachute Brigade (1st, 2nd and 3rd Parachute Battalions), considered to be the veteran paratroopers of the division, had earned the nickname 'Red Devils' from the Germans during the fighting in Tunisia. This was not only from their combat ability: while fighting in the hills of Tamara, skin and equipment became stained with the red mud of Tunisia.[8]

Lieutenant Colonel David Dobie DSO commanded 1st Battalion, formed in 1940 with men of No. 2 Commando. It first saw action in Tunisia after Operation TORCH, the Allied invasion of French North-West Africa, in Sicily, on Operation FUSTIAN and in Operation SLAPSTICK, the landings at Taranto in Italy. During fighting in Tunisia and Sicily the battalion took very heavy casualties and would do so again at Arnhem. Although one of the most experienced parachute battalions, in Operation MARKET it had a high number of new recruits with no battle experience; it saw no further action after Arnhem.

Lieutenant Colonel John Dutton Frost DSO MC commanded 2nd Battalion, formed on 30 September 1941. Its first action was Operation BITING, the Bruneval Raid of 27/28 February 1942, when C Company parachuted into France to seize German radar components. It, too, had fought well in North Africa and Sicily, but also had many new personnel. In addition, it included Lieutenant J.H. Grayburn who, as a platoon commander, would earn the Victoria Cross posthumously for his actions at Arnhem bridge.

Brigadier Philip Hugh Whitby Hicks commanded 1 Airlanding Brigade and has been criticised for his handling of the division when he stepped up while Urquhart was absent. Born on 25 September 1895, Hicks had served in the First World War as a lieutenant with the Royal Warwickshire Regiment, earning both the Military Cross and an MiD. He commanded 1 Airlanding Brigade in Operation LADBROKE in the invasion of Sicily in July 1943 and went on to Arnhem. When Urquhart was trapped behind German lines, Hicks took command of the division. Some consider this a mistake, especially his ordering 11th Battalion to head for Arnhem instead of allowing Hackett to select the battalion. However, Hicks was a veteran not only of the Great War,

Brigadier P.H.W. 'Pip' Hicks, commander 1 Airlanding Brigade, was an experienced and competent officer who was more than capable of commanding 1st Airborne Division during Urquhart's absence. (*IWM H 36654*)

the Blitzkrieg of 1940 and the battle for Sicily, but a brigadier who could read a map, which plainly showed 11th Battalion being closest to Arnhem bridge. After the battle Montgomery wrote to Brooke, 'There is no doubt Hicks did extremely well at Arnhem, but there is also no doubt that it has been too much for him and he is not now fit to fight again in battle in this war.'

Those units forming 1 Airlanding Brigade included 1st Border Regiment, which had seen service in France and Belgium in 1940 as a conventional infantry battalion before transferring to North Africa as part of 1 Airlanding Brigade and then landing by glider in the Sicily invasion. For MARKET GARDEN the battalion consisted of a headquarter company – which incorporated a headquarters, signal platoon, pioneer platoon, transport platoon and administration platoon; four rifle companies, each of four platoons, and a support company of two eight-gun medium machine-gun platoons, two mortar platoons, each with six mortars, one transported in jeeps, the other in handcarts; and an anti-tank group of eight 6-pounder guns.[9]

Known as the South Staffords, 2nd South Staffordshire Regiment was serving in India when war broke out. Returning to England in July 1940, in November 1941 it became a battalion of 1 Airlanding Brigade and served in North Africa and Sicily. The cap badge bore the 'Stafford Knot', or

Staffordshire knot. Legend has it that three criminals were to be hanged and an argument developed as to who should hang first, so the hangman devised a knot that would hang all three together; this is simply myth. The battalion would gain two awards of the Victoria Cross at Arnhem and suffer losses of eighty-six men killed, with eighteen still unidentified at the time of writing.[10]

The most inexperienced battalion of 1 Airlanding Brigade was 7th (Galloway) Battalion King's Own Scottish Borderers, referred to as the KOSBs (*never* Kosbies). From a regiment first formed in 1689, the 7th Battalion spent the early years of the war training and was for a time in 228 Brigade, serving with the Orkney and Shetland Defence Force (OSDEF). In summer 1943, the battalion moved to Woodhall Spa, Lincolnshire, to join 1 Airlanding Brigade.[11]

Divisional support units

The pathfinders of the division, 21 Independent Parachute Company, would mark the landing and drop zones (LZs and DZs) west of Arnhem for the troops scheduled to arrive on Sunday, Monday and Tuesday. The company, the brainchild of Major John Lander TD,[12] had been formed in June 1942 to act as pathfinders for any large-scale airborne landings. Despite action in North Africa, Sicily and Italy, where they had fought mainly as infantry, this was the first time the company would undertake its planned role (22 Independent

Pathfinders prepare to emplane in the Stirlings that would carry them to Arnhem to mark the DZs and LZs for 1st Airborne Division. (IWM C/01154)

Two Pathfinders of 21 Independent Parachute Company rehearse erecting a Eureka beacon in England. (*Peter Gijbles*)

Parachute Company had performed a similar role for 6th Airborne Division in Normandy). For this operation, command of the company went to Major Bernard Alexander 'Boy' Wilson, at forty-five years of age the oldest paratrooper in the division.[13]

Once on the ground the 'eyes' of the division were provided by 1 Airborne Reconnaissance Squadron under Major Charles Frederick Howard Gough MC. Formed from 31 Independent Brigade Anti-Tank Company, renamed 31 Independent Reconnaissance Company in January 1941, it became a glider-borne unit in November as 1 Airlanding Reconnaissance Squadron. Its first officer commanding was Major T.B.H. Otway. (Terence Brandram Hastings Otway, Royal Ulster Rifles, led the outstanding attack against the Merville Battery on D Day, earning a well-deserved DSO.) The squadron, equipped with jeeps and motorcycles, played its part in operations in Italy by landing from the sea at Taranto.

'Freddy' Gough was considered an old man by airborne standards; he celebrated his forty-third birthday the evening before the operation. At Arnhem bridge Gough would have the chance of earning not only further glory for his family, but also their fourth Victoria Cross. A midshipman in the

Major Freddie Gough MC commanded 1 Airborne Reconnaissance Squadron. Gough's advice on deploying the squadron in its true role was not heeded to the detriment of the battalions of 1 Parachute Brigade. (*Estate of the late Adrian Groeneweg OBE*)

Royal Navy during the First World War, he had commanded a provost section with the British Expeditionary Force in France in 1940 and was evacuated from Dunkirk. For action in Holland the squadron jeeps and their drivers would travel by glider, the remaining personnel parachuting in.[14]

Urquhart and Lathbury were responsible for the misuse of Gough's 1 Airborne Reconnaissance Squadron, deploying it in a *coup de main* attempt to seize and hold Arnhem bridge. Although recce *regiments* had performed such a role, it was not their intended role while Gough's squadron was a much lighter force than a standard recce regiment. In contrast, 6th Airborne Division had a full recce regiment in its orbat, including a squadron of light tanks.[15] Gough failed to persuade Urquhart that it would make more sense to deploy his squadron in its normal role with each of his three troops leading a battalion of Lathbury's brigade as it made its attack.[16] The squadron was equipped with unarmoured jeeps, each equipped with a single Vickers K machine gun, with a rate of fire of over 1,000 rounds per minute. Gough's attempts to have these replaced with twin mounts were turned down,[17] as was his suggestion of having a troop of light tanks from 6th Airborne Armoured Reconnaissance

A General Aircraft GAL49 Hamilcar glider in flight. With a wingspan greater than that of a Lancaster bomber and a fuselage of similar length, the Hamilcar could carry heavy loads such as the 17-pounder anti-tank gun or a bulldozer. It could also carry a light tank, but no tanks were transported to Arnhem, in spite of Freddie Gough's request. (*IWM E(MOS) 1357*)

Regiment flown in in Hamilcar gliders. Yet, for the second lift, two Hamilcars were unallotted.[18] Gough later blamed lack of interest in the higher command of 1st Airborne Division for failing to provide better weaponry or seek the loan of a troop from 6th Airborne Armoured Reconnaissance Regiment.

Apart from two 3-inch mortars, the only heavy weapons with the recce squadron were two 20mm Polsten cannon, a version of the Swiss-manufactured Oerlikon anti-aircraft guns. With a rate of fire of 450 rounds per minute, they had been adapted for ground use on probably the most complicated platform ever devised for a gun. On a light two-wheeled carriage, the weapons were towed by Support Troop jeeps.[19]

Artillery support for the division came from 1st Airlanding Light Regiment, Royal Artillery, formed on 13 February 1943. By May the regiment was in action in North Africa and American 75mm howitzers had replaced the original 3.7-inch pack howitzers. Despite its small size, the howitzer had a range of 9,600 yards and fired HE, smoke and anti-tank rounds. Although very accurate, the shell's explosive power was too light to deal with armoured vehicles or prepared emplacements. Nevertheless, the sight and sound of friendly artillery falling on enemy positions was a great morale-booster. For Arnhem, 1 and 3 Batteries were to fly in on D Day to lend immediate

The Polsten 20mm gun in towed configuration. A Polish development of the Oerlikon, it was simpler and cheaper to produce. Two were taken to Arnhem by Gough's Squadron, one of which was knocked out as its detachment was bringing it into action. (*Airborne Assault Museum, Duxford*)

support, with 2 Battery landing the following day. Forward Observation units would arrive with the parachute brigades and glider elements to ensure that all battalions could call on artillery support when needed. Each Horsa glider allocated to the regiment carried a jeep, gun and trailer or a jeep and two trailers, with one jeep-mounted radio per battery. This was the first time an entire Royal Artillery regiment had flown into battle although a battery had been delivered by air in Normandy. The gunners were allocated eighty-seven gliders, the first lift flying from Harwell, Keevil, Manston and Fairford, and the second from Down Ampney and Manston.

To kill enemy tanks, the division depended on the guns of 1 and 2 Airlanding Anti-Tank Batteries and the anti-tank platoons of 1 Airlanding Brigade's three battalions. The normal anti-tank gun for the division was the 6-pounder which, with its 57mm calibre, could penetrate up to 73mm of armour at just under 1,000 yards. Since the original 6-pounder was difficult to fit into a Horsa, an 'airborne' version was created with folding trail legs, narrower axle

The 6-pounder, its jeep tractor and detachment fitted neatly into a Horsa, as demonstrated in this image taken during an exercise in England. (*IWM H 37698*)

A 17-pounder anti-tank gun on the western side of the Hartenstein. (*David R. Orr*)

and smaller shield. Each airlanding anti-tank battery also had two troops of 17-pounder guns, the heaviest anti-tank weapons in British service and the only one in the divisional arsenal that could penetrate the armour of the Tiger tank. The guns would prove quite a surprise to the Germans at Arnhem. Each 17-pounder had its own towing vehicle which also carried the detachment[20] and a limited ammunition supply. Sixteen such guns were taken to Arnhem in the giant Hamilcar gliders. Some were lost, even while being landed, but the remainder played a vital part in defending the division's perimeter around Oosterbeek. They were continuously in action against German armoured and infantry attacks, particularly around divisional headquarters and in the lower part of Oosterbeek village.[21]

The Corps of Royal Engineers was represented by 1 and 4 Parachute Squadrons, 261 Field Park Company and 9 Field Company (Airborne). Capable of many specialist tasks on the battlefield, most would find themselves fighting as conventional infantry. Even greater engineer effort was assigned to GARDEN: 9,000 Sapper and Pioneer Corps personnel with 2,277 vehicles, half of which were RE, for a wide range of tasks that included bridgebuilding and repairing demolitions.[22]

A French Char B1 (bis). Captured by the Germans in 1940, many were converted by replacing the hull-mounted 75mm gun with a flame-thrower. This Char B1 served with Panzer Kompanie 224 at Arnhem. (*Bundesarchiv*)

Medical care was provided by 16th Parachute Field Ambulance RAMC, attached to 1 Parachute Brigade, with 133rd Parachute Field Ambulance attached to 4 Brigade; 181st Airlanding Field Ambulance would arrive by glider on 18 September. About 400 men would treat many times their own number, in conditions that were appalling.[23]

The division took its own police force to Arnhem – 1st (Airborne) Divisional Provost Company under Captain W.B. Gray. His sixty-one men were intended to guard prisoners and control traffic but, like nearly all others, would find themselves in the firing line.[24]

Except for 1 Airlanding Brigade, most infantry men were volunteers, having opted for parachute training; each parachute battalion had three rifle companies against the four of a standard infantry battalion.

Attached to the division was Major General Stanisław Sosabowski's 1 Polish Independent Parachute Brigade Group of just over 1,600 men, including three parachute infantry battalions, an anti-tank battery and medical, engineer, signals and transport companies. Arnhem was to be their first and last battle.

To get vehicles, equipment and other units to the battlefield required gliders. Three glider types were used: the General Aircraft Ltd GAL.49 Hamilcar

An Airspeed AS 51 Horsa glider. Built almost entirely of laminated spruce and plywood, it first flew on 12 September 1941, only ten months after its initial design. Practical and dependable, with a crew of two pilots, it could carry twenty-five fully-equipped troops, or a variety of loads, including jeeps and guns. (*Public domain*)

A Waco CG-4 Hadrian. Constructed of fabric-covered wood and metal and crewed by a pilot and co-pilot, almost 14,000 were eventually delivered. Known as Hadrian in British service, it could carry thirteen fully-equipped soldiers or a jeep, a 75mm howitzer or a ¼-ton trailer. (*Public domain*)

which could carry large heavy loads, including the Tetrarch and M22 Locust light tanks; Airspeed's Horsa which could carry a platoon of infantry, or a jeep and gun – either the 6-pounder anti-tank gun or the 75mm howitzer; and some American-built Waco Hadrian gliders which could also carry a jeep or an artillery piece.

A 6-pounder anti-tank gun ready for action on the corner of Klingelbeekseweg and Utrechtseweg in Arnhem, facing west and pointing at a German strongpoint on the high ground at Den Brink. The supporting infantry appear quite relaxed. (*Photograph via McFarlane*)

The gliders were flown by men of the Glider Pilot Regiment, all of whom were officers or NCOs with a minimum rank of sergeant. Unlike American glider pilots, once landed Glider Pilot Regiment personnel reverted to being infantrymen. The regimental motto was 'Nihil est Impossiblis' (Nothing is Impossible); at Arnhem some 1,100 glider pilots became infantrymen and lived up to the motto.

No. 38 Group RAF

Formed at RAF Netheravon on 15 January 1942, under command of Group Captain Sir Nigel Norman, No. 38 Wing included Nos 296 and 297 Squadrons, to which was added 295 Squadron that summer. In October 1943, with the addition of another six squadrons (Nos 190, 196, 298, 299, 570 and 620), No. 38 (Airborne Force) Group came into being.

Aircraft included Albemarles, operated by Nos 295, 296, 297 and 570 Squadrons, Stirlings, in 190, 196, 299 and 620 Squadrons, and Halifaxes in 298 Squadron. A second Halifax unit, No. 644 Squadron, joined the order of battle in February 1944.[25]

Squadrons of 38 Group deployed on Operations BEGGAR, LADBROKE and FUSTIAN during 1943. Operation BEGGAR, carried out by 298 Squadron, involved towing Horsa gliders from the UK to Tunisia in preparation for the Allied invasion of Sicily. Operation LADBROKE was the seizure of the Ponte Grande bridge in Sicily as part of the invasion, codenamed Operation HUSKY. A further operation, FUSTIAN, to seize the Primosole bridge over the Simeto river, followed.

In February 1944 squadrons of 38 Group began sorties over the European mainland to support the Special Operations Executive and Special Air Service detachments.

For the liberation of Europe, the group was operating from bases at Brize Norton, Fairford, Harwell, Keevil and Tarrant Rushton. As part of the overall NEPTUNE/OVERLORD plan, from 5 June the group carried paratroopers and towed gliders to Normandy; their operations included DEADSTICK, the seizure of the Caen canal and Orne river bridges in a *coup de main* attack, followed by the main insertion of British airborne forces in Operation TONGA and the follow-up Operation MALLARD on the evening of D Day. There followed a re-supply shuttle service that continued until the 16th.

By the time that First Allied Airborne Army launched Operation MARKET in September 1944, No. 38 Group was a highly-experienced and proficient organisation. In contrast IX Troop Carrier Command, for reasons explained on p. 28, had not had sufficient training and two decisions by

Brereton, the army commander, may have been due to that problem: that no tug aircraft would carry out double tows and the number of 'lifts' would be restricted, meaning that it would take three days to lift the complete airborne force. His rationale was that it was almost the autumnal equinox and daylight flying hours would be restricted. Nocturnal operations were ruled out following the experience of dispersion in Normandy. However, his decision, coupled with deteriorating weather in England and on the flight paths to the Netherlands, led to even more delays. It is very unlikely that 38 Group's senior staff and its aircrews would have been anything other than keen to carry out additional lifts.

No. 38 Group carried out a further major operation in Operation VARSITY in March 1945, an airborne operation in support of Operation PLUNDER, the Rhine crossing. Casualties were very heavy in VARSITY, but the airmen did not falter.

After VE Day most squadrons in 38 Group were sent to the Far East or disbanded and, on 1 June 1945, the group became part of Transport Command.

Second Tactical Air Force

Formed as HQ Tactical Air Force from the RAF's Army Co-Operation Command on 1 June 1943 with the intention of creating a force to support ground troops in the field, Second Tactical Air Force (2 TAF) included units from the existing Fighter and Bomber Commands. Light bombers from No. 2 Group Bomber Command formed the latter's contribution. Fighter Command was re-organised to the extent that its contribution to Second Tactical Air Force, Nos 83 and 84 Groups, meant that the remaining fighter force for home defence was renamed Air Defence of Great Britain.

Both 83 and 84 Groups provided the close air support element of 2 TAF while No. 38 Group was also assigned to it with the aircraft to tow assault gliders. A strategic photo-reconnaissance squadron, No. 140, was also placed under the new tactical air force; the photo-recce element grew to be No. 34 Wing with the addition of Nos 16 and 69 Squadrons. Ground-based units of the force, including airfield construction and air defence units, were controlled by No. 85 Group.

The first AOC of Second Tactical Air Force was Air Marshal Sir John d'Albiac who was succeeded by Sir Arthur 'Mary' Coningham in January 1944. Since Coningham had commanded the Desert Air Force, 1 TAF, in both North Africa and Italy, he was the ideal choice to take 2 TAF into battle and ensured that the lessons of the campaigns in Egypt, Libya, Tunisia and Italy were written into the DNA of his new command. Chief among those

Hawker Typhoon 1b. Designed as a Hurricane replacement in the interceptor role, the Typhoon proved unsuitable, except at low altitude. Adapted for the air-support role, for which its four 20mm cannon were ideal, the 'Tiffie' could also carry bombs and, from September 1943, rocket projectiles. Typhoons provided a valuable part of Second Tactical Air Force's capability. (*IWM CH 11578*)

was the adoption of the cab-rank system, begun in Tunisia and refined in Italy, which provided speedy and effective close air support for ground forces.[26]

By the late summer of 1944 the Luftwaffe was no longer the force it had been, and 2 TAF was able to devote most of its time to support the British and Canadian armies on the Allied left flank in France and the Low Countries. A notable exception to that support for ground forces was Operation MARKET with Brereton's decision to restrict the tactical air squadrons while drops or re-supply missions were underway. Adverse weather exacerbated the effects of that decision.

In January 1945 four Gloster Meteor jet fighters of No. 616 Squadron deployed to Belgium under 2 TAF command. The following month a transport group, No. 87, was created. After the war 2 TAF became the British Air Forces of Occupation with Nos 2, 83, 84 and 85 Groups. The name Second Tactical Air Force was revived in 1951 although it was renamed RAF Germany in 1959 with the RAF AOC-in-C becoming commander of NATO's Second Allied Tactical Air Force (2 ATAF).

Chapter Six

Operation MARKET GARDEN envisaged a rapid advance by Second British Army from its position on the Dutch-Belgian border northwards through Holland and into the area north of the Ruhr, Germany's industrial heartland. From there the Ruhr could be threatened, and the enemy deprived of most of his industrial capacity and, therefore, ability to continue the war. The operation consisted of two elements: from the air MARKET would see three airborne divisions, the US 82nd under command of Brigadier General James Gavin, the US 101st, commanded by Major General Maxwell Taylor, and the British 1st, commanded by Major General Robert Urquhart with Major General Stanisław Sosabowski's 1 Polish Independent Parachute Brigade under command, secure a number of river and canal crossings.

From south to north, the American 101st Airborne Division would take the bridges across the Wilhelmina Canal at Son, the Zuid-Willemsvaart canal close to Veghel, and at some other waterways. The American 82nd Airborne Division would take the crossing over the Maas at Grave, the longest road bridge in Europe, bridges over the Maas-Waal canal and the main road bridge at Nijmegen; it was also to take the Groesbeek Heights, overlooking the way to Nijmegen from the south, before taking Nijmegen bridge. Both US divisions had seen action in Normandy, while the 82nd, the proto American airborne division, had fought in Sicily and mainland Italy. The British 1st Airborne Division, with 1 Polish Independent Parachute Brigade Group, would capture the railway and road bridges at Arnhem, the last of five major water crossings, considered to be the final obstacle before entering Germany.[1*] Both Urquhart and Sosabowski were leading their commands into action for the first time.

In concert with this was GARDEN, an advance by ground forces of Second Army. Along the sixty-four miles of road would travel XXX Corps, consisting

---

* The principal water crossings were: Wilhelmina canal at Zon (80-100 feet wide); Willemsvaart canal at Veghel (average 80 feet); Maas river at Grave (normally 800 feet); Maas-Waal canal (200 feet); Waal at Nijmegen (September normal 850 feet); and Neder Rijn at Arnhem (summer normal 300 feet).

US 82nd Airborne Division paratroopers dropping at Grave. Within 30 minutes of landing, soldiers of Company E 504 PIR had taken the bridge which was reported 'secure' just over three hours later. (*NARA*)

of two infantry and one armoured division, its flanks protected by XII Corps on the left and by VIII Corps on the right.

XXX Corps was commanded by Lieutenant General Brian Horrocks, a man with Irish roots, who had shown much daring and innovation in North Africa. The corps comprised Guards Armoured Division under Major General Allan Adair, 43rd (Wessex) Division under Major General Gwilyn Thomas and 50th (Northumbrian) Division, commanded by Major General Douglas Graham. All three men were capable leaders, Thomas having acquired the soubriquet 'von Thomas' while training his division.[2] Graham had commanded in the Normandy landings, and, of all the assaulting formations, his division had come closest to achieving its objectives on D Day.[3] Adair had led his Guards with panache in the British *Blitzkrieg* that had taken Second Army out of Normandy and on to Brussels. He had also survived an attempt by Montgomery to have him removed before OVERLORD.[4]

Adair, another Irishman, commanded the 'mailed gauntlet', a combination of Sherman and Cromwell tanks, supported by artillery, that would punch a hole in the German defences. Guards Armoured was to be led by 5 Brigade which, in turn, would be led by the Irish Guards Group. Number 3 Squadron, 2nd (Armoured) Battalion Irish Guards would lead the Group with the leading tanks being those of Lieutenant Keith Heathcote's troop. Heathcote elected to lead Second Army into Holland and towards Arnhem and placed his tank in the vanguard, ready to drive north at a steady 8mph. Horrocks's advance would have support on the left from Lieutenant General Neil Ritchie's XII Corps and on the right from VIII Corps, commanded by fellow Irishman Lieutenant General Sir Richard O'Connor. XXX Corps' start line had been seized by Guards Armoured on 10 September when 2nd (Armoured) Irish

Lieutenant General Brian Horrocks, commander of XXX Corps. Highly regarded as a commander with considerable experience in North Africa, his corps was given the difficult task of punching through to Arnhem in Operation GARDEN. (*IWM B9532*)

Guards, with support from their 3rd Battalion, captured intact a bridge over the Bocholt-Herentals canal near Neerpelt and close to the border with the Netherlands. The bridge was promptly renamed 'Joe's Bridge' in honour of the Micks' commanding officer, Lieutenant Colonel J.O.E. Vandeleur.

The orders of battle of the three corps each included an armoured division with two infantry divisions in both XII and XXX Corps while XII Corps fielded an armoured division and an infantry division. Each division was operationally mature. In VIII Corps, Pip Roberts' 11th Armoured Division had begun arriving in Europe on 13 June and was complete the following day. Its GOC had commanded an armoured regiment and two armoured brigades in the Western Desert and Tunisia. Third Division, the infantry element of the corps, had served in France in 1940, under Montgomery, and was an assault division on D Day, landing on Sword Beach. XII Corps deployed 7th Armoured Division, the 'Desert Rats', with 15th (Scottish) and 53rd (Welsh) Divisions. The Desert Rats had considerable experience in the North African campaign and had been the first British formation to introduce the battlegroup system in Normandy, an innovation often, wrongly, attributed to Roberts. The two Celtic infantry divisions had already seen much action since arriving in France. Horrocks' XXX Corps had Guards Armoured Division with 43rd (Wessex) and 50th (Northumbrian) Divisions; all three divisions already had extensive experience in north-west Europe, to which the Northumbrian Division could add the North African campaign.

The plan for XXX Corps, GARDEN, which involved the entirety of Second Army, demanded a major logistical effort which Major General Miles Graham, chief administrative officer in Monty's HQ, considered possible with 21 Army Group's existing resources. Within the Q branch, however, there were doubts, since Second Army was still reliant on its reserves. This was despite the establishment on 6 September of a roadhead close to Brussels, and the opening of Dieppe port. Montgomery had already concluded that he needed more and broached the subject with Eisenhower at Brussels airfield on 10 September. This led to a series of exchanges regarding the date of D Day for MARKET GARDEN. Nonetheless, planning went ahead and, for XXX Corps alone, provision was made for the assembly of a 'vast amount of bridging' material on the assumption that the Germans would demolish the existing structures. To deal with the bridging some 2,300 vehicles and about 9,000 sappers and pioneers were to support XXX Corps' advance.

As Eisenhower and Montgomery conferred on the former's aircraft at Brussels airfield, Browning was at 21 Army Group's tactical HQ awaiting the outcome and possible orders for his I Airborne Corps. Montgomery returned with the news that First Allied Airborne Army was to have a major role in the forthcoming offensive. The cancelled Operation COMET had been for a reinforced division to seize the waterway crossings on the road between the Meuse-Escaut canal and Arnhem. Eisenhower had just given his approval for the full airborne army to deploy on what was basically the same operation. This time it was to be Operation MARKET GARDEN with the airborne element as MARKET while GARDEN was the ground thrust by Dempsey's Second Army to support the airborne forces, linking their landing areas, and advancing to make a junction with the British 1st Airborne Division at Arnhem.

First Allied Airborne Army included five airborne divisions, the airportable 52nd (Lowland) and the Polish 1 Parachute Brigade. However, 6th Airborne Division, unlike its American counterparts, had been retained in Normandy to fight as a ground formation, returning to the UK only in August. The division was still refitting and absorbing reinforcements and so was not available for MARKET. Neither was the US 17th (Golden Talon) Airborne Division ready, having only recently arrived in Britain; some of its equipment was still in packing cases at Liverpool.

We have already noted the landing areas of the three divisions with Flanagan commenting that 'these were based on where the divisions were located in England'. He quotes Gavin as saying that 'The British 1st Airborne was best positioned for the Arnhem drop, the 82d Airborne Division for the operation between Nijmegen and Grave, and the US 101st … for all the southern bridges'.[5] However, he goes on to record that, in 1954, General Anthony McAuliffe, who had commanded 101st Airborne's artillery, wrote to the US Army's chief of military history to explain how the decision to deploy 1st Airborne at Arnhem had been made.

> He stated that the original plan had the 101st attacking the Arnhem bridge, but the British 1st Airborne staff had already planned a drop in the area (Operation COMET) that had been cancelled. So Browning felt, wrote McAuliffe, that the British were more ready for that drop than the US 101st.[6]

Briefed by Montgomery, Browning flew to London from where he travelled to HQ First Airborne Army at Sunninghall Park, Ascot, where Brereton informed him that MARKET would be his responsibility and would be carried out by his corps. By early evening Browning was outlining the plan for the airborne forces. The two US divisions, 101st and 82nd, would be responsible, respectively, for the bridges across the Wilhelmina Canal at Son and the Zuid-Willemsvaart canal close to Veghel, and the crossing at Grave plus the main road bridge at Nijmegen. For 1st Airborne Division he declared the objective to be 'Arnhem bridge – and hold it'. Brereton's exhortation was that the bridges should be seized 'with thunderclap surprise'.[7] He also placed Sosaboski's brigade group under 1st Airborne Division command and gave 52nd (Lowland) Division a reserve role – to be flown in to reinforce 1st Airborne when the situation permitted. (It was doubly ironic that the first planned deployment of a Lowland division trained in *mountain* warfare should be to the lowest-lying part of Europe.)

For the staff of First Allied Airborne Army, Browning's outline of the plan was to lead to a period of hectic activity. Although they had considerable experience in planning airborne operations, albeit only to see them cancelled, 'the one he now outlined was not only of unprecedented complexity and boldness, but there were only seven days available in which to plan and launch it'.[8] While 1st Airborne Division and 1 Polish Parachute Brigade had planned for Operation COMET, which had targeted Arnhem bridge and so laid some of the groundwork, the task facing the planners was mammoth and was intensified by the proximity of D Day. (In fact, D Day might have been earlier, since Browning had indicated that the earliest date on which he could launch the operation was the 16th.) The staff work involved covered a daunting range and required consultation with the RAF and USAAF as well as drafting plans and producing information that would inform the planning of tactical commanders from general officers commanding divisions, to brigade and battalion commanders, right down to the junior NCOs commanding sections, troops or squads. The aim was to ensure that every individual would know his part in the overall scheme once his feet or his glider hit the ground.

What did the planners have to consider? These included the assignment of divisional-level tasks (we have already noted the differences between Gavin and McAuliffe on why the British division was given Arnhem bridge as its objective, and McAuliffe was almost certainly right), as well as the allocation of transport aeroplanes. Then came the identification and allocation of dropping zones (DZs) for paratroopers and landing zones (LZs) for glider-borne troops. Flight paths had to be planned, as did air re-supply since the airborne soldiers would need stores including ammunition and rations during the time it took for the ground force to reach them.

In planning for the air lifts, the flight paths and air re-supply, the fact that this was a multi-national operation with both ground and air forces involved had to be taken into consideration; three allies and two fighting services were involved with the air forces being from both the UK and USA. Not only were the transport aircraft under two different 'masters' but other elements of the RAF and USAAF were involved: photo-reconnaissance over the area of the objectives was a necessity; preliminary bombing of various targets was essential; escort fighters were needed to protect the slow, vulnerable streams of transport machines and glider tugs; anti-aircraft defences close to the DZs and LZs had to be knocked out or suppressed temporarily; close-air support for the airborne troops once they had landed was vital. Even the seemingly dull but critical role of meteorological reconnaissance had to be carried out by the RAF.

As we have seen, First Allied Airborne Army had been created in August (the official date of formation was 2 August) and thus its staff had been working together for less than a month. That created a further complication in the planning process. In total, Operation MARKET involved some 35,000 soldiers who had to be briefed on their tasks and moved from their camps or barracks to two dozen airfields across a swath of country between Lincolnshire and Dorset from whence they would take off for their part in the battles to come. There was simply no time for plans to be arranged and re-arranged. As Brereton proclaimed to his senior commanders on 10 September the decisions the planners reached had to be final.

Ironically, Brereton had no idea that Montgomery was asking for a delay in launching the operation. Considering the supply situation, he believed that D Day should be delayed by six days until the 23rd and signalled Eisenhower to that effect on the 11th. On the 12th, Major General Walter Bedell Smith, chief of staff at SHAEF, arrived with the news that Eisenhower had agreed to support MARKET GARDEN with transport re-deployed from three US divisions,

> to halt the Saar thrust, to give priority within 12th US Army Group to Hodges's First US Army on Monty's right flank and to allow Monty to deal directly with Hodges, rather than through Bradley. It seemed that the Northern Thrust was now becoming a reality and an exultant Monty advanced D Day for MARKET GARDEN to 17 September.[9]

However, Bradley was not pleased to learn of that development, which he did from Montgomery on the 13th. He lost no time in taking his perceived grievance to Eisenhower, objecting 'strenuously to it' (MARKET GARDEN). Although Bradley wrote that Eisenhower 'silenced my objections',[10] the net effect was that 'none of the promised support materialised'. However, preparations continued for D Day on the 17th, since Montgomery, Dempsey and Browning remained unaware of what Bradley had 'achieved'.[11]

One thing that the planners could not control was the weather. The date chosen for D Day, 17 September, was close to the autumnal equinox. It was also in the dark moon period, when the only moonlight came from the last visible crescent of the waning moon. Amongst other reasons, that ruled out a night operation. Other factors militating against a nocturnal drop were the problems of dispersion that had occurred on previous operations. Since MARKET was a strategic operation rather than a supporting one, it was essential that it be carried out in daylight. However, the pending equinox meant that daylight hours were restricted. And that equinoctial period also fell within the poet's 'season of mists and mellow fruitfulness'.[12] Unfortunately, the mists so eloquently lauded by Keats would play a baleful role in MARKET.

The period around the equinox is also noted for inclement weather, especially the possibility of equinoctial gales, which would have had a detrimental effect on the operation. Thus, the RAF's meteorological reconnaissance flights by Mosquitoes of No. 1409 Flight far out into the Atlantic were critical to providing information for the planners.

There was other planning to be carried out too, much of it mundane and well-practised, such as battle drills; or already standardised; or the subject of detailed loading tables, including equipment loads for individual transport aeroplanes, gliders and, of course, individual soldiers. That it was familiar made it no less important, and, of course, its scale did add to the burden on the planners.

Since Brereton commanded both the airborne troops and the USAAF element of the transport aircraft, with RAF machines coming under his command for the operation, his first pressing command decision was to choose between a nocturnal or daytime fly-in. Hitherto, operations had been carried out by moonlight, but this had resulted in problems that we have already seen – principally the widely-dispersed landings of Sicily and Normandy, the results of navigational errors. Eisenhower shared this concern about the navigational skills of the USAAF. Since Operation MARKET would be executed in the dark moon period, the absence of moonlight ruled out any major night-time landing. Brereton had no option other than a daytime assault.

Large numbers of slow transport aircraft and glider tugs would present excellent targets for German fighters and anti-aircraft guns. The C-47 (Dakota in the RAF; Skytrain in the USAAF) had a maximum airspeed of 224mph and cruised at 160mph, making it very vulnerable to fighters, while the glider tugs – while some were C-47s, most were RAF Short Stirlings, Armstrong Whitworth Albemarles and Handley Page Halifaxes – were equally slow, even before the burden of a towed glider was taken into consideration. However, by mid-September the Allied air forces had achieved almost complete mastery of the skies over Europe, which mitigated the threat to the air armada from Luftwaffe day fighters. The danger from anti-aircraft guns, or *Flak*, remained high, however, and part of the planners' task was to plot routes to avoid the

Douglas C-47 Skytrain/Dakota. The pre-war Douglas DC-3 airliner was adapted as a military transport for the USAAF as the C-47 Skytrain; the RAF named their C-47s 'Dakota'. The C-47 was the workhorse of the airborne forces. (*NARA*)

Waves of US paratroopers dropping in Holland from C-47s. (*NARA*)

heaviest AA artillery concentrations. (Had a nocturnal operation been possible, German AA guns would still have been a major threat since they were radar-controlled; night-fighters, fitted with radar but also directed by controllers on the ground, would equally have presented very serious danger.)

Brereton faced two real problems involving the transport aircraft. The first, and greater of the two, was the allocation of machines to the assaulting airborne formations. The second was the planning of fly-in routes that reduced as far as possible the danger from German anti-aircraft defences.

How many aircraft were available to Brereton and how many soldiers would those aeroplanes have to carry? To answer the second question first, there were 35,000 paratroopers and glider-borne troops to be conveyed to the Netherlands.[13] However, Brereton had available only enough aircraft to carry 16,500 men.[14] Therefore, only half of Browning's corps could be inserted in one lift. The manpower involved demanded no fewer than 3,790 transport aircraft, of which 2,495 would carry paratroopers and the other 1,295 would tow gliders. Combining all the resources of the USAAF's IX Troop Carrier Command and the RAF's Nos 38 and 46 Groups would not provide enough machines to carry the entire corps in a single lift.[15]

Landing the majority of I Airborne Corps on D Day would require two lifts, a fact that placed Brereton in a dilemma. The air officer commanding the RAF's No. 38 (Airborne Force) Group, Air Vice-Marshal Leslie Hollinghurst, was among the pioneers of airborne warfare and the first AOC of the group. Not one to remain at his desk, he chose to take part in operations, including flying in an Albemarle that dropped part of 22 Independent Parachute Company, the pathfinders of 6th Airborne Division, in Operation TONGA on the night of 5 June 1944.[16] Faced with Brereton's dilemma, the pragmatic Hollinghurst was prepared to countenance his airmen flying two missions on D Day with the first mission taking off in the pre-dawn darkness. However, his USAAF counterpart, Major General Paul L. Williams, commanding IX Troop Carrier Command, and Hollinghurst's senior for the operation, disagreed; the bulk of the transport fleet

Air Vice-Marshal Leslie Hollinghurst, a First World War fighter 'ace' and pioneer of airborne warfare, commanded No. 38 (Airborne Force) Group and was prepared to have his crews fly two missions on D Day. (*Taylor Library*)

was USAAF. Williams' rationale was that his command's aircraft strength had increased twofold in a matter of months with no commensurate increase in ground personnel, especially maintenance staff. He considered that, if two missions were flown on D Day, his ground crews would not be able to cope with the essential maintenance, plus battle-damage repair, in the turnaround time. Moreover, he opined, the airmen would suffer fatigue as a result of flying two missions. Of this reaction, Geoffrey Powell wrote:

> The advice was strangely out of character. Williams was known among both British and Americans for his general helpfulness and for his drive, and it was largely because of the respect in which the soldiers held him that they accepted what he had to say with little argument.[17]

Brereton decided that Williams' advice was sound and ordered that only one mission would be undertaken on D Day. The direct effect on 1st Airborne Division would be that its journey to Arnhem would be carried out over three days. Montgomery, on learning of this, immediately despatched his Brigadier General Staff (Operations), Brigadier David Belchem,[18] by air to Brereton's HQ to impress on him the importance of a second lift on D Day for 1st Airborne at Arnhem. Monty considered that Brereton, lacking the experience of ground combat to appreciate the adverse implications of a single lift to the Arnhem battle, had failed to recognise the difficulties that dropping Urquhart's division over three days would create. Belchem, who was deputy to Major General Francis de Guingand, had been the man who

Major General Paul Williams, commander of IX Troop Carrier Command USAAF and overall air commander for Operation MARKET, considered that two missions on D Day were not possible. (*NARA*)

had briefed the Field Marshal on Brereton's intentions, found the Airborne Army commander firm in his intention. As Powell suggested, it was probably too late anyway, and Brereton was sticking to his earlier resolution that there would be no change in plans once made. (Belchem was one of several officers, including Brigadier 'Bill' Williams, Monty's Intelligence 'guru', who had tried to persuade their commander not to proceed with MARKET GARDEN for reasons that we shall consider later.)

Thus was a major flaw formed in the plan for Arnhem from the very beginning. Further flaws were also present, and recognised by some of Montgomery's staff, as we shall see.

Although Hollinghurst had lost his argument for a second lift on D Day, he did not retire to his desk to ruminate. Instead, he inserted himself into the operation, maintaining direct control over his aircraft during the first lift; he did so in the air, from one of the Stirlings involved in the operation. Williams chose to exercise command from his command post at Eastcote in Middlesex.

Williams' IX Troop Carrier Command HQ was the location for a planning conference on the morning of 11 September. It was there that the routes to be used by the transport aircraft and glider tugs were decided and aircraft were allocated to each participating formation. In the division of transport resources in the air plan, the largest proportion went to 101st and the smallest to 1st. The reasons for that were logical: 101st had the first objective and the planners had to be certain that the southernmost bridges were seized so that XXX Corps' advance could maintain momentum. Urquhart, unhappy about the apportioning of aircraft, tried to persuade Browning to allocate more to 1st Airborne. Browning responded by pointing out that the priority in allocating transports had to be from 'bottom to top'. Even so, Urquhart was allocated 480 aircraft for D Day, a figure only forty fewer than 82nd, although more than 100 fewer than 101st. However, that was not the complete picture since Urquhart opted to take fewer infantry and more supporting arms than did either American commander. While Urquhart lifted a force slightly smaller than six battalions, both Gavin and Taylor dropped their nine parachute battalions on D Day. Urquhart took his field artillery on D Day while Browning chose to fly his own HQ in, using thirty-eight gliders. Had Urquhart left his artillery until D+1 and had Browning not chosen to deploy his own headquarters into the field, the aircraft and gliders thus freed would have been sufficient to allow all Urquhart's infantry to arrive on D Day. However, Urquhart's decision to include his artillery in the first lift was in line with British thinking that prioritised artillery over infantry on the basis that firepower saved lives.

Two routes were to be used by the aerial armadas and were described as the Northern and Southern routes. The former crossed over the occupied Netherlands, while the southern overflew Belgium; although the northern route was both shorter and simpler, the southern route was safer. Williams chose to use both; 1st Airborne and 82nd Airborne would take the northern route and 101st the southern. The paratroopers of 1st Airborne were flying from USAAF bases in Lincolnshire – Barkston Heath and Spanhoe – from whence 82nd Airborne would also depart; Urquhart's men were to be carried in 143 C-47s. However, 101st Airborne was flying from bases farther south in England while Urquhart's airlanding, or glider-borne, troops were departing from airfields in Lincolnshire and a group of airfields from Kent to the West Country,[19] their gliders towed by Stirlings, Halifaxes and Albemarles; in all, almost 500 aircraft carried 1st Airborne's paratroopers or towed its gliders.

In deciding the routes to be used, the planners also had to consider German anti-aircraft defences, not only at the target areas but also along the routes and, especially, crossing the coast. Plans were made to deploy RAF Bomber Command aircraft to raid the AA sites the night before D Day, followed by USAAF bombers of Eighth and Ninth Air Forces, and both British and US fighter-bombers. The locations of the various AA sites had been identified from aerial photographs taken by photo-reconnaissance aircraft. However, Hollinghurst was concerned that the concentration of AA guns around the Arnhem area (156 guns, of which forty-four were heavy), with mobile units nearby and AA barges on the river, presented a real danger to the transport aircraft *after* they had dropped their paratroopers or let go their gliders. The danger seemed to be greatest around Deelen airfield, seven miles north of Arnhem. This assessment contrasted considerably with an earlier report of AA defences for the aborted Operation COMET which suggested a lesser threat from the guns.

Geoffrey Powell commented that the source of the information on the increased gun defences was not known (but may have been the Dutch resistance) and goes on to note that, many years later, a map of the AA defences, dated 11 September 1944 and showing over 100 guns in the southern part of the city and south of the river, was given to Major General John Frost, as he had by then become. Although the bombing of the AA sites was planned, Hollinghurst recommended that DZs and LZs be chosen to avoid the danger.[20] Once again, Brereton's decree that when a decision had been made it could not be changed was felt.

Brereton was responsible for another decision that had a deleterious effect on the operation. He refused to countenance the C-47s double-towing gliders. He considered that IX Troop Carrier Command had not had sufficient training, partly because aircraft had been deployed in an intensive re-supply shuttle for the ground forces while others had been standing by for operations that had been cancelled. In this, Brereton had some justification, but the RAF airmen would have been willing and able to double-tow gliders. This was probably another example of 'one size fits all' by Brereton who was certainly risk-averse.

We have already noted that some of Montgomery's staff, including Bill Williams, had misgivings about 1sth Airborne's plan. Those concerns centred around the LZs and DZs and information from *Ultra* suggesting that two SS Panzer divisions were refitting close to Arnhem following the mauling they had received in Normandy. The armoured divisions were 9th *Hohenstaufen* and 10th *Frundsberg*, which formed II SS Panzerkorps, and were the major worry to Montgomery's Intelligence team. In the years since the war, the story of the two German armoured divisions has often been repeated and used as an argument against Montgomery. However, neither division was anywhere near full strength; each was about 3,000 strong and most of the tanks that had limped back from Normandy had been sent to workshops in Germany for repair and maintenance. Nonetheless, the soldiers were experienced, and other armoured vehicles were on hand in the area.

The presence of the panzer divisions had prompted Williams to make his appeal to Montgomery not to go ahead with the operation, in which he was supported by Colonel Oliver Poole, the staff officer in charge of plans, and by David Belchem. As already mentioned, Belchem was deputy to de Guingand, Montgomery's chief of staff. At this critical time, de Guingand was in hospital in England, although in telephone contact with 21 Army Group HQ. From his hospital bed, de Guingand telephoned his chief to express his 'fears that the proposed operation was too late, and that bad weather was likely and that the Germans might reinforce the target area'. Montgomery's reaction was to tell de Guingand that 'he was too far from the scene of action and was out of touch', in spite of the telephone connection provided by army group HQ.[21] It would appear that de Guingand would have been lobbying actively against MARKET GARDEN had he been in the HQ rather than hospital. After the war he wrote a note on the subject, outlining the reasons already given above and adding some other factors, including the restriction to one airlift on D Day, the poor weather and 'the enemy's powers of recuperation'. He wrote:

> We were, no doubt, influenced too much by the devastating defeat we had witnessed. Just as the enemy managed to produce forces to organise a defence at Arnhem, so do I believe he would have produced an answer to a single thrust into Westphalia as favoured by Montgomery. On the other hand, I consider that we might have held our bridgehead over the Neder Rijn if we had experienced really good weather … .[22]

At I Airborne Corps HQ Major Brian Urquhart, Browning's senior intelligence officer, had seen intelligence reports about German armour in the Arnhem area and became concerned and, on 12 September, requested oblique aerial photographs. When he received the photographs on the 15th, he was able to identify tanks in the vicinity of the LZs and DZs where 1st Airborne would be arriving. Browning's reaction was to dismiss the images and arrange for Urquhart to be sent on sick leave as a result of nervous exhaustion. There was suspicion of anything that came from the Dutch resistance which had earlier been infiltrated by the Germans, but the photographs were strong evidence of *some* German armour in areas that threatened the operation.

Powell referred to 'one puzzling aspect of these intelligence summaries' issued by Browning's HQ. That HQ had earlier drawn up an intelligence summary for Operation COMET which mentioned specifically a panzer division refitting north of Arnhem as well as SS training units in the Nijmegen area and about a division's worth of infantry in the operational area. He suggests that 'It is hard to find an explanation for this discrepancy'. He does, however, proffer some contributing factors for intelligence failures, such as the wide separation between planning teams and the short time involved in planning the operation. On the continent three HQs – SHAEF, 21 Army Group and Second Army – were involved while another two in England – First Allied Airborne Army and I Airborne Corps – had their parts to play. Several air force HQs were also contributing – not only those of Williams and Hollinghurst, but Bomber Command and the rump of Fighter Command (Air Defence of Great Britain) in the UK, as well as 2 TAF and Ninth Air Force.

Brereton's HQ was only receiving a small amount of *Ultra* intelligence, possibly because it was so new, but one of his staff, Wing Commander Asher Lee, found evidence of German tanks at Arnhem and, with access to *Ultra* elsewhere, consulted such files. As Powell records:

> Alarmed by what he found, Asher Lee took the information to Brereton, who told him to fly over to see Twenty-First Army Group. Asher Lee did so, but he seems to have been unable to make contact with anyone of adequate authority, and there the matter seems to have rested.[23]

The other concern felt by Monty's staff, including Williams, was caused by the locations of 1st Airborne Division's LZs and DZs at Arnhem. So critical was the element of surprise that dropping or landing airborne soldiers as close as possible to their objectives was imperative. Instead, the division's assigned area was eight miles from Arnhem's bridges and to the west of the city: LZs L and S were north of the Arnhem-Utrecht railway line; DZ Y was on Ginkel Heath; DZ and LZ X and LZ Z were on Renkum Heath, south of the railway. DZ K, south of Arnhem, would be used for the drop of the Polish brigade on D plus 3. Since there would be no second lift on D Day, elements of Urquhart's 1 Airlanding Brigade would have to secure and hold the DZs and LZs until the second day, reducing significantly the number of soldiers who could be deployed to seize and hold the divisional objectives.

The selection of DZs and LZs distant from the objectives was due to the RAF fears of heavy anti-aircraft defences in the area and, especially, around Deelen airfield, over which the turning transports and tugs would have to fly. However, not only was the intelligence on the AA guns wrong, but bombing raids were planned for the night of the 16th/17th and the morning of the 17th to suppress those defences. Thus, holding fast to Brereton's principle that plans would not be changed, Hollinghurst's fears led to those far-flung DZs and LZs.

The seven days of planning were crammed with activity but that was often activity not co-ordinated fully between planning teams. Nor did Montgomery have his eyes concentrated on the plans and the planners. Operation MARKET GARDEN was unique in that Monty allowed the planning to be conducted outside his HQ. It was also unique in being a plan of such boldness as to be completely untypical of him. As Richard Mead writes:

> He was generally meticulous in his preparation, refusing to move until he was absolutely ready, with the odds stacked in his favour. On this occasion, blinded by his determination to seize the opportunity to pursue his Northern Thrust strategy, for the first and only time he accepted a plan which had not been endorsed by his staff, but was firmly in the hands of others.[24]

And so, Operation MARKET GARDEN was launched on the morning of 17 September 1944. The first actions were those of airmen, bomber crews of the RAF followed by men of the USAAF.

Chapter Seven

On the night of 16/17 September, Lancasters and Mosquitoes of Nos 1, 3 and 8 Groups carried out missions to support Operation MARKET GARDEN. A force of 200 Lancasters and twenty-three Mosquitoes struck at airfields at Hopsten, Leeuwarden, Steenwijk and Rheine while fifty-four Lancasters and five Mosquitoes of Nos 3 and 8 Groups targeted a major AA position at Moerdijk. Two Lancasters were lost in the second mission. The strike on airfields was made by 1 Group and that on the AA defences by 3 Group. Each operation was led by 8 Group aircraft, that group being Bomber Command's Pathfinder Force. However, the AA position was not knocked out, although there were near misses and the approach road was cut.[1] All the airfields attacked in the first mission suffered severe damage to their runways, most of which 'were well cratered'; one of those airfields was home to some of the new German Me 262 jet fighters.[2] In addition, Bomber Command put up fourteen RCM (radio counter-measures) sorties, some of which may have supported the forthcoming Operation MARKET GARDEN.[3] The crews of the two Lancasters downed in the Moerdijk mission were thus the first casualties of MARKET GARDEN.

Bomber Command's missions were followed by attacks by bombers of the US Eighth and Ninth Air Forces, the former under the command of Major General Jimmy Doolittle, who had led the raid on Tokyo from the aircraft carrier USS *Hornet* in April 1942. Doolittle launched 821 B-17 Flying Fortresses which bombed 117 AA positions and a fifth airfield with 3,139 tons of bombs. The B-17s were escorted by 153 P-51 Mustang fighters but met no fighter opposition; the runways hit by the RAF during the night were so damaged that aircraft could not take off. Attacks on the AA positions were assessed as '43 good, 24 fair and 50 poor'. However, this was not the end of the air forces' contributions as 2 TAF attacked military barracks at Nijmegen, Cleve, Arnhem and Ede and 212 aircraft of Ninth Air Force, Brereton's former command, attacked the AA positions again. Ede barracks was close to 4 Parachute Brigade's DZ.[4] Powell also suggests that RAF Lancasters and Mosquitoes hit three coast batteries around Walcheren Island in the Scheldt estuary. This is not supported by RAF records: Middlebrook and Everitt note that the Walcheren operation was on the night of the 18th but had to be aborted by the Master Bomber after 8 Group's Mosquitoes had been unable to mark the target 'in poor weather conditions'. On the night of 17/18 September 241 aircraft had made diversionary sweeps to the Dutch coast and farther inland to draw Luftwaffe fighters away from southern Holland but the lure did not work, or perhaps there were no fighters able to react.[5]

As the USAAF bombers carried out their operations, the men who were to take part in the first drop were making their final preparations before boarding the 1,534 transport aircraft and 491 gliders that would carry them to Holland. Never before had such a huge assembly of transport aircraft been seen. The C-47s, Albemarles, Halifaxes and Stirlings with the Hadrian, Hamilcar and Horsa gliders, lifted off from two dozen airfields in England to make rendezvous at rallying points off the east coast from whence they formed into the two columns that would take either of the designated fly-in routes. Both the British 1st Airborne and the US 82nd Airborne followed the Northern route, overflying the offshore island of Schouwen-Duiveland in the province of Zeeland, while 101st Airborne used the Southern route which passed south of Antwerp before turning to the north-east in the direction of Eindhoven. Urquhart's and Gavin's formations would separate over 's-Hertogenbosch.

With a favourable weather forecast, at 1900 hours on Saturday 16 September Brereton made the decision to 'go'. H Hour was to be 1300 hours European time on the Sunday. The weather was favourable, as had been forecast, and ground mist had burned away by 0900 hours. As more and more aircraft took off and made for their rallying points, the sky seemed to be full of aeroplanes and the roar of their engines was deafening. At heights from 1,500 feet upwards they headed to the east coast, and thence to their destinations. For those on the ground looking up it was a sight never to be forgotten. It impressed even those airborne soldiers watching from their camps and who were due to fly on the Monday or Tuesday.

The flight was largely without incident as P-38 Lightnings, P-47 Thunderbolts and P-51 Mustangs of Eighth Air Force with Mosquitoes, Spitfires and Tempests of the Air Defence of Great Britain[6] flew escort sorties or engaged German AA defences. Only fifteen Luftwaffe fighters, Focke Wulf 190s, engaged any of the fighters; they met USAAF aircraft near Wesel where seven were shot down for the loss of a single American fighter. In all, the best part of 1,000 Allied fighters or fighter-bombers were engaged in shepherding the air armada across the sea. Claude Smith notes that 'The weather over England was far from ideal with the cloud base ranged from 500 feet to 2,000 feet, and before the English coast was reached twenty-three gliders had parted from their tugs.'[7]

Below, air-sea-rescue launches awaited the call to assist downed machines while marker boats also helped the aircrews maintain formation. As Smith notes, a small number of gliders cast off prematurely, generally due to faulty tow ropes, but there were few casualties; most of the passengers were taken back to their bases to join the second lift on the Monday. However, one Horsa broke up in flight not long after taking off and those aboard, half of No. 1 Platoon, 9 Field Company RE, died as a result; Smith notes that this was 'the unit which had provided the men for the ill-fated Freshman operation'.[8] Others crashed in the sea, but the soldiers were picked up by the rescue boats. Two landed close to the Dutch coast; one was carrying a platoon of 7th King's Own Scottish Borderers, who reached the shore but were captured following a short skirmish. The other carried some of Browning's Corps HQ and ditched close to a coast artillery battery manned by Russian conscripts who opened fire but kept missing deliberately; the men from the glider were picked up by a rescue boat after dark.

At 1240 hours the pathfinders of 21 Independent Parachute Company were the first to land at Arnhem, dropping from Stirlings of Nos 190 and 620 Squadrons. The tasks of the 186 pathfinders were to secure the DZs and LZs, set up Eureka homing beacons to guide the air armada to the correct zones, mark the ground with white indicator panels and prepare smoke markers. Twenty minutes later, the first gliders carrying most of 1 Airlanding Brigade began swooping down to LZ S. Only nineteen of the 153 gliders bound for LZ S failed to arrive. At 1319 the gliders for LZ Z began arriving, carrying Urquhart's HQ as well as divisional troops, including the jeeps and Polsten guns of 1 Airborne Reconnaissance Squadron, two batteries of 1st Airlanding Light Regiment and vehicles and anti-tank guns of 1 Parachute Brigade. Of 167 gliders destined for LZ Z, only seventeen failed to arrive.

There was only desultory opposition to the landings, although 21 Platoon of 2nd South Staffordshires had an unpleasant experience when they crashed almost on a German machine-gun position. As the Germans were slow to react, most of 2nd South Staffords were out of the glider before the gunners opened fire; two South Staffords were killed and seven wounded before the gun was knocked out. Other than those incidents, most disembarkation was carried out without problems. In all twelve men were lost to crashes or collisions. Two of the large Hamilcar gliders, carrying 17-pounder anti-tank guns, overturned with fatal results when their wheels dug into soft ground.[9] Both pilots and co-pilots were killed and both weapons were lost.[10]

The first of almost 2,300 men of 1 Parachute Brigade and parachute-trained personnel of divisional troops, including men of Major Freddie Gough's 1 Airborne Reconnaissance Squadron, began their descents over DZ X at

1350 hours. Heavy loads meant hard landings with several injuries, including broken legs, but such casualties had been anticipated. Also anticipated was the danger of being hit by someone else, or something else, coming down and upward observation had to be maintained; that had also been the case with the glider-borne personnel.

With 1 Parachute Brigade on the ground the first lift was complete. All had gone smoothly and seemed to augur well for the divisional operation. The airlanding troops, under Brigadier 'Pip' Hicks, began their task of securing the DZs and LZs for the next day while the parachute troops, including the Recce Squadron, made ready for the advance into Arnhem. Wolfheze village was cleared of enemy troops by the South Staffords who also began creating a defensive screen around the north-eastern sector of LZ S at Reyerscamp; two companies of the battalion had been assigned to the second lift. Meanwhile 1st Border, under command of Major Cousens since the glider carrying the CO had been one of those that cast off over England, was also in action. The task for 1st Border was to secure both DZ X and LZ Y. In doing so, the battalion's D Company liberated Heelsum, a village on the southern rim of the zones, following a brief skirmish with some German soldiers. C Company moved to Renkum to establish positions overlooking the main road to Arnhem and had a brief skirmish before setting up positions.

A Reconnaissance Squadron jeep destroyed in the ambush at Wolfheze.. (*IWM BU4132*)

The Memorial on Ginkel Heath, one of the landing zones for 1st Airborne Division on D Day. (*David R. Orr*)

Hicks' other battalion, 7th King's Own Scottish Borderers, were on their way to LZ Y, at Ginkel Heath, where 4 Parachute Brigade was due to drop the following day. The KOSB met more Germans than did the other battalions. Having set up positions on the main Arnhem-Ede road, the Amsterdamseweg, a platoon of A Company ambushed some Dutch SS troops who had been ordered to counter-attack the landing zones. The SS vehicles were shot up and heavy casualties inflicted on the SS men who fled when their commander was killed. For 1 Airlanding Brigade the night was to be generally quiet.

Meanwhile Urquhart was discovering the first frictions of the plan as he tried to keep in contact with the advance towards Arnhem of 1 Parachute Brigade and 1 Airborne Reconnaissance Squadron. The signallers in his HQ 'were having difficulty in raising anyone at all on their radios'. Urquhart, out of touch with his brigades and units and 1 Airborne Corps HQ as well as the US airborne divisional HQs, decided to make for Arnhem in a jeep with a signaller perched in the back, trying to make contact with any of the other elements of the division. After driving around for a time, he took the centre axis into Arnhem, that followed by 3rd Parachute Battalion and met Lathbury, commander of 1 Parachute Brigade. Lathbury had suffered similar problems and could not contact divisional HQ, nor did he have anything but intermittent contact with his own battalions. As the pair discussed their woes a mortar round struck Urquhart's jeep, wounding his signaller. He also realised that the Germans were between his position and his HQ and so decided to stay with Lathbury, 'where he could at least bring some influence to bear upon what was the vital section of the battle'.[11]

Whatever he believed, Urquhart's influence was restricted severely by his circumstances. He would have wielded more effective influence had he opposed the plan for landings so far from the objective. Dempsey believed that 'the distance of the DZs from the bridge was of course fatal'.[12] Nor was Dempsey impressed by Urquhart. Writing to the official historian in 1962, Dempsey stated that: 'It would, I am sure, be the opinion of all those who know the facts that Urquhart was the most vocal, though not the most able, of the divisional commanders.' This was not an opinion in hindsight. In an earlier War Office account, Dempsey is quoted:

> The primary reason was inept planning by 1 Airborne Division, loss of control by Divisional HQ, and the failure of their communications. They were never in the battle as a formation. Let me make it clear that the troops fought magnificently, and could not have done better individually. … I had 1 Airborne Div under my command in Sicily and Arnhem, and 6 Airborne Div in Normandy and the Rhine. The latter were better at the top. There was no comparison between the two divs in that respect.[13]

It is worth remembering that Dempsey had been responsible for more airborne operations than most of the airborne commanders. As his biographer notes, he 'had planned and launched more airborne operations than either'[14] Brereton or Browning, and he was also a 'huge admirer of Airborne Forces'.[15] Dempsey believed that a change of plan, as a result of a shortage of aircraft, proved fatal to the operation. When he discussed the MARKET plan with Browning on the 14th the intention had been 'to put one brigade down at Elst on the first day, and to land the other two brigades north of the river. But the lack of sufficient aircraft led to a change of plan which, despite Brereton's enjoinder to the contrary, combined with 'the failure to secure Elst plus the attempt to hold the DZ and LZ were fatal to the plan'.[16]

Urquhart was now going to be out of contact with most of his division, unable to influence or control the battle. Ronald Lewin, in his study of Montgomery as military commander, posed the pertinent question: 'How did it happen that a total of 10,095 men, 92 guns, over 500 jeeps, 300 motorcycles and 400 trailers – the bulk of what came down at Arnhem – could only deliver at the *point d'appui*, the Rhine bridge, about 700 men?' His answer was that Montgomery had asked too much, and that his strategic concept, while ambitious, had too many flaws. Eisenhower also came in for criticism for failing to provide the promised logistical support and for the failure of First US Army's supporting operation (which we shall look at in the light of GARDEN and XXX Corps).[17]

Lewin also commented on Urquhart's role stating that he, an infantry brigadier, 'had no notion – how could he have? – of how an airborne attack should be conducted'. He recorded that Dempsey would have preferred to have had Gale in Urquhart's place. Gale had commanded 6th Airborne Division in Normandy and believed 'that one should aim for a *coup de main* on the objective'. Urquhart's objective was Arnhem bridge, but he was landing his division miles away. Dempsey believed that Gale would not have accepted the RAF advice and would have landed at the bridge.[18]

The *Official History* is blunt about Urquhart:

It was certainly unwise … to leave headquarters in order to find out how the advance was proceeding; by being trapped in the fighting area he lost control for a vital thirty-six hours. It is moreover hard to find any real excuse for the fact that communications, both within the 1st Division at Arnhem and with I Airborne Corps or with 83 Group and Second Army, proved to be wholly inadequate. Good communications are of the first importance in airborne operations and the British airborne division had surely been long enough preparing for action to make certain of its equipment.[19]

How had the other formations involved in MARKET fared? Both 82nd and 101st Airborne Divisions landed at much the same time as their British counterparts, the main forces following their pathfinders in for textbook drops with very few casualties.

Since 101st's objectives in the southern sector were dispersed considerably, Major General Maxwell Taylor decided to land his initial assault force, of 6,809 men, in a central location from which his division's elements would move towards their specific objectives. Landing on DZ B, 502nd Parachute Infantry Regiment met no opposition and 1/502 was quickly en route for St Oedenrode where the Dommel bridge was soon in their hands following a brief skirmish. Although the road bridge at Best was seized by Company H of 3/502, the Americans were counter-attacked by *Kampfgruppe* Rink that evening but the remainder of 3/502 reinforced Company H and the bridge was firmly in US hands next morning. Taylor's tactical command HQ had also landed with 502 PIR and his command post was established in Son. His glider force followed an hour behind the paratroopers.[20]

DZ C saw 506 PIR land unopposed and set out quickly for the bridges over the Wilhelmina canal close to Son, but two of the three had already been demolished and Fallschirmjäger held the third bridge long enough to allow it to be demolished. However, the paratroopers of 506 PIR were able to cross the canal and establish positions south of it, some four miles north of Eindhoven. Although the landings of 501 PIR to either side of Veghel were not accurate, the regiment was quickly in possession of its objectives, four bridges over the Aa river and the Willemsvaart canal. Engineers put a second bridge across the canal. There was only light and disorganised resistance to the regiment.[21]

The 'Screaming Eagles'' role in MARKET had begun well, in marked contrast to that of Urquhart's 1st Airborne Division. In between those two formations, in the Nijmegen sector, Brigadier General James Gavin's 82nd Airborne Division landed almost 7,500 paratroopers and glider infantry (but only 209 of the latter) at DZ and LZs N, O and T. From DZ O, near Overasselt, 504 PIR advanced to seize crossings over the Maas-Waal canal and the eastern side of the Grave bridge from the Heuman direction. One company of 2/504 landed in DZ O-1, just west of the Grave bridge, while the remainder of the battalion dropped on DZ O and marched to the bridge. The battalion was fortunate in that, although the bridge had been prepared for demolition, a main fuse had been found to be faulty that day and two soldiers had gone to obtain a new one, leaving one member of the demolition party at the bridge. That man failed to set off the charges himself and the bridge was soon in 2/504's hands, the few defenders having been overcome in a short engagement. As well as the bridge at Grave, 504 was also charged with taking the west sides of four other bridges along the canal, co-operating with other elements of Gavin's division from the other side. Of those bridges, the southernmost one was captured, those north of Malden and Hatert were demolished by the enemy and the final one was taken, although damaged, next day.[22]

Gavin's other two regiments, 505th and 508th, were also down with the former landing in two zones around Groesbeek before establishing a defensive perimeter facing south-east towards the Reichswald. Along the Maas-Waal canal 505 had linked with 504. Meanwhile, 508 had dropped in DZ T, north-east of Groesbeek, to seize the Groesbeek Heights to the west of Berg-en-Dal. The Heights dominated the landscape in the area and would also be the location for Browning's I Corps HQ, which came in when the area had been secured by 508. The HQ included 105 personnel who travelled in thirty-eight gliders (thirty-two Horsas and six Hadrians), of which twenty-eight arrived safely. Those gliders could have carried either an anti-tank unit or the two companies of the South Staffords who had been left behind to await the second lift.

By the end of D Day, the bulk of the three airborne divisions was on the ground and the first phase of MARKET was complete. The ground element,

GARDEN, was also underway. For XXX Corps, that meant an advance along sixty-four miles of road by a force that included about 20,000 vehicles. However, there was only one road and some of it ran above the level of the surrounding countryside, which was polder land. The first 'leap' to be covered in the breakout was one of those stretches raised between four and six feet above the countryside. To make matters worse, deep drainage ditches on either side would funnel vehicles into ideal ambush areas for anti-tank guns, for which they would be perfect targets. Much of the road ran through heavily wooded areas and it was narrow, varying from twenty- to forty-feet wide, the latter close to Arnhem. The road surface was either tarmac or concrete, that darling of 1930s engineers, with parts of the stretch from Nijmegen to Arnhem being of compressed cinders – hardly suitable for heavy tracked vehicles. From Grave to Nijmegen, vehicles on the road would be overlooked from the Groesbeek Heights, part of the rationale for seizing the feature.

Horrocks was unable to set an accurate H hour for XXX Corps to cross its start line, the Meuse-Escaut canal, since this depended on the air armada. However, when the airborne divisions appeared overhead, he gave the order to advance at 1435 hours. Although he was aware of the many problems, he 'was confident that we would win through. The troops were in great heart. I had an experienced and very able staff, and the end of the war seemed to be

Two armourers load 60lb high-explosive rockets onto a Typhoon while a third checks the cannon ammunition. The unguided rockets had a tremendous psychological effect that far outweighed their physical effect on enemy armour. (*Public domain*)

approaching rapidly.'[23] One qualm that he did have was that the operation was starting on a Sunday and 'no assault or attack in which I had taken part during the war which started on a Sunday had ever been completely successful'.[24]

At 1400 the artillery opened fire: 350 guns began their counter-battery programme and the Irish Guards Group[25] tanks moved into position, ready to cross the start line. Lieutenant Keith Heathcote of No. 3 Squadron ordered 'Driver, advance' and Second Army's part in the operation was underway. Artillery fire pounded the terrain 100 yards ahead of Heathcote's tank in a rolling bombardment and in front of the gunfire 'an endless stream of RAF Typhoon fighters [were] pouring their rockets into the German defences'.[26]

Hardly had the Guards' Shermans moved off than nine were knocked out in rapid succession by German anti-tank gunners who were dealt with by Typhoons. The advance continued but met further opposition from enemy troops using both *Panzerfauste* and 76mm guns, but the Typhoons were again on call and the road was cleared, the artillery also lending their support. A German self-propelled gun was knocked out by Sergeant Cowan's Sherman Firefly and the gunners not only surrendered but persuaded another gun team to join them; both groups then happily pointed out further German positions which were dealt with either by artillery or the Typhoons.[27] Valkenswaard, seven miles from the start line, was reached at 1930, just as light was fading; more enemy personnel came in to surrender. There the advance stopped, although Eindhoven was but another six miles distant. The Germans had begun counter-attacking 'the hinges of our breakthrough' but 50th (Northumbrian) Division was dealing with those attacks. Casualties had been lighter than might have been anticipated.

An unexpected obstacle was reported at Valkenswaard: the bridge at Son had been blown and engineers would have to be called forward. In twelve hours, the sappers built a 190-feet-long Class 40 Bailey bridge which would allow the advance to continue, but not until Tuesday morning.

And so D Day had ended. While XXX Corps was at the heart of the GARDEN thrust, VIII Corps on its right and XII Corps on its left were to protect Horrocks' flanks by advancing to either side. However, VIII Corps, which had been 'grounded', was still having supply problems and at the beginning of the advance could only maintain a single battalion forward; it was to advance to Helmond, east of Eindhoven. XII Corps was to seize bridgeheads across the Meuse-Escaut canal and then protect XXX Corps' flank by extending its own positions to the Maas.[28]

Chapter Eight

Brigadier Seán Hackett,* commander of 4 Parachute Brigade and a man who had already seen much active service, was unimpressed by the way in which the airborne planners made their plans. He shared this concern with the commander of 1 Polish Independent Parachute Brigade, Major General Stanisław Sosabowski, who had famously commented on the COMET plan, 'But the Germans, General, the Germans.' Maurice Tugwell, who jumped with 6th Airborne in Operation VARSITY, wrote of Brereton's staff

> producing plans that were apt to be somewhat remote from the harsher realities of airborne soldiering. Every factor that could affect an operation was taken into account except, it would seem, the German army. Air Power enthusiasts who turn their attention to airborne warfare are inclined to think of these actions in terms of bombing missions – get the force to the target area and set it down accurately and intact and success is assured.[1]

Likewise, Powell quotes Hackett describing the planning, commenting that it was set up as a 'sort of "airborne picnic"', to which the enemy were added 'as salt and pepper to taste'.[2] We shall learn more of Hackett and his brigade in the next chapter.

The speed with which the Allied armies had powered across France after the closing of the Falaise Gap seemed to have indicated a breakdown in the German armies, both in cohesion and morale. That success encouraged Allied generals to believe that the war might be ended by Christmas, or even earlier. In their minds the once mighty German army had become but a shadow of its former self. In the race across France, commanders had been conscious of the German capacity for improvisation, for creating ad hoc *Kampfgruppen*,

---

* Hackett, who was Irish-Australian, used the Gaelic version of his first name, John. Often incorrectly written 'Sean' and pronounced 'Shan', it is as shown here and pronounced 'Shaun'. Sean, pronounced 'Shan', is Gaelic for 'old'.

Paratroopers in a training balloon in the UK: paradoxically, 4 Parachute Brigade recorded that more men refused to jump from a balloon than from an aircraft. (*Airborne Archive*)

or battlegroups, that could fight as effectively as a well-established unit or formation. However, the speed of the Allied advance had denied the Germans the opportunity to create such groups. Inevitably, the Allied momentum had decreased, as had the mass of forward formations, as the logistical tail back to Normandy was stretched almost to breaking point and General Lee's COMZ HQ continued paying more attention to its own comfort than to the needs of the advancing armies.

A certain degree of what might be termed complacency seems to have crept in at the higher levels. It was almost as if the high command was congratulating itself on having gained the upper hand on the enemy and believed that the Germans were finished. Indeed, even Dempsey, an astute commander, told officers of the Sherwood Rangers Yeomanry that 'there was almost nothing to oppose us once we reached Germany'.[3] Stuart Hills, then a troop leader, continued: 'Some believed this kind of guff from on high, but not many. We had seen how the German Army had defended France and Belgium, and it seemed very unlikely that their resistance would suddenly disintegrate when they were defending their own homeland.[4]

The German retreat had been ended by the determination and inspiring energy of Lieutenant General Kurt Chill, commander of 85th Division, 'an audacious and prescient commander',[5] who, appreciating that the only way to avoid complete collapse was to form a solid defensive line, ordered what was left of his division, together with individuals and units from other formations, to establish such a line on the Albert canal. There Chill's *Kampfgruppe* was reinforced by Fallschirmjäger from Generaloberst Kurt Student's First Parachute Army, which was then being created.[6] Before long a strong line had been created and bridges prepared for demolition. Second Army encountered that line on 6 September when Guards Armoured Division, in the van of XXX Corps, was ordered to capture two bridges over the canal. Although one bridge was destroyed, the second was taken and a bridgehead, albeit small, established. On the 9th Dempsey recorded that 'It is clear that the enemy is bringing up all the reinforcements he can lay hands on for the defence of the Albert Canal, and that he appreciates the importance of the area Arnhem-Nijmegen.' Since it appeared to Dempsey that the Germans were determined to hold that area, he thus deemed unlikely 'any question of an advance to the

Fallschirmjäger leaving Mook to counter the Allied attack. A shortage of transport led to wheelbarrows and stolen bicycles being pressed into service. (*Airborne Archive*)

North-East'. Moreover, since the supply situation meant that Second Army would not be in a position 'to fight a real battle for perhaps ten days or a fortnight, he questioned whether it would be right 'to direct Second Army to Arnhem, or would it be better to hold a LEFT flank along the Albert Canal and strike due East towards Cologne in conjunction with First Army?'[7]

What was the German situation and what were the German commanders thinking? We have already seen that Chill had acted quickly to establish a blocking line and that Kurt Student's soldiers had joined the defence. Although Student's formation had the impressive title of 'army' it was not composed of veteran paratroopers, but of disparate units gathered to create a defence, including some who happened to have been trained as paratroopers. On 4 September Student had been telephoned by Jodl, OKW's chief of staff, and told to gather all available units together to build a new front on the Albert canal: 'This front is to be held at all costs!'[8] As Robert Kershaw comments:

> the German penchant for organisation and improvisation, even in the face of disaster, coupled with a professionally effective staff network, began to make itself felt. *General der Flieger* Friedrich Christiansen, the Wehrmacht Supreme Commander of the Netherlands, filled the immediate vacuum by pushing a thin security screen made up of Luftwaffe fortress personnel forward to the Albert canal.[9]

On 6 September Allied intelligence decrypted an order from Hitler that subordinated First Parachute Army to Army Group B. Student's army was to include

> all Parachute Army formations from the Reich, including 5th, 6th and 7th Parachute Divisions, which were to be brought up to strength by 1st [Luftwaffe] Training Division; LXXXVIII Corps with 719th and 344th Infantry Divisions; battle groups from the Netherlands formed from SS training units and Training Regiment Göring; and ten Flak battalions equipped with heavy anti-tank guns and short-range weapons.[10]

By the 9th Second Army intelligence was aware of the deployment of units and formations along the Albert canal, including elements of four infantry divisions (136th, 119th, 347th and 176th), two companies of 2nd Fallschirmjäger Regiment, 51st and 53rd Luftwaffe Regiments and 6th Fallschirmjäger Regiment. Stiffening resistance along the waterway was preventing the enlargement of Second Army's bridgeheads across the canal.[11]

Almost as Jodl gave Student the order to gather forces to create a new line on the Albert canal, the advancing Allies were coming to a stop, having all but outrun their logistical supply lines. Thus, they granted the Germans a breathing space. It was a short breathing space, but it was enough, even though the Germans had no idea how difficult the Allied supply situation had really become. Field Marshal Walter Model, commander of Army Group B, was lunching with his staff in Oosterbeek, near Arnhem, when one officer spotted 'bombers'. He had seen the transport aircraft bringing 1st Airborne Division to nearby Arnhem, and also to Oosterbeek. To avoid being captured by British paratroopers, Model and his staff made a hasty departure in the direction of SS *Obergruppenführer* Bittrich's II SS Panzerkorps HQ at Zutphen, less than thirty miles north-east of Arnhem.[12] Although taken completely by surprise, Model was soon issuing orders to deal with the Allied attack, although, as Powell recounts, he did waste time 'relating to [Bittrich] the details of his personal escape from the British assault'.[13] As more information became available, including the news that the British had failed to seize Arnhem bridge, Model turned his attention southwards, and especially to the Nijmegen-Eindhoven sector which he had quickly identified as the critical area. Model was possibly the best general that the Germans could have had in situ, as Horrocks explained:

> It was also particularly unfortunate that Model should have had a grandstand view of the 1st Airborne drop, because he was thus able to take immediate steps to deal with this unexpected situation. He was used to plugging gaps as he had come from the eastern front, so, where a less experienced commander might have panicked, Model did nothing of the sort. He made a first-class appreciation of the situation and started active counter-measures at once.[14]

Moreover, the two armoured divisions of II SS Panzerkorps had been trained specifically to deal with airborne assaults. That the surviving elements of both divisions were not concentrated was not a problem, since their anti-airborne role meant that this was sound operational practice as those elements formed quick-reaction groups.

Student was another man placed ideally for such a situation. Among the pioneers of airborne operations, he was also taken by surprise but reacted as the thorough professional he was. He also had an unexpected stroke of luck. 'Two hours after the air armada first appeared in the skies over Holland, the Allied operation order for MARKET GARDEN was on my desk.' Contrary to orders, the plans had been carried by an American officer whose glider had

Field Marshal Otto Moritz Walther Model. The son of a music teacher, he joined the army, served during the First World War and was retained in the small force permitted to Germany between the wars. An outstanding commander in the Second World War, he was more than a match for First Allied Airborne Army's Lewis H. Brereton. (*Taylor Library*)

been shot down and, according to Student, were recovered from his body.[15] Badsey suggests that the glider was one that was 'almost certainly missing from Browning's headquarters'.[16]

Bittrich's armour was ordered to deal with the British forces at Arnhem and secure the important bridges at Nijmegen. Bittrich had anticipated the nature of Model's orders since he already knew of the British landings and that Nijmegen and Arnhem were the enemy's main objectives. Arnhem was assigned to 9th SS Panzer Division *Hohenstaufen* and Nijmegen to 10th SS Panzer Division *Frundsberg*. Neither formation was at full strength: both were effectively *Kampfgruppen* with minimal armour, most of the tanks and other AFVs that had made it from Normandy having been loaded onto railway flats for the journey back to workshops. Hohenstaufen, preparing to move to Siegen in Germany to refit and re-form, had already handed much of its heavy equipment over to Frundsberg. However, the personnel were still near Arnhem, Model having ordered that the fighting element be last to depart for Siegen. Both Kampfgruppen were ready for action very quickly; Hohenstaufen was the smaller, much of its equipment having gone to Frundsberg, and

Obergruppenführer Wilhelm Bittrich. A highly-decorated SS officer, and veteran of the First World War, he was given command of II SS Panzerkorps in July 1944 and was overseeing its re-organisation in the Arnhem area when the first Allied troops dropped near his HQ. (*Taylor Library*)

numbered about 2,500 soldiers, mostly committed to moving on foot or by bicycle. However, its acting commander, *Obersturmbannführer* Walter Harzer, had turned a Nelsonian eye to some of Model's orders and held on to a number of Panther tanks.

Other elements of the German defence included an SS depot battalion, an SS NCOs' school and an SS *panzergrenadier* training and depot battalion, the last-noted under *Sturmbannführer* Josef 'Sepp' Krafft who had alerted his men for action following the air attacks on the morning of D Day. Thus, three-quarters of an hour after the gliders began arriving, he had deployed a company to attack the LZ and sent the remainder of his force to take up positions on the line of the Oosterbeek-Arnhem road, since he realised that the attackers were making for the Arnhem bridges. It was Krafft's men who attacked the LZ and ambushed Freddie Gough's Reconnaissance Squadron along the railway line and who also inflicted delays on 1 Parachute Brigade's battalions. Yet the men Krafft commanded, about 435 including thirteen officers and seventy-three NCOs, were only half-trained with the majority in their late teens 'and a high proportion … unfit'.[17] The delay inflicted by Krafft's force allowed Kampfgruppe Hohenstaufen to reach Arnhem in time to stop the progress of 1st and 3rd Parachute Battalions. Krafft agreed with Student's later assessment that 1 Parachute Brigade 'lost too much time whilst overcoming the resistance by weak German garrison and units of the Luftwaffe'.[18]

Other major elements of the defences included 719th Infantry Division, its high number indicating that it was not a first-line formation. It had spent its time since formation in 1941 on coast defence duties until becoming part of Student's new army, as did 176th Division, a training and replacement formation made up of convalescent soldiers and known as the '*kranken* division' (sick division). A further division that joined Student's command was 347th, a fortress formation that had been deployed

General die Infanterie Hans von Tettau. His Kampfgruppe attacked the airborne forces from the west. Tettau, who served on the Eastern Front in 1945, died in Mönchengladbach in the then Federal German Republic on 30 January 1956, aged 67. (*Public domain*)

in Normandy and had suffered considerable loss. Sometimes known as von Tettau's Division, Kampfgruppe von Tettau was under command of Lieutenant General Hans von Tettau, the commander of training in the Netherlands. Tettau proved a capable commander, able to make a cohesive command from disparate units; he had commanded an infantry division on the Eastern Front and was descended from a Dutch general in the army of King William in Ireland in 1690.[19] His 'new' command included Luftwaffe and artillery units deployed as infantry.

In drawing together a defence force at such short notice, Model's command included more than a dozen divisions from the army, the Luftwaffe and the SS, as well as diverse units such as the Luftwaffe 6th Penal Battalion which proved ineffective (recently moved from the Italian front, it arrived clad in tropical uniforms), a naval manning unit (*Schiffstammabteilung* 10) and a Luftwaffe *fliegerhorst*, a battalion of ground crew. The last two units proved as ineffective as the penal battalion and could be used only in a support role since they lacked training in infantry tactics.

Not all of those units and formations went into action on D Day, but they were drawn together very quickly, emphasising Kershaw's comment about the German 'penchant for organisation and improvisation'. Hackett, commander of 4 Parachute Brigade, which was yet to arrive, emphasised that particular German attribute:

> I had abundant experience myself, from the other side, of the high competence of German command and the responsiveness of the machine it handled, none more vividly than what happened in Operation MARKET GARDEN … . Some of our own commanders and staff, who may have had less first-hand experience of fighting Germans than others, thought that since defences were weak in the area around Arnhem we in the British First Airborne Division could expect to seize fairly easily a bridgehead across the lower Rhine there, and hold it for long enough for Allied ground troops to get up to us. Older hands, who had seen the swiftness and violence of German reaction to a threat to anything that really mattered were not so sanguine.[20]

The loss of momentum in the Allied advance and the delay created by the logistical problems provided a boon to the German defenders, and one that they would exploit to the full.

Chapter Nine

On Monday 18 September, D plus 1, Hackett's 4 Parachute Brigade was due to fly out to Arnhem at 0600 hours, but Keats' seasonal mists had arrived to disrupt the plan. What shrouded the airfields was more than autumnal mist, however; it was thick fog that kept aircraft on the ground, and it was to be followed by heavy rain. Nor were the unpleasant conditions confined to England. Fog also covered airfields in northern France and Belgium, grounding the tactical support aircraft for the morning.

At 0600 hours Guards Armoured Division resumed their advance, the armoured cars of 2nd Household Cavalry Regiment (2 HCR) probing ahead. In Valkenswaard, 231 Brigade of 50th (Northumbrian) Division provided a holding force as the armour moved on. The Irish Guards Group still led, but at Aalst, halfway to Eindhoven, the Micks were held up by a single SPG covering the single-carriageway road to which the armour was restricted. The Grenadier Group took over the lead, following 2 HCR who were trying to by-pass Eindhoven to link up with the Americans. The Welsh Group had moved off on a new axis, Heart Route, towards Helmond which came to naught against stout resistance from Kampfgruppe Walther, prompting Adair to order the group to re-join the main axis at Son. Fog in Belgium had kept the aircraft of 2 TAF on the ground and deprived the units of XXX Corps of close air support; since Dutch skies were clear, the tanks and infantry were exposed fully.

In Eindhoven Colonel Robert E. 'Bounding Bob' Sink's 506 PIR had cleared the last Germans from the town, including a brace of 88mm SPGs, and secured the bridges across the Dommel river. Thus, Eindhoven became the first significant Dutch city to be liberated. Meanwhile, the Irish Group liberated Aalst and overcame further obstacles to reach Eindhoven where the Grenadiers re-joined. One pleasing sight for the tank crews had been that of at least six 88s that had been abandoned by their gunners.[1] With XXX Corps aiming to punch through to Arnhem, what was the situation at Arnhem bridge?

Urquhart had planned to deploy 1 Airborne Reconnaissance Squadron in a *coup de main* assault on Arnhem bridge. Although Gough tried to explain that his squadron's role was 'information, not assault', and that he had intended to

On the morning of 18 September, two members of No. 2 (Dutch) Troop, 10 (Inter-Allied) Commando, Private Jef van der Meer and Corporal Tom Italiaander, met local women Mrs Tjoonk and Maarte van der Poel and displayed the Dutch national flag. Italiaander carried a Thompson sub-machine gun. Both soldiers escaped in Operation BERLIN. (*IWM BU1156*)

deploy each of his three troops ahead of a parachute battalion, both Urquhart and Lathbury insisted on the *coup de main*. The squadron was to travel some eight miles 'in … jeeps at top speed to the road bridge … at Arnhem, avoiding if possible any contact with the enemy and hold the bridge until the arrival of the parachute force'.[2] That plan ground to a halt at Wolfheze railway crossing where the leading section was ambushed and several men were killed, wounded or captured. Further clashes as the squadron continued towards the bridge killed off the *coup-de-main* plan. Some of the squadron reached the northern end of the bridge and joined with elements of 2nd Parachute Battalion, under Lieutenant Colonel John Frost, a number of sappers and other divisional troops, including some of Lathbury's HQ, to hold the bridge against German efforts to push them off. However, the divisional objective had been to seize the entire bridge and hold it until the arrival of XXX Corps. (The railway bridge had been destroyed by the Germans while the pontoon bridge had been partially dismantled to facilitate river traffic.)

The bridge had been defended very lightly by about twenty-five 'old soldiers most of whom had served in the First World War and all of whom had run away as soon as it seemed likely that they might be called upon to fight'.

According to a Dutch policeman, the bridge had been undefended for a period of less than half an hour before SS troops arrived.[3] A landing on or close to the bridge would have helped shape the subsequent battle more favourably for 1st Airborne Division by creating Brereton's 'thunderclap surprise'.

Frost's command numbered about 700 from his own A and B companies, part of C Company 3rd Parachute Battalion, five 6-pounder guns of 1 Airlanding Anti-Tank Battery, two jeeps from the Reconnaissance Squadron, including Major Gough, 100 sappers from 1 Parachute Squadron and 9 Field Company RE, plus elements of Royal Signals, Glider Pilot Regiment, Royal Army Service Corps (RASC), Royal Army Ordnance Corps (RAOC), Royal Electrical and Mechanical Engineers (REME), MPs and 1 Parachute Brigade headquarters. Wireless communication was established between the forward observation officer at the bridge and 1st Airlanding Light Regiment in Oosterbeek. The remainder of 1 Parachute Brigade was fighting through the town suburbs while 1 Airlanding Brigade was guarding the LZs and DZs for the second lift.

An attempt was made to cross the bridge that evening. Lieutenant John 'Jack' Grayburn, born in India of Irish descent, was commanding 2 Platoon in A Company and had already shown his mettle on the advance to the bridge. He took his platoon, with faces blackened and boots muffled, onto the bridge ramp but the resistance was so strong that he had to withdraw. Already wounded, Grayburn was last to pull back.

The adverse weather conditions in England meant a four-hour delay in the departure of Hackett's 4 Parachute Brigade and further elements of the divisional troops, including 2 Battery of 1st Airlanding Light Regiment and 2 Airlanding Anti-Tank Battery, known as the Oban Battery.[4] Both US divisions also executed second lifts on the 18th, their commanders having chosen to drop three regiments of parachute infantry on D Day and bring in the glider infantry and heavier weapons on the second lift.

North of the Rhine 1 Airlanding Brigade prepared for the arrival of the second lift, 4 Parachute Brigade and the remainder of the divisional troops. The airlanding soldiers were also coming under stronger attacks from those enemy forces, and armoured vehicles were arriving in greater numbers as the hours passed. Throughout the western suburbs of Arnhem, the remnants of 1 Brigade continued fighting towards the bridge against increasing opposition. Frost's men, still holding the north end of the bridge, were confident that relief would soon arrive in the shape of XXX Corps.

Brigadier Hackett's 4 Parachute Brigade arrived over DZ Y at 1500 hours. On the fly-in, the brigade had suffered losses from enemy anti-aircraft fire and fighter aircraft, 156th Battalion in particular losing some key elements. Brereton's order to keep the close-air-support aircraft on the ground while

A supply container hanging in the Dreijenseweg. There were many times when the recovery of the containers required considerable extra effort. (*Bundesarchiv 722-4 K.B. Höppner*)

transport aircraft were delivering men and equipment undoubtedly had a detrimental effect – and would continue to do so. There was some fire from enemy troops on the ground who were engaging 1 Airlanding Brigade, but the arrival of 4 Brigade caused most of them to withdraw.

Once on the ground some confusion developed. Urquhart, cut off in Arnhem with Lathbury's brigade, had devolved divisional command to Brigadier Hicks[5] who ordered Hackett's 11th Battalion to proceed straight to Arnhem. It was 1700 before the advance began. At 2000 it was stopped: the Germans had formed a strong defensive line along the Dreijenseweg, a north-south road barring the way into Arnhem. Without previous reconnaissance, attacking during darkness was out of the question. The brigade settled down for the night; leading platoons had come under fire from SS troops, something the remainder would discover to their cost the following day.

Meanwhile US 101st Airborne Division had secured the landing zones for the second lift, which consisted of its glider infantry and artillery. The 'Screaming Eagles' then went on to secure a fifteen-mile stretch of the road between Veghel and Eindhoven. That strip of road would become known as 'Hell's Highway'.[6] Between 101st and 1st Airborne Divisions, Gavin's 82nd had the critical and complicated task of taking the main Nijmegen bridge and securing ground for defence. At Nijmegen later in the day, as we shall see, Gavin planned to capture the bridge in a two-pronged assault, but Browning,

US airborne units enjoyed considerable success on D Day, 17 September. The censor has obliterated divisional and unit badges in this image of paratroopers receiving a final briefing before emplaning. (*US Army Signal Corps/NARA*)

who had asked Gavin to draw up the plan to seize both bridges (road and rail), vetoed this, considering defence of the Groesbeek Heights to be more important.[7] At Son, Royal Engineers were arriving to begin constructing a Bailey bridge to replace the bridge blown by the Germans. However, it would be Tuesday morning before the new bridge was complete.

The programme for XXX Corps' advance was: Eindhoven by 1715 on D Day, Veghel by midnight, Grave by noon the following day, Nijmegen by 1800 and Arnhem by 1500 on D plus 2. That programme was already proving optimistic. Although taken by surprise the previous day, the Germans had recovered quickly and reacted just as quickly. Kampfgruppe Hohenstaufen had rapidly deployed much of its reconnaissance battalion – about thirty vehicles – across Arnhem bridge prior to Frost's arrival. Its destination was Nijmegen. Another Kampfgruppe, equipped with armoured cars and some light tanks, had passed through Arnhem towards Oosterbeek.

As already noted, further improvised units had deployed to Arnhem and were to be joined by additional ad hoc units on D plus 1. Chill's men had imposed delay on Guards Armoured Division, including that already mentioned at Aalst.

Gavin's men had encountered troops from training or base units in their area, many of whom had surrendered almost enthusiastically close to Groesbeek. However, at Nijmegen's Keizer Karelplein the leading American airborne company had encountered the vanguard of Hohenstaufen's reconnaissance unit, who proved a much tougher proposition. Overall, the German defence of Nijmegen, although chaotic, was effective and 82nd Airborne was thwarted in efforts to reach and seize the bridge.

Generally, Taylor's 101st Airborne had met second-line troops, other than those close to Best and the bridge across the Wilhelmina canal. At the canal the company from 502 PIR assigned to seize the bridge had been seen off by troops of 59th Division. At St Oedenrode and Veghel, where the Americans had taken the bridges, Student had even ordered two battalions of airborne soldiers recovering from wounds or illness to recapture the bridges. In spite of American efforts to secure the bridge at Best, it was blown an hour before noon by soldiers of 59th Division, leaving the Bailey bridge at Son the sole option for the advance of Guards Armoured Division. For 101st Airborne, the sharpest fighting on D plus 1 was that around Best.

That so many bridges had been taken undamaged on D Day was a boon to the Allies, provided by the mixed quality of the defenders and the shock and disruption caused by the sudden descent of the airborne divisions. Most bridges had already been prepared for demolition but the orders to destroy them were not carried out in many cases. Although German troops broke and ran, as at Groesbeek, the sinews of command and control had not been disrupted. As Powell described the situation:

> Nowhere was there any delay in preparing or launching counter-attacks against the Allies. The British and Americans were out of luck in being faced with officers of the calibre of Model, Bittrich, Chill, Walther, Harzer and Student.[8]

On D plus 1 Colonel John H. Michaelis, commanding 502 PIR, pushed two battalions towards Best, intending to capture the bridge there after the failure to take Son bridge the day before. Lieutenant Colonel Robert G. Cole, CO of 3/502, who had earned the Medal of Honor in Normandy, was shot en route to Best but Lieutenant Edward L. Wierzbowski, commanding a platoon of Company H, with fifteen men, worked his way forward until he was less than 100 yards from the bridge where he was forced to take cover from enemy fire.

Once again, a bridge was blown up with men of the 101st close to it. At 1100 some 100 feet of the steel-and-concrete structure fell into the Wilhelmina canal. Wierzbowski then ordered Privates Mann and Hoyle to destroy a nearby German 88mm gun position. Both paratroopers returned before long to report that they had accomplished their mission. With bazooka fire, they had knocked out the gun and blown up an ammunition store, as well as engaging the gun detachment with rifle fire. During the engagement 'Mann was shot twice, although neither of his wounds was serious enough to incapacitate him'.[9]

That afternoon the Germans attacked Wierzbowski's platoon, killing one man and wounding two others. Private Mann was one of the wounded and was hit twice, with both arms 'ripped open by German bullets'.[10] Seeing that Mann was bleeding badly, a medic bandaged him, placing both arms in slings. Unexpectedly, the Germans then withdrew.

> At daybreak on D plus 2, Wierzbowski's group found itself enveloped in a thick morning mist. Out of this mist emerged a German assault team that was bent on destroying the little cluster of Americans. Throwing potato-masher hand grenades as they advanced, the Germans worked their way to within twenty yards of the paratroopers before halting for the final attack. Then one of Wierzbowski's squad leaders, Sergeant Betras, and several paratroopers rose from their foxholes and threw grenades back at the Germans.[11]

Private Joe Mann in civilian clothes.
(*US Army Don F. Pratt Memorial Museum*)

Private Joe Mann in uniform. This image of him in uniform was created for 101st Airborne Division, 'the Screaming Eagles', since no photograph of him in uniform is known to exist. Private Mann's heroism led to a posthumous award of the Medal of Honor. (*US Army Don F. Pratt Memorial Museum*)

Hardly had Betras and the others ducked back into their foxholes than more grenades began falling on them. Two fell among the wounded, but Betras threw one back before it detonated. A third blew up beside the machine gunner who was blinded. Even so, he felt another grenade hit him; feeling about at the bottom of the hole, he grabbed it and returned it to the Germans.

With ammunition almost exhausted, the situation was dire but Wierzbowski's men fought hard to repel the attackers in spite of the shower of grenades.

One of the grenades bounced into a large trench in which Private Mann was sitting with both of his mangled arms taped to his body to prevent further loss of blood. Six other paratroopers were in the trench with Mann, but they were so busy shooting at Germans that they never saw the grenade land behind them. Knowing full well that when the grenade exploded it would kill everyone in the trench, Mann shouted 'Grenade!' Then he threw himself down on [it] absorbing the full blast with his body.

... however, some of the fragments passed through Mann's body, lightly wounding Privates Atayde, Paxton and Wienz. Lieutenant Wierzbowski reached Mann just in time to hear him say, 'My back's gone ...'. With those words, Mann died.[12]

Joe Mann, from Washington State, received a posthumous award of the Medal of Honor. The concluding sentence of the citation read: 'His outstanding gallantry above and beyond the call of duty and his magnificent conduct were an everlasting inspiration to his comrades for whom he gave his life.'

Battles had raged all day on the 18th. Frost's command had created strongpoints in houses and commercial buildings at the north end of the bridge while the Dutch families took shelter in the cellars of those buildings. Having already knocked out German vehicles that had tried to cross the bridge during the night, Frost's men were prepared to deal with any further attempts in daylight. Not long after dawn a German convoy of troop-carrying lorries crossed the bridge and ran into fire from HQ 2nd Parachute Battalion.

Thus began a brutal encounter of some two hours' duration as German troops, under cover in neighbouring buildings, and Frostforce exchanged fire. Then Hohenstaufen's Reconnaissance Battalion arrived, en route back from

Many Germans seemed to covet the Sten gun while the iconic wooden-handled grenade, the *Stielhandgranate* or 'potato masher', was always in evidence. These soldiers are advancing along the Utrechtseweg. (*Bundesarchiv 497/3531A/31a*)

Nijmegen and unaware of the immediate tactical situation. Although the four leading vehicles sped through without harm, those that followed were hit by rounds from 2 Airlanding Anti-Tank Battery's 6-pounders or from PIATs fired from houses overlooking the road.

Those attacking Frost at the bridge were from Hohenstaufen, forming Kampfgruppe Knaust. Before long the SS realised that the airborne troops were determined and well-armed, and heavier supporting weapons were called up. On the eastern side of the road sappers dropped grenades into open-topped half-tracks. Supported by self-propelled artillery and armoured cars, German infantry advanced from the city side, but made no significant inroads. Although their main effort died out, small parties tried infiltrating the area and shells and mortars continued to bombard the British positions. Although a 150mm SPG, capable of destroying the houses sheltering Frost's men, arrived, it was knocked out quickly.

Among the defenders were Jack Grayburn's 2 Platoon of A Company, who had attempted to cross the bridge. The platoon subsequently occupied a house in a location critical for the defence of the bridge. Through D plus 1 and the night that followed, Grayburn led its defence against attacks supported by artillery and mortars as well as AFVs. That the house did not fall into German hands was attributed to Jack Grayburn's 'great courage and inspiring leadership'.[13]

In the course of the day, much of Frost's B Company arrived, strengthening the force somewhat, but ammunition was running low while information on the overall situation was lacking. A radio message brought news that 1st Parachute Battalion was just beyond the railway line on the city outskirts. Frost also realised that the intelligence briefing he had been given on the opposition to be expected in Arnhem was wrong when he discovered that some of his prisoners were personnel from 9th SS Panzer Division Hohenstaufen.

The information about 1st Parachute Battalion was accurate. Commanded by Lieutenant Colonel David Dobie DSO, the unit, formed in 1940 with men of No. 2 Commando being trained in

Lieutenant John Grayburn VC, 2nd Parachute Battalion. Born in India of Irish descent, he was commissioned in the Oxfordshire and Buckinghamshire Light Infantry. He was posthumously promoted to captain. (*Public domain*)

parachuting, first saw action in Operation TORCH, the invasion of French North-West Africa. After Operation FUSTIAN in Sicily, it fought briefly in Italy before returning to England to prepare for Arnhem, as part of Lathbury's 1 Parachute Brigade.

In Tunisia and Sicily, the battalion had suffered very heavy casualties. Thus, despite being one of the most experienced parachute battalions, part of the original 'Red Devils', it arrived at Arnhem with a high number of recruits who lacked battle experience. That lack of experience is exemplified in a post-battle report by *SS-Sturmmann* Alfred Zeigler, whose unit ambushed a column from the battalion, killing a large number and taking prisoner about thirty.

> They were so beaten and submissive that it only needed one man to march them off to the rear. We were not too impressed by this lot. They were completely surprised. I ask you, they came marching straight down the road in a company file! What nonsense! We were so few! They should have taken a route through the trees.

Dobie's men had clashed with enemy armoured cars and light tanks on the Ede-Arnhem road soon after landing and had then made for Johannahoeve through the woods. As it moved southwards, the battalion had a series of

Prisoners from 1st Airborne Division being marched into captivity, some of whom look happy to be 'in the bag'. It may have been a scene such as this that prompted *SS-Sturmmann* Ziegler to make his dismissive comment about the British paratroopers. (*Public domain*)

Known to British soldiers as 'Moanin' Minnie', the *Nebelwerfer* was a multi-barrelled rocket launcher of various calibres. SS Mortar Group Nickmann deployed Nebelwerfers at Arnhem. (*Public domain*)

encounters with the enemy and lost men killed, wounded or captured. At the Utrechtseweg, 1st Parachute Battalion turned in the direction of Arnhem; this was also the route 3rd Battalion was taking. It was about dawn on D plus 1 that radio contact was made with Frost's group at the bridge. Responding to a request for reinforcements, Dobie decided to make for the bridge. To do so, he side-stepped his unit to the south and the riverbank where German positions were encountered along the railway line and near the higher ground at Den Brink. A similar manoeuvre had been performed by 3rd Parachute Battalion, commanded by Lieutenant Colonel J.A.C. Fitch, who would be killed in action on D plus 2. (The CWGC site notes that he was killed *between* 19 and 23 September.) The Germans opposing both 1st and 3rd Parachute Battalions were from SS Kampfgruppe Spindler.

Fitch's battalion had moved off at 0430, when it was still dark and, before long, had split as a result of the leading men moving too quickly. Both Urquhart and Lathbury, who were with the battalion, were separated from their radio vehicles. Any control either of them might have been able to exercise was lost at that point. More confusion was to follow.

Although the leading elements of Fitch's battalion, about 170 strong, evaded the Germans at Den Brink and reached the area of the St Elisabeth Hospital, they were then attacked by a small force of German infantry, armoured cars and a tank. While this was happening, Dobie's battalion was trying to force its way past Den Brink. The fighting that followed was so confused that both parachute battalions were firing at each other and, possibly, the Germans. Lathbury was wounded not far from the hospital entrance while Urquhart, with his batman and two other officers, took cover in a house nearby. However, they could not leave the building since a German SPG was in front of the door. By nightfall neither 1st nor 3rd Parachute Battalions survived as complete units, each having not many more than 100 personnel. (Formed in September 1941 with volunteers from numerous different units, 3rd Parachute Battalion's first CO was Lieutenant Colonel Gerald Lathbury, later brigade commander. It captured the German airfield at Bone in Tunisia on 12 November 1942 in what is said to be the first battalion parachute operation; it was there that the battalion, and later the brigade, adopted the war cry *Waho Mohammad*.[14] In Sicily the battalion was involved in capturing Primosole Bridge, suffering many casualties.)

Although the battle was not going to plan, the situation was not considered hopeless. The arrival of 4 Parachute Brigade was awaited, in anticipation of its three battalions helping to create circumstances in which the divisional objective could still be achieved. Not only would the second lift bring Hackett's battalions, but also more artillery and engineers. Most importantly, it would mean that 1 Airlanding Brigade could move from defending the DZs and LZs to a more active part in the battle. The situation prevailing on the morning of D plus 1 made it clear that the decision not to have two lifts on D Day was wrong. Flying the entire division in in two lifts on the 17th would have allowed Urquhart's full strength to be directed to seizing the bridge. Powell makes the argument that even flying in both parachute brigades on D Day would have been a better option since there would have been no need to deploy protective forces for the DZs and LZs.[15]

Command of 4 Parachute Brigade was held by Brigadier John 'Shan' Winthrop Hackett, born in Australia in 1910, the sole son of five children in a wealthy Irish family. His father, Sir John Winthrop Hackett, owned two Western Australian newspapers and had founded the University of Perth. After schooling in Australia, Hackett attended London Central Art School before going up to New College, Oxford, to read Greats, intending to be a don. However, an under-par degree led him to join the Army. Commissioned into The Queen's Bays (2nd Dragoon Guards) he transferred to 8th King's Royal Irish Hussars, his grandfather's regiment. As a junior subaltern, Hackett continued his studies, producing a thesis on Saladin and the Third Crusade (1189-1192) and earning the degree of Bachelor of Letters. Powell describes him as 'fighting soldier;' who was 'an outstanding linguist, historian and classicist, a rare combination in the pre-war British cavalry'.[16] Service in Palestine brought a Mention in Despatches for his part in anti-terrorist operations while a secondment to the Transjordan Frontier Force in 1937 resulted in two further Mentions. In 1941, during operations against the Vichy French in Syria, he was wounded for the first time. The following year, in the Western Desert, he received a second wound while GSO1 Raiding Forces. Described by his contemporaries as 'slim, dapper, energetic and friendly', he would eventually be able to converse fluently in nine languages.[17]

Hackett's command was entering its first and last battle. Of its three battalions (156th, 10th and 11th) only 156th and 10th had seen action before, this being limited skirmishing in Italy; in 11th Battalion one company had made a combat jump, onto the Greek island of Kos, but had not seen any fighting, instead being greeted as liberators by the Italian garrison.

Departing from England in poor weather, the brigade arrived over Arnhem at 1500 to a 'welcome' from heavy AA fire while Luftwaffe fighters tried to engage the transport aircraft but were fought off by RAF fighters, twenty of which were shot down in battle against ninety enemy fighters. Hackett's paratroopers dropped on top of the Dutch SS attacking their DZ who fled when the new arrivals made their entrance. Even so, some men were killed or wounded in the engagement. In addition, the remaining South Staffords came in by glider, as did the balance of the divisional troops. In an apparent confirmation that the Germans did have a copy of the complete orders for MARKET GARDEN some thirty German fighter-bombers had attacked the gliders' LZ at the very time they had been scheduled to land.

Lieutenant Colonel Sir Richard Des Voeux, fated to be killed in action on 21 September, commanded 156th Battalion at Arnhem. Formed in India as 151st Parachute Battalion under Lieutenant Colonel Martin A. Lindsay, Royal Scots Fusiliers, it attracted volunteers from twenty-three different British units, most of which were serving in India at the time. It was part of 50 Indian Parachute Brigade (151st British, 152nd Indian and 153rd Gurkha Battalions) before being transferred to the Middle East and renamed 156th to confuse the enemy. Following limited action in Italy, it 'returned' to England. Despite its high numerical designation, it was the senior battalion of the brigade. (A battalion affectation was the use of the cardinal rather than the correct ordinal designation.)

Lieutenant Colonel K.B.I. 'Kidney' Smyth OBE MiD, another battalion CO who would lose his life,[18] commanded 10th Parachute Battalion, formed at Kabrit, Egypt, in December 1942 with a majority of its volunteers from Eighth Army units, in particular 2nd Royal Sussex. It accompanied 156th Battalion to Italy, where Eighth Army veterans and raw recruits gained some

Lieutenant Colonel Ken Smyth, CO of 10th Parachute Battalion, with HM King George VI and Brigadier Hackett. (*IWM H36704*)

King George VI with Brigadier Hackett and Lieutenant General Browning inspecting 156th Parachute Battalion. Second right is Major George Lea who was soon to command 11th Parachute Battalion. (*IWM H36711*)

battle experience. Among the veterans was Lionel Queripel, of the Royal Sussex, who would earn the Victoria Cross at Arnhem.

Lieutenant Colonel George Lea commanded 11th Parachute Battalion, also raised in Kabrit; the first men enrolled in March 1943. When 4 Parachute Brigade left for Italy, the battalion was still in training. Prior to Arnhem, its only action was when a reinforced A Company parachuted onto Kos on 14 September 1943 to secure the airfield.

Although 4 Brigade had already been delayed by over four hours, it was to endure a further delay before advancing, even though the battalions were ready to move within an hour of their arrival. Moving off at 1700, led by 156th Battalion, the line of advance was a path running along the north side of the railway. At 2000 a KOSB officer stopped the leading troops to advise them that the Germans had established a defensive line along the Dreijenseweg. That enemy line ran north-south and led into Oosterbeek. In the darkness Des Voeux's 156th Battalion was the first to encounter the line and met a storm of rifle and machine-gun bullets. Since it was impossible to see the layout of the line, Des Voeux chose to draw his leading troops back about 1,500 yards and prepare to make an attack on the enemy positions. In fact, those positions were held by elements of Kampfgruppe Hohenstaufen, but neither Des Voeux nor his officers and men knew that as they set about their preparations. It would be D plus 2 before 156th and 10th Battalions attempted to renew their advance.

Meanwhile, Brigadier Pip Hicks, who had assumed command of the division, had deployed those South Staffords who had arrived in the first lift into Arnhem to reinforce 1 Parachute Brigade. Hicks knew of Frost's predicament through the only working radio net, that of the gunners. He decided to deploy in the same reinforcing role the remainder of the South Staffords who arrived in the second lift and Lea's 11th Parachute Battalion. Soon after his arrival, Hackett learned of this decision from Urquhart's senior staff officer, Lieutenant Colonel Mackenzie. He also learned that Hicks was acting GOC and was not pleased by either piece of news. Powell considered that the removal of Lea's battalion was the more unwelcome news, especially as Hackett regarded 4 Brigade as his creation.

To remove a battalion, and to decide, without consultation, which battalion it was to be, was bad enough, but to feed units into the battle as night was approaching with no clear orders and no coherent plan, to fight in a strange built-up area where the enemy appeared to be gathering strength, was not, in Hackett's opinion, in any way sound.[19]

Nor did Hackett's unease end there. He was unhappy with Hicks' orders for the balance of 4 Parachute Brigade and summarised matters as 'a grossly untidy situation'. When Hackett and Hicks met, there were tensions but those were eased when Hackett briefed Hicks on his own plans for the brigade's deployment. Hicks concurred and it was agreed that, on the morning of D plus 2, 4 Brigade, less 11th Parachute Battalion but plus 7th King's Own Scottish Borderers, would attack in the direction of Arnhem. The brigade's first objective was high ground at Koepel, to the east of the Dreijenseweg, the area where the Airborne Cemetery was later created.

Once again Urquhart's absence was having a baleful effect on the battle, although some might question that as his overall performance was poor. The arrival of 4 Brigade *should* have provided an opportunity to reshape the battle. However, Hicks had made two major mistakes: deploying newly-arrived units willy-nilly into a messy tactical situation and failing to provide Hackett with clear information and instructions. Powell suggested a further option that Hicks might have considered.

> It was a time when major decisions were needed. With the situation as it was on the second day, before the second lift arrived, one possible option would have been to change the plan for the use of 4 Parachute Brigade and drop it south of the Arnhem road bridge on the DZ planned for use by the Poles on the third day; this was something that could, admittedly with difficulty, have been arranged, since one of the few radio links still working was that to Browning's rear headquarters in England.[20]

Since the advantage of surprise had gone completely by that stage, Powell also posited the possibility of abandoning efforts to force an advance to the bridge in favour of creating a bridgehead based on the ferry crossing at Heveadorp and the nearby high ground at Westerbouwing. Such a bridgehead might have been sustainable until XXX Corps arrived with heavy bridging equipment.[21]

Today, this period can be recognised as the most critical of the battle. That would not have been clear at the time to Hicks, and it is probable that he considered himself only to be 'holding the fort' until Urquhart's return. It was not known if the GOC was a casualty and so it was possible that he could appear again at any time. The fault, according to Powell, lay more in the fact that, in contrast to its US counterpart, a British airborne division did not have a deputy commander who could have immediately assumed the responsibilities and role of the GOC and made such a major decision. (The lack of a deputy GOC was not unique to the British airborne divisions since it also applied in armoured and infantry divisions.)

Not every Nebelwerfer rocket exploded. Captain G.E. Hemelryk of No. 1 Company Divisional Signals examines one that failed to explode. Hemelryk was one of those who were later captured. (*Public domain*)

While the Germans were still reacting on D plus 1, they were also pulling in reinforcements while the excellent staff work for which the German army was renowned was showing itself at its best. Among the arrivals were elements of LXXXVI *Armeekorps*, commanded by General Hans von Obstfelder, a highly decorated soldier, but one of those responsible for the Babi Yar massacre of

A Panther, the most effective German tank of the war. This example has lengths of track hung onto the turret to augment its armour. (*Bundesarchiv Bild 101I-244-2306-14*)

Jewish civilians in Ukraine in 1941. Under his command von Obstfelder had two weak divisions, 176th Infantry and Division 'Erdmann'. The former, the 'kranken division' already mentioned on p. 88, included 7,000 personnel who were either trainees or personnel unfit for normal duties due to illness or injuries while the latter numbered only 3,000 men who were recruits for the planned 7th Fallschirmjäger Division. Obstfelder's command was deployed to improve the defences between Weert and Helmond. Since Arnhem was close to the border with Germany, it was a relatively simple task to deploy formations from the Fatherland. The German military district closest to Arnhem was *Wehrkreis* VI whose commander had, in the summer, been ordered to improvise an infantry division from units in his district. Earlier in September Korps Feldt, under General Kurt Feldt, had also been organised in the district to serve as a defensive force along the border. Following Operation MARKET GARDEN, Korps Feldt was assigned the task of attacking towards Nijmegen, deploying an improvised formation, Division z.b.V. 406.

Perhaps the most effective of the 'fire brigade' formations deployed was Panzer-Brigade 107, which would engage the US airborne soldiers. Created in summer 1944 in Poland from the surviving elements of 25th Panzergrenadier Division, 107 Panzer Brigade was intended for service on the Russian front. However, on 15 September, two days before the Allied landings in the

Netherlands, it had been subordinated to Model's Army Group B and began arriving in the Netherlands on D Day plus 1, as we shall see below. Under Major Berndt-Joachim Freiherr von Maltzahn, the brigade had a strength of 2,117 personnel with thirty-six Panther tanks, eleven Jagdpanzers and 157 armoured half-tracks.

Browning and Brigadier General Gavin, commanding 82nd Airborne Division, agreed that the priorities around Nijmegen were the high ground of the Groesbeek Heights, the bridge at Grave, the three smaller bridges over the Maas-Waal Canal, and, finally, the bridge at Nijmegen. Browning also told Gavin not to make any attempt to move towards Nijmegen until the Heights had been secured. Gavin agreed but was confident enough in his plan to allow one battalion to head for the bridge immediately after landing. The Groesbeek Heights served as the division's main drop zone and dominated the entire area, so there is no question that the position of 82nd Airborne Division, and the right flank of Second British Army, when it arrived, would be placed under considerable pressure if the area remained in enemy hands. However, the priorities of any airborne formation had to be the capture of its ultimate objectives – the bridges. All other concerns were entirely secondary. Browning defended his decision after the war, but it was a great mistake not to give higher priority to Nijmegen Bridge since, without it, 1st Airborne Division would be marooned behind two large rivers and thirteen miles of hostile

A column of Shermans from XXX Corps stopped on the road north. Included is a captured SdKfz 251 half-track, which has been claimed for the divisional RHA regiment, with its MG42 replaced by a Browning .50-calibre machine gun. (*Public domain*)

territory. Had the bridge been taken in strength and quickly then it is entirely possible that Guards Armoured would have reached Arnhem bridge before the British defence collapsed. This oversight, however, was not particular to the Nijmegen plan, but a further product of the blind optimism which dogged Operation MARKET GARDEN.

On D plus 1 Korps Feldt attacked towards the Groesbeek Heights with Division z.b.V.406 and, in spite of the motley nature of the formation, made good progress with the support of armoured cars and some mobile quad 20mm AA guns. Such was the penetration made by the attackers that two LZs were overrun and 508 PIR's ammunition dump was in German hands. Gavin organised and led a counter-attack that regained the LZs. It had included Lieutenant Colonel Warren's 1/508 PIR which had just made an unsuccessful attempt to seize Nijmegen bridge; Gavin had called the battalion back to help protect the LZs. The arrival of Gavin's second lift saw the gliders come in to land through fire from enemy AA units. Only 385 of 454 gliders landed safely with some overshooting and landing elsewhere and others destroyed. As a result, only 40 per cent of the division's artillery arrived in good order. However, the effect of the gliders appearing and Gavin's counter-attack caused the collapse of the German attack.[22] Only a battalion of Gavin's 325th Glider Infantry Regiment (325 GIR) was included in this lift which, in addition to field artillery, also brought in anti-tank artillery, a battery of AA guns, engineers and signallers.

After his second lift had arrived, Gavin was asked by Browning to lay a plan to seize both the road and railway bridges at Nijmegen. Although this had been 82nd's main task it had yet to be executed and, according to the original schedule, XXX Corps was due to reach Nijmegen at 1800. (Problems with communications continued to plague Browning's HQ and that of 1st Airborne, whose commander was still missing.) Gavin drew up plans for assaults by a battalion of 504 PIR on both bridges while 508 PIR attacked at the same time from either flank. Presented with the plan, Browning demurred, reminding Gavin that his priority was retaining the Groesbeek Heights. 'This decision was one of the very few Browning was called upon to make during the battle. … There is little any senior commander can do to influence the course of events in the early stage of a battle, and this Browning was to discover.'[23] The gliders used to carry Browning's HQ could have been better employed to carry an additional infantry battalion in for either 82nd or 1st Airborne.

Throughout the day there was constant fighting and confusion as the Germans sought to contain the Allies who fought to take and consolidate their objectives. Amid all this, the Germans were preparing their counter-attack, another element of their reaction, to which the Allies were well accustomed. That counter-attack would be launched on D plus 2.

As well as the second lifts for all three airborne divisions, aircraft had been involved in re-supply missions. These had followed the second-lift flights and, in the Arnhem sector, included Stirlings and Dakotas of 38 and 46 Groups. However, the area designated for re-supply drops remained in German control and the Germans simply copied the 'friendly' recognition signals. As a result, much of the eighty-seven tons dropped fell into enemy hands. Urquhart's command received only twelve tons. As if to make matters worse, thirteen of the 145 aircraft deployed were shot down while almost all received damage from AA fire. Knowing that the airborne troops could only be maintained by air, the Luftwaffe was also reinforcing AA defences in the area. In addition, IX *Fliegerkorps* was ordered to carry out strikes against the Allied positions and related targets. We have already noted the Luftwaffe attack on the LZ for the gliders in the second lift. On the night of the 18th about twelve Do.217 bombers of I./KG 2 took off to attack bridges over the Meuse-Escaut canal in the Neerpelt area, but some missed their target and the raid was far from effective.

Some re-supply did reach the soldiers inside the 'Cauldron'. This pannier of .303 ammunition landed in the garden at No. 16 Van Lenneweg. The soldiers, from 1st Border Regiment, include CSM G. Stringer (L), with Corporal James Swan (in the beret), who earned the Military Medal. Corporal James Webster, smoking a cigar in the centre, was later awarded the US Silver Star. Helping Webster is Private Eric Blackwell, the section Bren gunner. (*James Swan/ Border Regiment Museum*)

Brereton's injunction against the close air support aircraft operating while drops or re-supply were underway had continued to affect adversely the situation on the ground. Poor weather had also played its part, since fog, followed by heavy rain, had closed airfields in Belgium where the British tactical aircraft were based: 2 TAF's No. 83 Group had been able to fly fewer than 100 sorties in support of 82nd Airborne and none in support of 1st Airborne. The US XVIII Airborne Corps commander, Major General Matt Ridgway, had decided to join his troops in the Netherlands but his aircraft could not land in Brussels because of the conditions. (On D Day both he and Brereton had flown in B-17 Fortress bombers to observe the 101st Airborne Division drop, Brereton's aircraft suffering damage from AA fire.) He would have been unable to exercise command in any event since his 82nd and 101st Airborne had been placed under Browning's I British Airborne Corps for the operation; in fact, when XXX Corps reached 101st, that division passed to Horrocks' command. At the same time, 50th (Northumbrian) Division passed to Lieutenant General Sir Richard O'Connor's VIII Corps. As the witching hour struck, VIII Corps moved off on its delayed supporting advance. The first phase of that move was an assault crossing of the Meuse-Escaut canal at Lille St Hubert (now St Huybrechts Lille). Making that crossing was 3rd Division, the tail of which was still on the road from Brussels, with 9 Brigade leading across the forty-yard-wide canal. VIII Corps' task was to form a bridgehead before advancing to protect the left flank of Horrocks' corps. With support from the artillery of three divisions, the infantry made their crossing in assault boats and, after some sharp fighting, secured their bridgehead. Sappers built a Class 9 bridge for 9 Brigade's jeeps and carriers, followed by a Class 40 bridge for the tanks of 11th Armoured Division, this latter being completed by 1930 on the 19th, allowing 11th Armoured to attack across the canal on the morning of the 20th.[24]

The Bailey bridge at Son was open for business at dawn on Tuesday. Household Cavalry armoured cars were first to cross, followed by the Grenadier Guards Group. The HCR arrived at the bridge at Grave at 0820, where both Browning and Gavin awaited Horrocks. At about 1000 the Grenadiers reached the bridge, held by men of Colonel Tucker's 504 PIR.[25] Thus Gavin's division also passed to Horrocks' command, leaving Browning with only 1st Airborne Division under his command, although he had virtually no contact with the division or its commander. Both Browning and Horrocks, with Adair and Gavin, established a joint HQ close to Heumen 'and agreed to command by a form of mutual agreement'.[26] Horrocks recorded his delight at finding that Gavin's soldiers 'had captured intact the road bridge over the Meuse at Grave. Had the Germans succeeded in destroying this bridge our advance might easily have been delayed for several days, for the broad river would have proved a formidable obstacle.'[27]

The arrival of Guards Armoured and 8 Armoured Brigade was a boon to Gavin since he was short of infantry: the two battalions of 325 GIR due to arrive that day were grounded in England by fog and rain. However, a break in the weather allowed the last battalion of Taylor's glider infantry to take off, with the artillery, in 385 gliders; only 196 gliders landed in the Netherlands, the remainder being lost or forced to turn back.[28]

While the weather had prevented Gavin's glider battalions from taking off, Ridgway managed to get into the air again and fly to Antwerp, this time accompanied by Brereton. Both men had 'decided to see for themselves how the battles across the airborne carpet were progressing'.[29] Brereton added a touch of theatre by 'wearing his dress uniform complete with medals', presumably believing he was about to witness a victory.[30] From Antwerp, both generals travelled by jeep to Eindhoven. However, Brereton's 'theatre' turned to farce when 'they found themselves under a Luftwaffe bombing run' on the edge of Eindhoven.[31] Both took cover in a ditch, the dive into which destroyed Brereton's dress uniform; he also lost his personal firearm.[32]

That air raid on Eindhoven, by some 120 bombers, had caused considerable damage to roads and buildings in the city, blocking some roads and setting parts of the city aflame. As well as damage to railway lines and ammunition dumps, the effect was to create even more delay for XXX Corps as it tried to make its way to Arnhem. Significantly, the deployment of a force of Ju 88 bombers at Eindhoven 'was the sole major strike in the west by long-range bombers during the autumn of 1944, a mark of the German determination to smash this Allied offensive'.[33]

The re-supply flights mentioned earlier were several hours late in arriving, a fortuitous delay since that meant that the German fighters had departed. However, there remained the threat of intense anti-aircraft-gun fire. In Geoffrey Powell's words, 'As the slow-moving Dakotas throbbed into view, German light flak hammered at them from the surrounding hills and woods, fire far more intense than anything seen on the Sunday or Monday.' The pilots simply flew their machines straight into the enemy fire, making directly for their dropping zone. Dakotas exploded in mid-air, their cargoes spilling down into the German lines. Although men on the ground fired Very pistols and spread parachutes on the earth to attract the pilots' attention, their efforts failed. Among the Dakotas was one of No. 271 Squadron, flown by a 30-year-old Irishman who had planned to become a priest, Flight Lieutenant David Lord. Powell commented that his aircraft seemed to catch the attention of everyone: 'Although one wing was blazing, it made a second circle, its pilot clearly determined that his cargo should be delivered with precise accuracy.'[34]

It was the starboard wing that was blazing, having been hit twice. Although Lord would have been justified in abandoning his aircraft (the C-47 had unprotected fuel tanks and thus was vulnerable to fire) Lord continued with his mission. With his starboard engine burning furiously,

> Lord came down to 900 feet, where he was singled out for the concentrated fire of all the anti-aircraft guns. On reaching the dropping zone he kept the aircraft on a straight, and level course while supplies were dropped. At the end of the run, he was told that two containers remained.
>
> Although he must have known that the collapse of the starboard wing could not be long delayed, Flight Lieutenant Lord circled, re-joined the stream of aircraft and made a second run to drop the remaining supplies. These manoeuvres took eight minutes in all, the aircraft being continuously under heavy anti-aircraft fire.[35]

Cork-born Flight Lieutenant David Lord VC DFC of 271 Squadron. His VC, the only one ever awarded to RAF Transport Command, was earned through remarkable courage and an exemplary sense of duty, which had marked all his service. (*Authors' collections*)

The headstone of David Lord VC in Arnhem (Oosterbeek) Cemetery. (*David R. Orr*)

David Lord then ordered his crew to bale out but remained at the controls with the Dakota down to 500 feet. Then the starboard wing crumpled, the aeroplane fell from the sky and exploded in a ball of flames. Only one crew member survived; he had been thrown out while helping other air despatchers to put on their parachutes.[36]

The citation for David Lord's Victoria Cross concluded with the comment:

By continuing his mission in a damaged and burning aircraft, descending to drop the supplies accurately, returning to the dropping zone a second time and, finally, remaining at the controls to give his crew a chance of escape, Flight Lieutenant Lord displayed supreme valour and self-sacrifice.[37]

With his division under Horrocks' command, Gavin outlined his plan to secure Nijmegen bridge and allow the British armour to continue the advance to Arnhem. At 1500 Lieutenant Colonel Ben Vandervoort's 2/505 PIR would attack the south end of the bridge. However, he wanted to deploy another force across the river in small boats to attack the north end, but he had no small boats. Horrocks agreed to provide an infantry company and a battalion of tanks for the first element of Gavin's plan and thirty-three assault boats for the second element. However, the boats would not be available until the following day. Nonetheless, Vandervoort's attack went ahead that afternoon, as Horrocks wrote:

The Grenadier Guards Group and a battalion of the 505th US Parachute Regiment combined in an immediate attack on the road bridge, which to our astonishment, was still intact; but in spite of the utmost bravery little progress was made. The Germans had fortified the open squares and had constructed a tight perimeter of defences around the southern end of both the vital bridges. Huner Park, which dominated the southern end of the road bridge, was particularly strongly held. ... By midnight it was obvious that the bridges could not be captured by direct assault.[38]

At 1715, however, 107 Panzer Brigade launched a surprise attack that resulted in the crossing at Son being denied to XXX Corps for the next twenty-four hours. It had taken seventeen trains to move the brigade to its deployment area. The first elements, a company of Panther tanks, one of panzer-grenadiers and another of pioneers, had been unloaded at Venlo the previous evening. At dawn the brigade moved out to secure the bridge now erected by Allied engineers at Son. After taking the bridge they were to move towards St Oedenrode to prevent XXX Corps reaching Nijmegen. Maltzahn, the brigade commander, decided to attack with the forces available to him. Since the roads in the area did not allow a conventional attack, he launched a reconnaissance in force. His advance party crossed the Maas and the South Wilhelmina canal to advance on Helmond. The weather favoured the Germans since cloud cover enabled them to move towards Son without being spotted by Allied fighters. In Helmond the brigade was reinforced by I. Batallion Fallschirmjäger-Regiment 21, under Hauptmann Vosshage, the men riding on the backs of the Panthers.

German attacks also continued to be delivered against the 101st perimeter from the direction of Best, which remained the focus of savage fighting. The 'Screaming Eagles' mounted a counter-attack, supported by British tanks, of 15th/19th King's Royal Hussars,[39] and artillery. When, at 1415, 1/502 PIR and a squadron of the Hussars launched a new attack to take Best bridge, the support of the tanks proved crucial and the bridge, although demolished, was in Allied hands by 1800. The town was also taken, netting 1,056 enemy soldiers, mostly from the recently arrived 59th Infantry Division, which lost 300 dead.

In 82nd Division's area Gavin learned that Nijmegen was 'not strongly held' and that a display of force, including tanks, would prompt an enemy withdrawal. The information came from the Dutch resistance but was in error. A battlegroup including 2nd (Armoured) Grenadier tanks, a company of 1st Grenadiers and 2/505th PIR attacked the two Nijmegen bridges that afternoon but met strong opposition from SS troops and Fallschirmjäger, who outnumbered the attackers considerably. A halt to the attack was called at 1900 as darkness descended.

All this effort was aimed at getting XXX Corps to Arnhem to relieve 1st Airborne Division. That morning, while Frost's men hung on by their fingernails, the remaining battalions of 1 Parachute Brigade, severely reduced in numbers, with the South Staffords and 11th Parachute Battalion, battled through the streets of the town attempting to reach the bridge. Their advance began at 0330, when it was still dark, and fog added to their difficulties. However, the fog also provided some cover from observation and when it lifted, just after dawn, the paratroopers on the road by the river were exposed to vicious fire from both sides of the river. The appearance of enemy armour as the battalions tried to form up for a fighting advance to the bridge surprised them and caused some confusion. However, some support was at hand in a side street near the St Elisabeth Hospital where the gunner FOO with 11th Battalion, Captain P.A. Taylor, ordered a 6-pounder anti-tank gun into action. Since the detachment had suffered from German machine-gun fire, Taylor acted as both No.1 (detachment commander) and loader and scored a direct hit on the SPG which had appeared.

Throughout the day, Captain Taylor continued to be an inspiration to all present in his behaviour and leadership. Gunner F.R. 'Dickie' Bird, a signaller with 2 Battery, arrived shortly after the vehicle had been knocked out and saw another enemy armoured vehicle half-concealed behind the first. Taylor enquired if Bird could remember his gun drill for a 6-pounder? Thankfully, this was not put to the test, and later, both men made their way back towards Oosterbeek by jeep. Gunner Bird would become a prisoner of war; Captain Taylor would be killed on 24 September.[40]

In that area of the Netherlands there was no shortage of AA weapons of all calibres since it lay under the bomber 'autobahn' between Britain and Germany and multi-barrelled 20mm AA guns sited on the southern bank were brought to bear on the men of 1st and 3rd Parachute Battalions. They were also engaged by the remnants of 9th SS Reconnaissance Battalion, located in the brickworks across the Rhine, for whom the paras were 'an unbelievable target'. The recce men 'were able to lay at short range over open sights with an uninterrupted traverse up and down the road'.[41] At the same time Kampfgruppe Spindler fired on them from positions on the embankment to the north. 'Spindler's men, occupying the houses and gardens bordering the high ground to the left overlooking the low road, grenade and fired at anything that moved.'[42] By 1000 both battalions had ceased to exist; between them they numbered only 156 men. The South Staffords, leading, and 11th Parachute Battalion were also assailed by heavy fire from rifles, machine guns, flame-throwers and even *Panzerfauste*. Although they fought with determination and even had one SS officer worried for a time, the end result was still the same.

As the four battalions were trying to reach the bridge, Urquhart had at last been able to escape from his hideaway, thanks to their efforts. He was quick to realise that those battalions could not hope to reach Frost and his command; he ordered 11th Battalion to break off and withdraw and despatched a messenger to the CO of the South Staffords to do likewise. That message never arrived and the South Staffords continued to fight. Their surviving PIATs were keeping the SPGs of Assault Gun Brigade 280 at bay but once ammunition was exhausted the SPGs pressed on and the battalion was forced to scatter. Worse still, 11th Battalion had formed up for its withdrawal, unaware of what was happening behind them, and 'were caught in the open with catastrophic results'. The afternoon was spent by the survivors of all four battalions trying to make their way, often in small fighting groups, to Oosterbeek.[43]

Meanwhile, concerted attacks on Frost's positions continued and intensified. The house defended by Jack Grayburn's platoon was attacked again and again

Major General 'Roy' Urquhart outside 1st Airborne Division HQ in Arnhem's Hartenstein Hotel. The flag beside him is that of Airborne Forces. As with everyone else in the Division, Urquhart was in danger from German shells, mortar rounds and machine-gun fire. (*IWM BU 1136*)

but every attack was repelled, largely due to Grayburn's 'valour and skill in organising and encouraging his men'. When the house was set on fire, however, there was no alternative but to evacuate. Lieutenant Grayburn then assumed command of a group that included survivors of 2 Platoon but also elements of other arms, creating a defensive force and organising defensive positions to cover the bridge approaches.[44]

Sturmbannführer Ludwig Spindler, who had commanded the *Panzer-Artillerie* regiment of 9th SS Division, was ordered to form an ad hoc group to prevent 1st Airborne Division entering Arnhem. His Kampfgruppe not only succeeded in that task but also launched a counter-offensive that forced Urquhart's command out of the city. Spindler was killed in action in the Ardennes in December 1944. (*Public domain*)

To the west, near Oosterbeek, Hackett's Brigade, less 11th Battalion, prepared to attack the positions along the Dreijenseweg where the Germans had established a *wand aus stahl*, a 'steel wall' of resistance, or *Sperrlinie* (barrier line), with a combination of tanks, self-propelled guns and strong infantry positions 'that no single battalion in the British Army was ever going to pierce'. Such was the German firepower, with more than adequate supplies of ammunition, that not even a brigade supported by armour would be able to break through to reach Arnhem bridge. On one end of the line a crossroads marked its northern cut off. There stood a hotel, the Leeren Doedel, which was incorporated into the line. The Oosterbeek Hoog railway station marked the southern end, where the Dreijenseweg crossed the railway cutting on a bridge. Hackett's 4 Parachute Brigade would be smashed on that blocking line.[45]

The Sperrlinie was held by Kampfgruppe Spindler commanded by Obersturmbannführer Ludwig Spindler, commander of Hohenstaufen's armoured artillery regiment. The 34-year-old Spindler was an experienced officer with much combat experience. His practice of leading by example gained him the respect of his soldiers. He had been awarded the Iron Cross Second Class in Poland in 1939 and the Iron Cross First Class in Russia. With II SS Panzerkorps he was transferred to Normandy where he earned the German Cross in Gold. When the Allied airborne drops started on 17 September, he was given command of a number of 'alarm' companies formed from units of Hohenstaufen. By force of personality, he was able to create a cohesive unit from such disparate groups. At 1730 on D Day, Kampfgruppe Spindler was ordered into action, its task to attack from east to west using the main routes from the centre of Arnhem to Oosterbeek.[46]

By the time the depleted 4 Parachute Brigade was launched against the Sperrlinie, Kampfgruppe Spindler was a well-led and well-equipped force, determined to prevent any British advance. Under his command, Spindler had the survivors of his own artillery regiment, about 100 assault pioneers from the Hohenstaufen engineer battalion, a light AA battery, and Sepp Krafft's battalion of some 300 men. In fact, Spindler had so many units under command that he formed two more Kampfgruppen, one built around the anti-tank battalion of Hohenstaufen under its commander Klaus von Allworden, the other from 9th Panzer Regiment under Untersturmführer Harder, which included three companies of infantry, one of them composed of naval personnel. It was Kampfgruppe von Allworden that stopped 1st and 3rd Parachute Battalions' attempt to by-pass Kampfgruppe Krafft on D Day. Allworden's command was later assigned to Kampfgruppe Bruhns, a Wehrmacht group, when it arrived.[47]

Before daybreak on the 19th, the soldiers in the Sperrlinie were aware of the sounds of battle on their left flank as the ill-fated British units made their

Two Flakpanzer IVs, supported by infantry, on the Dreijenseweg on 20 September. Known as the *Möbelwagen* (moving, or furniture, van), the Flakpanzer IV used the chassis of a Panzer IV on which was mounted a 37mm Flak 43 light AA gun and an MG34 machine gun. Intended as a stop-gap to counter ground-attack aircraft until better weapons could be produced, only 240 were built. (*Bundesarchiv 2KBK 771-15*)

way towards Arnhem bridge. An attack on the line was expected soon. It came as dawn broke. Both 156th and 10th Parachute Battalions, having occupied the high ground north of Arnhem, advanced during the evening and night, clashing as they did so with outposts of the Sperrlinie. Companies of both British battalions made determined attacks along the west-east-running woods north and south of the Dreijenseweg. Although the attacks were supported by some light artillery and mortars, the paras were trying to take a line that more than matched their firepower and numbers. In places, however, it looked as if the British might succeed. Sturmmann Alfred Ziegler, a despatch rider, was with Kampfgruppe Bruhns as some of the outlying posts were overrun. He recalled that Captain Bruhns was concerned that, without reinforcements, a further attack would lead to a withdrawal. Such was Bruhns' concern that Ziegler was sent towards Arnhem to hurry forward reinforcements that were believed to be on their way.[48]

Among the reinforcements found in a nearby wood was an SS battery of self-propelled light anti-aircraft guns. Mounted on half-tracks, the unit was commanded by an officer-cadet. Then a further mobile light AA unit

Infantry supporting StuGs of Kampfgruppe Möller advance towards Oosterbeek on the Utrechtseweg. (*Bundesarchiv 497-3530-32a, P.J. Jacobsen*)

arrived. Commanded by a major, its half-tracks mounted 20mm guns, either *Flakzwilling* (twin) or *Flakvierling* (quadruple) weapons. Although relatively slow-firing in their intended role, both were lethal against unprotected infantry. They were deployed into the line promptly. Although their sites had

Flakvierling, or quadruple 20mm anti-aircraft guns. With a practical rate of fire of 800 rounds per minute, it was a devastating weapon when used against low-flying aircraft and even more devastating when deployed against infantry. (*Public domain*)

been reconnoitred quickly, the weapons' arcs of fire were such 'that nothing could move in the open, and attacking infantry would only be able to penetrate with difficulty through the wooded areas'.[49]

The multiple AA guns were turned on the two leading companies of 156th Battalion and the paras were cut down in the horrific hailstorm of 20mm shells.

As 10th Parachute Battalion withdrew across the landing zone on 19 September, the gliders carrying the Polish anti-tank guns arrived. (This view is looking north across LZ L.) although supply containers had been dropped an hour earlier, they remained uncollected; most of the soldiers responsible for their collection had been killed, mainly at Oosterbeek railway crossing. (*Photograph via Jasper Booty*)

This sudden crescendo of heavy-calibre fire was apparent even to the … companies moving up to support in depth, as 20mm rounds exploded and ricocheted among top branches and from tree trunks. … Attacks petered out, mown down by this sudden increase in the concentration of fire. Exhausted survivors stumbled and exfiltrated back through the trees, and began to dig in around the vicinity of the start line.[50]

There was no possibility of breaking through in the face of such firepower. Although it had yet to become clear, the tide of battle at Arnhem was turning against 1st Airborne Division. The point at which reinforcement or re-supply could influence positively the flow of battle for Urquhart's formation had been passed and the Sperrlinie had been the critical element in the German defence of Arnhem and its bridge. From being a steel wall or blocking line, Spindler's defence line would become the start line for a German advance on Oosterbeek, which was to become the final bastion for 1st Airborne Division.

Hackett's 4 Parachute Brigade had advanced into battle for the first and only time. The survivors would fight a defensive battle in Oosterbeek to which they withdrew, having been repelled by Spindler's Kampfgruppe.

As both battalions withdrew from the Dreijenseweg, the Polish glider lift arrived carrying the brigade's artillery and engineers (the Polish paratroopers were still in England) and there was much confusion, with the Poles caught in crossfire between 10th Parachute Battalion and Germans. As men of 7th King's Own Scottish Borderers came to help unload the gliders there were some instances of 'friendly fire'.[51]

Such was the ferocity of the battle that day that another posthumous award of the Victoria Cross was earned. Captain Lionel Queripel, an officer of the Royal Sussex Regiment, was serving with 10th Parachute Battalion. That afternoon he had been commanding a composite company composed of soldiers from

Captain Lionel Ernest Queripel VC, of 10th Parachute Battalion, commissioned in the Royal Sussex Regiment, earned a posthumous Victoria Cross for his actions in organising a composite company from all three battalions of Hackett's 4 Parachute Brigade. Although wounded, he also carried an injured NCO to the aid post. A veteran of the North African campaign, he is wearing the ribbon of the Africa Star. (*IWM HU 2030*)

all three battalions of 4 Parachute Brigade in an advance towards Arnhem when they came under heavy machine-gun fire and sustained heavy casualties. The company was also split up on either side of the road. Queripel began re-organising his command under sustained fire. Not only did he cross and re-cross the road to do so, but he also carried a wounded NCO to the aid post although wounded himself.

Captain Queripel then led a successful attack on a German strongpoint that was holding up the advance. Later he and his men were cut off and under machine-gun and mortar fire. Although wounded in both arms he continued to inspire his men but, deciding that the position was untenable, ordered his soldiers to withdraw. He provided covering fire with a pistol and hand grenades. He was not seen again. The citation for the VC states that during a nine-hour period he 'displayed the highest standard of gallantry under most difficult and trying circumstances. His courage, leadership and devotion to duty were magnificent, and an inspiration to all.'[52]

Chapter Ten

On D plus 3, Wednesday 20 September, German attacks continued against the crossings at Son and Veghel, but vigorous counter-attacks by 101st Airborne, supported by British armour, checked them. On that morning, too, contact was established between Browning's HQ at Nijmegen and Urquhart in Oosterbeek and, for the first time, the world outside Arnhem became aware of how serious the situation was north of the Rhine. It was clear that 1st Airborne Division was so weak as to be no longer capable of punching through to Frost at Arnhem bridge.

Of Urquhart's nine infantry battalions, only 1st Border Regiment survived as a coherent unit:[1] the other battalions had suffered heavy casualties that, in other circumstances, would have led to their withdrawal. In the circumstances, Urquhart decided to withdraw the division towards Oosterbeek, leaving Frost's command isolated at the bridge.[2] The Germans attacking Frost's positions were by then well supported by tanks and self-propelled guns.

Urquhart's new intention was to create a defensive perimeter around Oosterbeek, secure the ferry crossing at Driel and hold out until XXX Corps

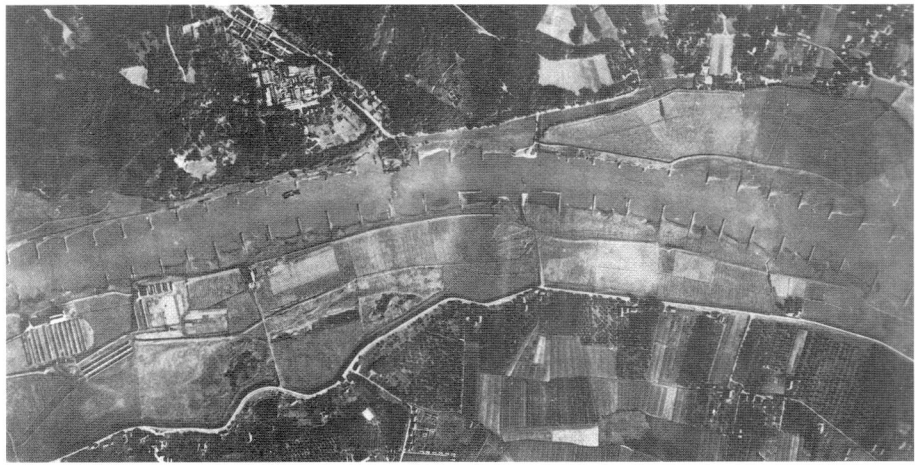

An aerial photograph, taken earlier in 1944, showing the Driel ferry in the centre of the image. The stretch of the Rhine included is from west of Heveadorp to the eastern side of Oosterbeek, just beyond the church. (*Border and King's Own Royal Border Regimental Museum*)

arrived. Some sources suggest that, using the local telephone system, Urquhart informed Frost of his decision, although Frost's account of the conversation was that Urquhart did 'not [have] anything really encouraging about the ability of the Division to get through to us'. He also wrote that Urquhart's HQ 'came on the air', suggesting a radio rather than a telephone conversation.[3] By that time, Frost's force had suffered very heavy casualties and was short of food, water, and medical supplies for the many wounded. There was also a grave shortage of ammunition, including anti-tank rounds, which allowed German armour to come closer and demolish systematically British positions from close range; flame-throwers were used to clear any defenders from the rubble. With many buildings on the point of collapse, a truce was arranged to allow British wounded to be evacuated into German hands. Those evacuated included Frost, injured by a mortar round; he had handed over command to Major Freddie Gough, OC of 1 Airborne Reconnaissance Squadron.[4]

Meanwhile Lieutenant Jack Grayburn continued his defensive stance, using a system of fighting patrols to stop German access to nearby houses which would have threatened the defence of the bridge. To counter this measure, the Germans deployed AFVs, including tanks, and subjected the positions to such intense fire that Grayburn was compelled to move farther north. Realising that the enemy was trying to lay demolition charges under the bridge, he organised a fighting patrol to drive them away, allowing time for the charges to be defused. Wounded again, he refused to be evacuated. When a tank closed on the position, Grayburn stood up in full view and directed his men to withdraw to the main perimeter. He was killed that night. As Frost wrote, 'Though hit several times, he refused to leave his men and died in action with them'.[5]

The citation for Lieutenant Grayburn's Victoria Cross concludes:

From the evening of September 17th until the night of September 20th, 1944, a period of over three days, Lieutenant Grayburn led his men with supreme gallantry and determination. Although in pain and weakened by his wounds, short of food and without sleep, his courage never flagged. There is no doubt that, had it not been for this officer's inspiring leadership and personal bravery, the Arnhem bridge could never have been held for this time.[6]

As the day wore on, German pressure overcame British resistance until the northern approaches to the bridge fell under German control, allowing reinforcements to cross the bridge and move to support the Germans fighting farther to the south around Nijmegen. Although four Tiger tanks crossed the bridge at 1800 on their way south, continuing resistance prevented any further

A Tiger I tank. Tigers were railed to Arnhem and thus were not present in the early phase of the battle. The King Tiger, or Tiger II, also made an appearance but the earlier version proved more effective in the built-up area. (*Public domain*)

vehicles from following.[7] Although British resistance at the bridge continued throughout the day, the end was inevitable and, by early Thursday morning, most of Gough's command had been made prisoners. By 0500 on Thursday resistance at the bridge had all but ceased. As the struggle came to an end, a radio message was sent from Gough's men. Although not received by the British, it was heard by German forces; it ended with 'Out of ammunition. God Save the King!' However, some British troops continued fighting and would not fire their final shots for another two days. Gough and his men even tried to break out in the face of Kampfgruppe Knaust at 0900.[8]

The initial intention had been for 1st Airborne Division to seize and hold Arnhem bridge for two days. Although the bridge was never wholly in British hands, a small force of some 740 men had denied its use to the Germans for twice that time – against opposition significantly stronger than expected.

Since the remnants of many shattered units had already withdrawn to Oosterbeek from Arnhem, the eastern section of the new perimeter was already in place. Company commanders had improvised ad hoc sub-units to deny the enemy the approaches to Oosterbeek. Among them was Major Richard Lonsdale DSO MC,[9] second-in-command of 11th Parachute Battalion, who assumed command of a number of groups and their positions. Having fought off several German attacks, Lonsdale's men withdrew to the new divisional perimeter. Renamed Lonsdale Force, they became the mainstay of the

'Gallipoli', an anti-tank gun of No. 26 (Anti-Tank) Platoon 1st Border, in action against a German flamethrower on 20 September. The flame-thrower, a converted Char B, was less than 100 yards away. (*IWM BU 1109*)

defensive effort on the south-eastern perimeter of Oosterbeek.[10] The greater part of the western defence would be provided by 1st Border Regiment, whilst a miscellany of units covered the northern portion of the line. With more units falling back, a re-organisation resulted in a perimeter shaped as a thumb with the Nederrijn as its southern base.[11] Along the top of the 'thumb' were men of 7th King's Own Scottish Borderers, while the eastern flank was held by the remnants of 10th and 156th Parachute Battalions and Pathfinders with, as we have seen, Lonsdale Force close to the river in the south-east.[12] Included in Lonsdale Force were those survivors who had been withdrawn from the vain attempt to reach the bridge in Arnhem – men of 1st, 3rd and 11th Parachute Battalions. Within the perimeter were 1st Airlanding Light Regiment's guns and several anti-tank guns.

Units in the Wolfheze area also began withdrawing to Oosterbeek on D plus 3 but came under heavy pressure from the Germans. Several groups were encircled and taken prisoner, one of which numbered 130 men.[13] A further group of 150 from 156th Parachute Battalion led by Brigadier Hackett was pinned down in a hollow about a quarter-mile from the Oosterbeek perimeter. That they reached the hollow, later known as Hackett's Hollow, was due largely to the leadership of Major Geoffrey Powell, who led a platoon-strength charge to gain the objective, followed by the remainder of the group, which

Soldiers of C Company 1st Border behind a hedgerow as they prepare to meet an enemy attack. (*IWM BU 1103*)

Prominent in the Oosterbeek defence was Major Richard 'Dickie' Lonsdale (third from the left). Born in County Leitrim, Ireland, he had served in India with the Leicestershire Regiment and is pictured at Razmak on the North West Frontier with, among others, (left to right) an unknown sepoy, Sergeant William 'Bill' Stevens, Sergeant A. Horrocks and Lieutenant Hillen. (*Stevens' family photograph, courtesy of Mr and Mrs Martin Cassidy*)

included some German prisoners.[14] Late in the afternoon, having spent most of the day in the cover of the hollow, the group made their breakout with about ninety reaching 1st Border's positions.[15]

Another posthumous Victoria Cross was earned on D plus 3. Sergeant John D. Baskeyfield of 2nd South Staffords was in command of a 6-pounder anti-tank gun which was brought into action during a determined German attack on Oosterbeek. In the early stages of the attack, Baskeyfield's gun knocked out two tanks and an SPG. In each case, Baskeyfield had allowed the AFV to approach within 100 yards of his position before giving the order to fire. He was wounded but refused to be evacuated. His gun detachment members had been killed or injured. When the Germans renewed their attack under artillery and mortar fire, Baskeyfield manned his gun

Sergeant John Daniel Baskeyfield VC of 2nd South Staffords, the only non-commissioned VC laureate of the Arnhem battle. His courage in manning a 6-pounder anti-tank gun was inspirational. (*Taylor Library*)

alone and continued firing until his weapon was knocked out. Even then, he crawled under fire to another gun with which he continued to engage the enemy. Although another soldier tried to crawl to his aid he was killed almost immediately. Daniel Baskeyfield fired two rounds at an SPG, crippling it, but was killed by shellfire as he prepared to fire a third. The citation for his VC noted that he 'spurned danger, ignored pain and, by his supreme fighting spirit, infected all who witnessed his conduct with the same aggressiveness and dogged devotion to duty which characterised his actions throughout'.[16]

A crucial element of the MARKET plan had been the aerial re-supply of the airborne formations. However, the heavy concentrations of German AA guns had adversely affected the plan and disrupted supply dropping. Although the recovery rate for air-dropped supplies began improving on D plus 3, it remained poor with 101st Airborne retrieving less than half of its supplies. Gavin's 82nd had considerable help from Dutch civilians but, even so, their recovery rate was under 70 per cent. According to Gavin, collecting all airdropped supplies would have required about a third of his overall strength; such numbers could not be assigned to the task amid a battle. The unfortunate 1st Airborne Division retrieved under 15 per cent of its supplies. Overall,

IX Tactical Air Command undertook 4,242 aircraft and 1,899 glider sorties for the loss of ninety-eight aircraft and 137 gliders. The RAF's Nos 38 and 46 Groups of Transport Command carried out 1,340 aircraft and 627 glider sorties for the loss of fifty-five aircraft and two gliders.[17]

For 1st Airborne the afternoon supply drop on D plus 3 was not much improvement on that of the previous day. Although a message had been sent to Britain to arrange a new supply DZ close to the Hartenstein Hotel, some aircraft flew to LZ Z where their supplies fell into German hands.[18] For those at Oosterbeek there was the galling experience of watching critical supplies also falling into enemy hands: the Germans were using British marker panels and flares, which the airmen assumed indicated British positions. Of 164 aircraft deployed, ten were shot down in the Arnhem area.[19] According to one source, only 13 per cent of the supplies reached Urquhart's soldiers.[20] A note from Brereton's chief of staff, Brigadier General Floyd Parkes, in England to the army commander suggested that the 'British lost 18 out of 190 planes trying to drop resupply to 1st British A/B'. Whilst inaccurate in that respect, the note also confirmed that radio contact had been established between 1st Airborne HQ and the UK. The link, the sole one between the division and Britain, was via a BBC set in the Hartenstein Hotel.[21]

The flanking operations to support XXX Corps were also proving slow. Although 15th (Scottish) Division of XII Corps had forced its way to the Wilhelmina canal line, the Germans stubbornly held on to the village of Best. Before deploying in Operation GARDEN, the division had been involved in a hard battle to secure the Gheel bridgehead; in three days of fighting 8th Royal Scots of 44 (Lowland) Brigade had lost 230 officers and men killed, wounded or taken prisoner, of whom the dead numbered thirty-one. It could be said that the division was engaged in GARDEN before the operation even began since they were fighting to extend the Gheel bridgehead. On the night of D Day for MARKET 2nd Argyll and Sutherland Highlanders made an assault-boat crossing to relieve 6th Royal Scots Fusiliers in the Aart bridgehead; the fusiliers had suffered over 170 casualties in three days, including eighteen killed. By the 19th, when the fighting in the Gheel/Aart bridgehead was closed down, 15th Division had lost 900 casualties, the majority (over 500) in 44 Brigade.[22] Thus the division had already endured several days of hard fighting and suffered heavy losses before it crossed the Wilhelmina canal unopposed on 21 September to advance to Best. On the 22nd D Company 7th Seaforth Highlanders entered Best, believing it to be unoccupied. However, the town had a German garrison that reacted sharply after its initial surprise and a bitter battle followed in which D Company lost thirty-three men and was forced to withdraw. That withdrawal was followed by further attacks, launched by

46 Brigade and 15th (Scottish) Reconnaissance Regiment, which evolved into a bitterly-contested five-day battle that featured house-to-house fighting.[23]

Although 44 Brigade had been held in reserve to protect the route along which XXX Corps advanced, it was released on the 24th to re-join 15th Division. With 227 Brigade, 44 Brigade launched an attack to the north in which they cleared the ground up to the Dommel river. The division remained in action in the Best area until relieved by 51st (Highland) Division at the beginning of October.

VIII Corps was also finding the going hard but was deploying 69 Brigade of 50th (Northumbrian) Division to support 101st Airborne.

To the south, the American airborne divisions continued their advances against determined opposition. Gavin's plan for a waterborne assault came closer to reality with the arrival of the promised assault boats from XXX Corps. The assault across the Waal would be made by two companies of 3rd/504th Parachute Infantry Regiment with fire support from British and US artillery, British tanks and 2 TAF Typhoons, the aircraft bombing and strafing the enemy just before H Hour, 1400 on D plus 3.

Using the British-supplied Goatley[24] canvas assault boats, 27-year-old Major Julian A. Cook led two companies of his 3rd/504th across the Waal at Nijmegen in the face of strong enemy opposition that inflicted heavy casualties on the paratroopers. As Gavin wrote:

> [They] had a hard time getting the boats into deep water while they climbed over the sides with their weapons. To add to their difficulties, German small arms fire began to intercept the fragile flotilla. Never having rowed together, the troopers sometimes worked against each other, and boats were spinning in the river. The German fire steadily increased, heavy artillery fire joining the machine-gun and mortar fire.[25]

The American paratroopers, having rowed across the river using paddles and rifle butts, landed on the north bank, cleared it of enemy and advanced on the village of Lent and the railway and road bridges. A troop of Grenadier Shermans, led by Sergeant Peter Robinson, rushed the bridge from the southern end, crossed despite enemy fire and joined the American paratroopers in the village. The crossing, known as the 'Hail Mary Crossing', filled witnesses with admiration for Cook's men.

> Lieutenant John Gorman, an Irish Guards tank commander, was pumping shells at the north bank as fast as his crewmen could unleash them. The little American armada struck him as almost pathetically small against

the formidable backdrop of the river, the opposite bank and the hulking bridges looming a couple miles to the right. ... 'It seemed to me the Germans must have had their guns firing two or three feet above the water level, catching the Americans across the chests,' he later said. ... Major Edward Tyler was worried about the safety of his own tanks ... perched out in the open, along the dike road, on the river side of the power station.[26]

The squadron's Shermans had been silhouetted against the skyline, firing their main guns and machine guns, as well as smoke shells. From the nearby power station Browning and Colonel Reuben Tucker, of 504 PIR, also observed as the boats made their way through enemy fire. Browning described Cook's men as 'magnificent troops'[27] while Sir John Gorman told both authors that the crossing was the bravest thing he had witnessed during the campaign in North-West Europe.[28] As a result of their courage, Nijmegen railway bridge was in Allied hands. The road bridge also fell to an attack by 3/504 PIR, who had followed the assault crossing, and by 505 PIR and the Grenadiers advancing through the town. Horrocks was prompted to write in his memoirs: 'Of the many battle honours which the Grenadier Guards can claim, none can have been more richly deserved than Nijmegen.'[29]

In addition to the work of the Grenadiers and the American paratroopers, Lieutenant A.G.C. Jones, reconnaissance officer of 14 Field Squadron RE, 'succeeded in seeking out the charges and in rendering them harmless', thus preserving the bridge from demolition.[30]

A squadron of Grenadier Shermans and two companies of Irish Guards which crossed during the night made no further advance. This was indeed a missed opportunity; the road to the Rhine was defended only by detached picquets from 9th SS Panzer Reconnaissance Battalion at Elst and on the road towards Arnhem. Given this leeway, the Germans had set up a blocking position north of Lent by the time darkness fell.

D Day plus 4 was the day on which a second posthumous Medal of Honor was earned by a paratrooper, this time by one of Gavin's men. In the ranks of Company C of 1/504 PIR was Private John R. Towle, a native of Ohio, who had enlisted in March 1943. By September 1944 he was a veteran of North Africa and Italy, having dropped at Salerno.

The previous day, Private Towle and Company C, as part of the third assault wave across the Waal, were subject only to sporadic enemy fire, mostly from the railway bridge area. A bridgehead, albeit weak, was established, against which several counter-attacks were made. With that bridgehead on the north side of the Waal, Arnhem and 1st Airborne Division were only a stone's throw away. Guards Armoured tanks had crossed Nijmegen bridge to spend the night at Lent, a small town just north of the road bridge. They had to wait for 43rd (Wessex) Division, with whom they could clear the area between Nijmegen and Arnhem of German forces and reach their brothers in arms at Arnhem bridge.

One counter-attack against 82nd Airborne at about noon on the 21st consisted of two tanks, 100 infantry and a half-track. Flanagan described the engagement:

> With extraordinary courage for even a paratrooper, Pvt. John R. Towle, a bazooka man … climbed out of his foxhole, ran across an open field, knelt, and fired two bazooka rounds at the tanks. He got two direct hits and forced the tanks to back off. Still in no man's land by himself, Towle saw nine Germans race to a nearby house.

Private John R. Towle, a Bazooka man in Company C, 1/504 PIR, a native of Ohio, showed 'extraordinary courage, for even a paratrooper' when he engaged enemy tanks and forced them to pull back. He was posthumously awarded the Medal of Honor. (*NARA*)

> He ran up to the house, fired a bazooka round through the door, and killed all nine. Towle had one target left – the half-track. He ran towards the vehicle and, in plain sight, got down on one knee and took aim. Unfortunately, just at that moment, a mortar round landed right beside him and killed him. For his unusual valor, Towle was awarded the Medal of Honor posthumously.[31]

Shortly afterwards the Germans broke off their attacks. The citation for John R. Towle's Medal of Honor concludes with the observation:

> By his heroic tenacity, at the price of his life, Pvt. Towle saved the lives of many of his comrades and was directly instrumental in breaking up the enemy counter-attack.

It seems that the Germans expected Urquhart's force to break out from Oosterbeek as Model subordinated von Tettau's group to check any such attempt. Reinforcements continued arriving for Model's command while the recently-formed XII SS Corps, with 180th and 190th Infantry Divisions, both understrength, was expected over the following week. Bittrich was also ordering counter-attacks against the Americans.

A StuG operating in a built-up area. Such mobile artillery pieces proved very effective as support to the German infantry who, in turn protected the AFVs from Allied infantry with close-range anti-armour weapons. (*Public domain*)

However, only three depleted battalions of Frundsberg barred the way from Nijmegen to Arnhem and it seemed that XXX Corps might reach Arnhem bridge that night. It was not to be: Guards Armoured, which had been fighting hard, faced difficult going in the dark and, without infantry support, Horrocks allowed them to halt for the night.[32] That halt would prove to be a mistake on Horrocks' part.

Less than perfect weather in England again delayed the third lift, carrying 1 Polish Parachute Brigade and the US 325th Glider Infantry Regiment; the latter was due to land close to Groesbeek. However, 43rd (Wessex) Division had crossed the Meuse-Escaut canal and, after a short delay around Eindhoven, its leading brigade, 130, reached the bridge at Grave, where it stopped for the night.

Time was running out in more ways than one for those engaged in both MARKET and GARDEN. Eisenhower's HQ had moved from Granville in Normandy to Versailles, close to Paris, thereby improving SHAEF's communications considerably. It seems that a change of location and scenery had affected Eisenhower's memory for he sent a telegram to Montgomery's HQ in which he re-affirmed the northern thrust's priority while denying the plans for a broad-front strategy. By this stage of the battle deadlock had set in,

Paratroopers of Major General Sosabowski's 1 Polish Independent Parachute Brigade emplane at RAF Saltby in Leicestershire. (*Public domain*)

but it was clear that the objective of taking Arnhem bridge could no longer be achieved. As Badsey comments, 'The whole nature of the Battle of Arnhem was about to change.'[33]

The morning of Thursday 21 September, D Day plus 4, was one of unpleasant weather with fog and rain predominating, and the air was chillingly cold. Since Nijmegen bridge was in Allied hands, Model reviewed the situation and his dispositions, ordering Korps Feldt, which had taken considerable punishment on the Groesbeek Heights, to hold its positions. II SS Panzerkorps was given command of all forces as far south as Elst and was also to clear the British out of Arnhem while preventing any Allied drive north from Nijmegen. As already noted, Gough's men tried unsuccessfully to break out of Arnhem that morning but to no avail and, save for isolated small groups and individuals, the British force at Arnhem bridge ceased to exist; it had been intended to hold the bridge for two days but the small force had denied its use to the enemy for almost twice that time. Meanwhile Student's First Fallschirmjäger Army was ordered to prepare a pincer attack against the main road, by this time known as Hell's Highway to the Allies, on Friday. The pincers were to be provided by LXXXVI and LXXXVIII Corps.

Urquhart had re-organised his command in the Oosterbeek pocket, creating two zones, a western and northern zone under Hicks and an eastern one under Hackett. The divisional perimeter, about three miles in all (4.8 kilometres) was a series of defended localities using houses and slit trenches. Divisional

Several members of Urquhart's HQ staff carried the US M1 carbine, including this soldier firing from the front of the Hartenstein towards nearby parkland. However, the presence of a soldier tempting goats into the undergrowth suggests that the image may have been posed. (*IWM 1122*)

HQ was in the centre in the Hartenstein Hotel. Kampfgruppe von Tettau had pushed 1st Border off the Westerbouwing Heights to positions along the western side of the new perimeter. From the Heights the Germans could bring fire down on any attempted crossing of the river. However, throughout the day, the airborne positions held firm.

The Germans had dubbed the Oosterbeek pocket 'Der Kessel', the 'Cauldron', in military parlance an encircled area but, as Powell comments, 'at Oosterbeek an accurate metaphor indeed'.[34] At 0900 the day's first onslaught was launched by infantry with tank and SP artillery support. In the course of the fighting Major Robert Cain, a Manxman and officer commanding a company of the South Staffords, distinguished himself in fighting off the attackers. Using a PIAT, he knocked out a German SPG that was later destroyed by a 75mm howitzer. Cain was wounded in the engagement but continued to command his company and fight off German AFVs with a PIAT, showing complete disregard for his own safety. He was awarded the Victoria Cross and was the only VC laureate to survive the battle. The citation for his award noted that 'Major Cain was everywhere where danger threatened, moving amongst his men and encouraging them by his fearless example to hold out.' Although wounded several times he refused medical attention.[35]

Urquhart had fewer than 4,000 men who would defy German efforts to overrun the perimeter for the next five days. In that effort they were supported by the artillery of XXX Corps, and especially 64th Medium Regiment, a London TA regiment. That morning at 0935, the regiment arrived at Nijmegen, eleven miles from Arnhem, where its radio net picked up signals from 1 Forward Observation Unit in Arnhem.[36] This was 1st Airborne Division's first contact outside the Arnhem/Oosterbeek area since the initial drop on the 17th. Together with 419 Battery of 52nd (Bedfordshire Yeomanry) Heavy Regiment, equipped with 7.2-inch howitzers, 64th's guns (eight 4.5- and eight 5.5-inch weapons in 211 and 212 Medium Batteries) provided support for the airborne from then until

Manxman Major Robert H. Cain VC, 2nd South Staffords, the sole VC laureate to survive the battle, continued leading his company although wounded and engaging enemy tanks with a PIAT. He is shown wearing the ribbons of the Victoria Cross and the 1939-43 Star (later 1939-45 Star). (*IWM H 40971*)

A PIAT team in cover on an exercise in England. The PIAT had the advantage of not revealing its firing position since it produced neither flame nor smoke when fired. (*Airborne Museum Hartenstein*)

the withdrawal. (Urquhart later addressed 64th Medium Regiment, telling the gunners that, without their support, 'We would almost surely have been wiped out'. With HQ XXX Corps' approval, the unit was styled 'Airborne Medium Regiment' and every gunner was given a 'Pegasus' badge, which was worn on the bottom of the left sleeve, a privilege also extended to 419 Heavy Battery. However, 'higher authority' decided otherwise and 64th was ordered to remove their badges and drop the 'Airborne' title. Strangely, 419 Heavy Battery continued wearing the Pegasus badge and its descendants do so today as 201 (Hertfordshire and Bedfordshire Yeomanry) Parachute Battery.) For most of that time 64th's radio link provided 1st Airborne Division's only link with XXX Corps. A battery of 7th Medium Regiment and two field regiments from 43rd (Wessex) Division would also add their firepower to the artillery support for the Oosterbeek defenders.

Another easing of pressure on Oosterbeek, albeit temporary, came with the arrival later that day of the paratroopers of Sosabowski's 1 Polish Parachute Brigade. Of 114 C-47 Skytrains[37] that took off, forty-one returned to their bases on orders from IX Troop Carrier Command which had decided that if the aircraft were in the air too long then landing would be too dangerous, due to adverse weather conditions. That removed almost a complete battalion from the brigade's order of battle. The aircraft that continued did so because their

A 5.5-inch medium gun such as those used by 212 Battery of 64th Medium Regiment. By 1944 the range of the weapon had been increased to 18,100 yards; the 4.5-inch medium gun, which equipped 211 Battery, and shared the same carriage as the 5.5, had a range of 20,500 yards. (*Private photo*)

crews, who had been given incorrect transmission codes, failed to understand the message. However, in another fortuitous turn, a rare message from Arnhem had warned the Poles to drop on the polder east of Driel since DZ K was not secure. By doing so, they could secure the ferry at Heveadorp on the east bank of the Rhine.

At 1700 the Poles dropped, sustaining casualties from enemy fire, much of it from Luftwaffe fighters attacking the aerial formation; of over 100 aircraft waiting to intercept the C-47s, about a quarter evaded the escorts to attack the Skytrains; thirteen were lost to fighters and AA fire. Once on the ground, Sosabowski's paratroopers assembled quickly and moved to the riverbank. There was no ferry.[38] The ferryman had sunk it to prevent the Germans using it. The Poles' arrival prompted a redeployment of German troops to the south of the river. Two battalions and other elements were moved across during the night. To the Germans the Polish landing appeared to be an attempt to capture Arnhem bridge from the south. With Kampfgruppe Knaust moving to counter Guards Armoured at Elst, a blocking force, *Sperrverband* Harzer, of hastily-organised units, was placed west of the road from Nijmegen between the bridge and Sosabowski's men.[39]

Major General Stanisław Sosabowski whose Polish brigade's entry into the battle was delayed by poor weather so that it became piecemeal, thus depriving the Poles of their opportunity to make a significant contribution. (*Public domain*)

Although the Polish drop had been witnessed by Urquhart's men, radio contact was impossible. Private Ernest Archer swam across the river to let the Poles know that they were needed on the northern bank and that rafts would be provided. At 0300 on the 22nd, with no rafts having appeared, the Poles moved to Driel and established defensive positions.

An RAF 38 Group re-supply mission after the Polish drop also fell foul of Luftwaffe fighters with ten Focke Wulf 190s penetrating the escort screen to attack the slow transport machines. In the ensuing melee, twenty-three of the aircraft were shot down while almost forty were damaged by either the Fw 190s or AA fire. Of 300 tons of supplies intended for 1st Airborne Division only 41 tons fell in the divisional area.

A Focke Wulf 190D fighter. Introduced in 1941, the 190 was popular with pilots, performed well and was better armed than the Messerschmitt Bf 109. Much improved by 1944, Fw 190s took a heavy toll of Allied aircraft in the battle area. (*Public domain*)

Taylor's 101st Airborne, supported by British armour, continued to battle German interdiction along Hell's Highway. Limited attacks were launched to deter the enemy. Gavin's 82nd were also engaging with support from British armour, which led to the first instance of British troops entering Germany when Recce Troop of the Sherwood Rangers 'crossed the Dutch border … between Beek and Wyler'. Their reconnaissance under fire produced useful information on German strength and dispositions and the award of the MC to the troop leader, Captain McKay.[40]

Horrocks wrote that 'almost a miracle had been achieved' by the evening of the 21st with the capture of the two bridges at Nijmegen by British and American troops 'whose co-operation on this occasion should be an object lesson to all allies in the future'. Although he retired to bed 'a happy man' he commented that it was almost the last such occasion 'in this battle'.[41]

However, his fellow corps commanders, O'Connor and Ritchie, probably did not have the same sense of contentment that night. O'Connor's VIII Corps had been dispersed over 250 miles from the Seine and his leading units at the beginning of GARDEN. By the 19th, 3rd Division plus two independent brigades had arrived in the corps area and 50th (Northumbrian) Division was transferred to VIII Corps that night. On the afternoon of the 21st, Pip Roberts' 11th Armoured Division 'fought a fierce battle with 107 Panzer Brigade,

Lieutenant General Sir Richard
O'Connor. Although his VIII Corps
was spread out over 250 miles
when it was ordered to deploy for
Operation GARDEN, it made a
major contribution to the operation.
(*IWM B 10600*)

Lieutenant General Neil Ritchie commanded XII
Corps. His command faced tough opposition, with
53rd (Welsh) Division sustaining heavy losses
north of the Wilhelmina canal. (*IWM B 8222*)

which had counter-attacked from the north towards Eindhoven'. O'Connor
considered that Roberts' success in that battle had prevented the Germans
re-capturing Eindhoven.[43] Ritchie's XII Corps had experienced some tough
opposition with 53rd (Welsh) Division suffering heavy casualties in clearing
the ground south of the Wilhelmina canal, 71 Brigade having a stiff fight in
taking the village of Wintelre where German losses included forty-four dead
and 144 captured.[44] For both flanking corps, however, the situation at the end
of 21 September was that they had come almost to a halt.[45]

   On the broader picture, Dempsey was beginning to move his HQ to St
Oedenrode while Montgomery was relocating Tactical HQ of 21 Army
Group. Monty's new Tac HQ was south of Eindhoven, putting him closer to
the battle. The field marshal had also responded to Eisenhower's message (see
p. 135) asking that the supreme commander underline his commitment to the
northern thrust through a halt order to Patton and Third Army and putting
Hodges' First Army 'at least under some form of British control'.[46]

Chapter Eleven

North of the Rhine, D Day plus 5 dawned misty with light rain, continuing the unpleasant conditions that were to remain for the final days of the operation. Ground conditions were appalling, restricting even further the ability of heavy armour to move off the roads. Within the Oosterbeek perimeter there was a shortage of food to accompany the lack of sleep while ammunition had to be husbanded carefully. At the gun positions near Oosterbeek church the Germans made several attacks. On at least one occasion, they penetrated the defences and were ejected only after vicious hand-to-hand fighting.

Heavy fighting continued around the divisional perimeter while incessant shelling and snipers added to the number of casualties taken to the aid posts in the town. With Bittrich determined to destroy the British bridgehead north of the Rhine, major attacks began at 0900; Kampfgruppe Hohenstaufen attacked from the east while von Tettau's units came in from the west.[1] Only small gains were made before a lull and then, in the afternoon, the Germans made co-ordinated attacks on both northern and eastern faces of the perimeter. In the north they briefly pushed back 7th King's Own Scottish Borderers but the Scots launched a counter-attack and restored the situation, forcing the Germans out of their temporary gains.[2] However, Urquhart then grasped the fact that the northernmost tip of the perimeter held no tactical importance whatever and pulled back the units there, creating a shorter line.[3] On the eastern perimeter, the survivors of 10th Parachute Battalion were suffering heavily in their position on the main Arnhem road. Lieutenant Colonel Ken Smyth, wounded the previous day, was one of those taken prisoner; paralysed below the waist, he died over a month later. Although Hackett's HQ thought that the defenders had been wiped out, survivors appeared the following morning, led by a Gunner officer. The Germans had not gained any significant ground.[4]

Urquhart's Polish liaison officer, Captain Ludwig Zwolanski, swam across the Rhine during the day to tell Sosabowski's HQ that it was planned to widen the bridgehead at the Westerbouwing Heights while Sappers would prepare boats to ferry the Poles across close to Oosterbeek church. However, this did not work out as planned and a Sapper officer from Urquhart's staff swam across with the news. The Poles were to cross the river and come into the Oosterbeek perimeter.

At Driel the Poles were also fighting off German attacks. During the night Sperrverband Harzer had taken up positions along the railway to screen the road bridge at Arnhem from Sosabowski's soldiers. While the Allied ground advance was hampered by weather and the terrain, that same ground was working to the Poles' advantage. Without their anti-tank guns, which had landed north of the Rhine on the 19th, the Polish paratroopers depended on PIATs to combat German tanks. Since the enemy armoured vehicles were unable to manoeuvre off the narrow dyke roads, the PIAT teams scored several notable successes. The Poles had dug in and were well-positioned to deal with any threat. This day, Friday 22 September, brought the first direct contact with XXX Corps, when three Household Cavalry scout cars arrived at 0830, having used the cover of the mist to avoid being spotted. Another troop, also from C Squadron, got through that morning.

During the great MARKET GARDEN airborne operation to take the large bridges at Grave, Nijmegen and Arnhem, 2nd Household Cavalry were constantly on forward patrols. Two troops managed to get through

Soldiers of 5th Duke of Cornwall's Light Infantry, 43rd (Wessex) Division, formed part of the mobile column deployed by Horrocks that pushed through to Driel. (*IWM BU 935*)

heavy German defences on the Neder Rijn and made contact with the Polish airborne near Driel, Arnhem.[5]

Thanks to the HCR wireless sets, Sosabowski was able to make direct voice contact with Horrocks and Browning.

Later in the day, tanks of 4th/7th Royal Dragoon Guards appeared, part of a mobile column deployed by Brigadier Essame of 214 Brigade. That column included 5th Duke of Cornwall's Light Infantry (5 DCLI), a machine-gun platoon of 8th Middlesex Regiment, in universal carriers, and two DUKW amphibians carrying ammunition, medical supplies and other essentials for 1st Airborne Division. However, it proved impossible to launch the DUKWs into the river. En route, the column, which was in two elements, was 'split' by a German force that came onto the same route. The Germans were engaged and their AFVs knocked out by PIATs. By 2359 another battalion of Essame's brigade, 1st Worcesters, had reached Driel.

This was part of XXX Corps' renewed effort to reach Arnhem and it had begun early in the morning with Horrocks ordering 43rd (Wessex) Division to take all risks to reach their objective. Thomas's division attacked north from Nijmegen with 214 Brigade advancing towards Driel and 129 Brigade, with the Irish Guards Group of Guards Armoured, attacking at Elst. It was this

Shermans of XXX Corps continue their advance, passing a knocked-out 88 which had probably been deployed in the anti-tank role. (*Public domain*)

action that led to the arrival at Driel that day of the Household Cavalry scout cars and, later, the relief column from 214 Brigade.

At Oosterbeek crossroads three hotels had been taken over as dressing stations by the RAMC. On several occasions those dressing stations came under German control but, irrespective of who controlled them, British and German wounded were treated.

Between the surges of extreme violence, the battle died down and both sides patrolled aggressively. The Germans sought out weak points in the British defences, while the defenders tracked down the bothersome snipers and stalked enemy tanks and self-propelled guns. Inevitably, casualties occurred, one such being Dubliner Private James Fiely of 21 Independent Parachute Company. One of the first to arrive on D Day, Fiely was killed on the 22nd.

Enemy artillery fire, on at least one occasion, brought a bounty to the defenders. In a house close to Oosterbeek church a shell cracked open a section of wall, revealing a hoard of food. Lance Sergeant Jack Fryer, a former Royal Ulster Rifleman, recalled:

> there were tins of hot-pot, strawberries and condensed milk. Now at about that time there was a Polish anti-tank gun crew set up at the corner outside the garden. Our medic collected all the rations and made a big pot of stew, but just as he finished, a shell meant for the Poles hit … and stew went everywhere. … Still the strawberries and condensed milk tasted fine.[6]

To the south, Student launched his attacks against Hell's Highway at 0900 with, from the west, Kampfgruppe Huber, of 59th Infantry Division, and, from the east, Kampfgruppe Walther, most of which was 107 Panzer Brigade. Both forces broke through to cut that stretch of the road between Uden and Grave, which was virtually undefended. Although 101st Airborne had received some information about the attack from the Dutch Underground and the Americans were ready, the German forces were still able to disrupt the Allies. Forewarned, Taylor deployed 150 men of 506 PIR to Uden; they arrived just before the Germans. Taylor was also able to obtain support from 2 TAF, with Typhoons from 83 Group flying 119 sorties along Hell's Highway that day; the Typhoons fired rockets as well as their cannon.[7]

Elsewhere, 501 and 502 PIRs had been due to make an attack to the north-west but this had to be abandoned as Kampfgruppe Huber reached Veghel at 1400. In the ensuing battle at Veghel, the CO of 501 PIR was wounded seriously and the defence of the town, under Brigadier General McAuliffe, was reinforced to eight battalions, American and British, as the day wore on.

Horrocks was forced to divert tanks and infantry from his force to return south. The Grenadier and Coldstream Groups, under HQ 32 Guards Brigade, turned around to drive south from Grave to Uden to clear the road of Germans. Although the German pincer movement failed to close, the overall effect of Student's attacks was to stop any northward Allied movement for a day at Veghel.[8]

At 2100 the Poles began an attempt to cross the river to Heveadorp. In this operation the DUKWs used to bring supplies to the brigade should have played a critical part, but they were no longer available, having been hit by enemy fire or become bogged.[9] Only four small two-man rubber reconnaissance boats were available, plus 'an unwieldy RAF dinghy'; these were to be tied together and 'run' across by signals cable. Unfortunately, the cables broke or snagged and the oars provided were inadequate for the fast-flowing current. In addition, the Germans were firing on the crossing area. The solution reached was for Polish sappers to row the boats with a single passenger on each journey. As a result, only fifty-two Poles crossed before the operation was halted at 0400 on Saturday, D Day plus 6.[10] According to Waddy, of those who made the crossing, only thirty-five reached the perimeter.[11] They were sent to reinforce 1st Border.[12] Some were shocked at the condition of the defenders; men who had been deprived of sleep and adequate food for days had lost weight and appeared gaunt and exhausted.[13]

It had been a very difficult day, as indicated by Urquhart's exhortation to Browning that evening that relief within twenty-four hours was imperative. He cannot have known that Bittrich planned the destruction of 1st Airborne Division the following day.[14]

The weather in England remained poor with visibility restricted by mist and thus there were no re-supply missions. Poor conditions also prevented RAF Bomber Command from carrying out any major operations, Middlebrook and Everitt noting that 'Bad weather – rain and low cloud – prevented any major operations during the next 48 hours'.[15] However, US Ninth Air Force aircraft carried out missions over the German frontier town of Kleve, not far from Arnhem while Allied close support aircraft were unable to carry out their mission at Arnhem. Ironically, as Badsey comments, 'Only at Arnhem and Nijmegen did the Luftwaffe continue to enjoy air superiority.'[16]

Saturday brought bright sunshine that, finally, heralded an improvement in the weather which allowed the tactical air forces to execute their mission with 2 TAF's No. 83 Group and IX Tactical Air Command attacking the enemy forces surrounding 1st Airborne Division in the Oosterbeek perimeter. British Typhoons and American P-47 Thunderbolts hit German ground positions throughout much of the day while also engaging those Luftwaffe

Captain F. Robson MC, No. 16 Flight, Glider Pilot Regiment, was taken prisoner after suffering a broken leg. Two men, one of them Staff Sergeant Edwards, are seen assisting him. The crew of the StuG have added track links behind the armoured shields as additional protection against PIAT and Bazooka rounds. (*Bundesarchiv 487-3527-19A KP Wenzer*)

aircraft that made an appearance. As well as supporting the defenders of the Oosterbeek perimeter, the fighters struck at German positions along the airborne corridor leading towards Oosterbeek.[17] However, Urquhart's view, and that of some others in the Oosterbeek redoubt, was different; he wrote of being disappointed bitterly by the lack of fighter support.[18] Against this, Ryan notes that the attacks were 'heartening' to men 'who had not seen a fighter since D Day'.[19] There were, inevitably, difficulties in communicating between the ground forces and the aircraft – another outworking of the radio problems – resulting in a limit to what the airmen could do. Despite this, the presence of close air support fighters provided another problem for German gunners and mortarmen.

The guns of 64th Medium Regiment and the heavies of 410 Heavy Battery continued lending their support to the defenders of Oosterbeek, engaging German artillery positions that were bombarding the British ground troops. Field guns from 43rd (Wessex) Division were also involved in XXX Corps' artillery fire-plan. Nonetheless, Saturday proved 'to be the hardest day to bear' for 1st Airborne Division, according to Powell, who was one of those within the Oosterbeek perimeter. 'The weight of metal poured into the small area by the German mortars and guns seemed to be heavier than ever, and there were few anti-tank weapons of any type left to halt the German armour.'[20]

The German main effort was made in the north, where a British force (it included a company of 1st Border, some glider pilots, the KOSB and surviving men from 156th Parachute Battalion, the Recce Squadron and the Pathfinders) held out in 'a rough half-circle'. In doing so they denied the Germans the possibility of cutting off 1st Airborne Division from their comrades on the south bank of the river. The Germans made the error of attacking Urquhart's 'thumb' from the tip rather than driving at it from either side of the base.[21]

The improved weather allowed the RAF to fly a re-supply mission from England during the afternoon, but at a cost of eight aircraft lost from 123 despatched (mostly Stirlings, although fifty were C-47 Dakotas); more than half the aircraft that returned to base had been damaged. However, little of their cargo was recovered by the defenders of Oosterbeek.[22] (Over the next two days there would be some small-scale re-supply missions flown from airfields in Belgium but, again, most supplies dropped failed to reach their intended recipients.)

On Saturday morning, at 1025, Dempsey's HQ had given I Airborne Corps permission to use a grass airfield that had been captured at Oud Keent, two miles north-west of Grave, for the landing of supplies, an altogether more effective way to deliver supplies than dropping them by parachute or simply pushing them out of the doors of aircraft. In Britain the Airborne Forward Delivery Airfield Group (AFDAG) was awaiting orders to move to the continent and prepare such airstrips for operational use. XXX Corps allocated a light AA regiment (with forty-eight Bofors 40mm guns) to defend Oud Keent, but AFDAG was not to be deployed there until the 26th, by which time Operation MARKET GARDEN was being shut down.

In the evening I Airborne Corps HQ received another signal from Second Army HQ. This signal granted permission for the withdrawal of 1st Airborne Division should circumstances demand it. Twenty minutes later, at 2100, yet another signal stipulated that the airportable 52nd (Lowland) Division would not be flown in without Dempsey's clearance. On D plus 3, Browning had turned down an offer from Major General Edmund Hakewell-Smith, 52nd's GOC, to deploy a brigade by glider to reinforce 1st Airborne.[23] Browning had very little to do. He could not influence the battle in any way: Taylor's 101st Airborne had passed to XXX Corps while Gavin's 82nd was away from the main fighting and Sosabowski's brigade was under 43rd Division command. The folly of flying in the corps HQ was being underlined in tragic fashion.

Brereton, with his uniform damaged and dirty following his redundant trip to the Netherlands, seems not to have had a clear grasp of what was happening.

Indeed, Powell avers that his diary entries suggest that 'his ignorance … seemed to be complete'. Powell quotes those diary entries, including one showing that Brereton was 'encouraged' by Browning's rejection of Hakewell-Smith's offer of a glider-borne brigade on the Wednesday, another claiming that 'Troops and supplies were sent to' 1st Airborne[24] and by a signal to Eisenhower that there were signs of improvement in the situation. Eisenhower forwarded that signal to Marshall in Washington.[25]

Brigadier General Anthony 'Nuts' McAuliffe of 101st Airborne Division commanded the division's artillery and the defence of Veghel. He would achieve greater fame at Bastogne during the German offensive in December when he earned the 'Nuts' soubriquet. (*NARA*)

As well as the re-supply mission to 1st Airborne, other aircraft were aloft to carry men to Gavin and Taylor's divisions, plus the remainder of Sosabowski's brigade. Gliders that had been grounded since D Day plus 2 carried Gavin's 325th Glider Infantry Regiment, reinforcing him with 3,385 personnel; almost 3,000 men arrived for Taylor, as well as his field artillery, 907th Glider Field Artillery Battalion.[26] During this mission the only aircraft lost was a USAAF C-47 Skytrain. However, Sosabowski could not be reinforced at Driel and his men had to be dropped on Oud Keent in Gavin's area. With this large-scale operation, an airlift of 35,000 men came to an end. It was an airlift which Brereton had planned to execute in three days, but it had taken seven.[27]

Meanwhile Brigadier General McAuliffe had continued the fight to secure the main road at Veghel. On Saturday morning the Germans had resumed their offensive, again deploying a pincer movement. Kampfgruppe Huber, which had taken a hammering the day before, was relieved on the western side of the 'pincer' by 6th Fallschirmjäger Regiment. The paras proved less than effective, having been on the march for two days while their commander considered one battalion unreliable, since it was poorly led and ill-disciplined. Kampfgruppe Walther was the other arm of the pincer, but 107 Panzer Brigade had, by then, 'been fighting and moving without respite' since Monday. Walther had also to consider a threat to his rear. VIII Corps had crossed the Willems canal the day before and thus Walther had to think about O'Connor's force.

In spite of Bittrich's determination to smash the British that day, his own men were tired and attacks were not pushed home as might have been the case with fresher troops. Outside Veghel, two battalions of 501 PIR broke the attack from the west and, by 1200, Walther had also stopped his attack. However, fighting had been bitter with heavy casualties on either side. By 1300 McAuliffe knew that he had wrested the initiative from the enemy and went onto the offensive. Two battalions of 506 PIR were sent to link with the Grenadier Group, which was attacking down the road from Uden. Both groups met two hours later: the road was open again. The Coldstream Group had also been involved in heavy fighting, losing some tanks and men, as they attacked towards Volkel that morning. During the afternoon the Coldstream had achieved their objective, nearby woods had also been cleared and the main road cleared.[28]

In Arnhem the men of Frost Force, who had been defending the bridge, were loaded onto trucks for the move to prison camps in Germany. They still faced danger, including the risk of their convoys being attacked by Allied aircraft as James Sims noted:

> I could not help wondering, however, about air attack from our planes. This was noticeably lacking during the battle but was now to be an ever-constant threat to our survival. With the Allies' absolute command of the skies nothing that moved by road, rail or river was safe from their attentions.[29]

The author of the history of XXX Corps noted that, on the night of the 23rd, an attempt was made to get supplies across the river to the airborne troops at Oosterbeek. However, it failed due to the steepness of the banks and intense fire from the Germans.[30] The same writers also recorded the RAF re-supply mission that evening: 'long lines of Stirlings flew in at zero feet to make sure of dropping their supplies in the right places. The bravery of these pilots was magnificent, for the flak was intense and losses high.'[31]

Once again, Sosabowski's men prepared to cross to the north bank of the river. Assault boats were to be provided by XXX Corps, but the boats were delayed and it was after midnight before they reached the Polish positions where many were found to be without oars. At 0300 on the 24th, the crossings began, the guns of 43rd (Wessex) Division providing support.[32] Between then and daylight, only 153 men (from Brigade HQ, 3rd Parachute Battalion and the anti-tank battery) were conveyed across the river; that was less than a quarter of the number it had been hoped to bring across.[33]

Sunday morning, D Day plus 7, began with more autumnal mist, which cleared to give fine weather with good visibility. The weather conditions permitted the aircraft of 2 TAF to fly close-support missions for the men in the Oosterbeek pocket. Sorties were flown from mid-afternoon but were constrained by the difficulties of identifying targets and the risk of hitting British positions rather than German. However, twenty-two missions were flown and, at least, had the effect of keeping German heads down. Even so, German artillery, mortars and machine guns continued harassing the surviving airborne soldiers in the perimeter, but support from XXX Corps' artillery, including the mediums and heavies of 64th Medium Regiment and 419 Battery, ensured that the battle was not one-sided. Harzer, commanding Hohenstaufen, later commented that the more 'the perimeter shrank, the more stubbornly the British troops defended every heap of ruins and every inch of ground'.[34]

On this eighth day of what had been planned as a two-day operation at most, the plight of the wounded was a major concern. In Oosterbeek, Colonel Graeme Warrack, senior medical officer of 1st Airborne Division,[35] and Urquhart's Dutch liaison officer, Lieutenant Commander Wolters (who adopted the pseudonym Johnson for the occasion), approached the Germans at the Schoonoord Hotel under a Red Cross flag and with Urquhart's permission. They met Sturmbannführer Egon Skalka, the doctor in charge of Hohenstaufen's medical personnel, and told him that they would like to arrange the evacuation of the wounded under a temporary ceasefire.[36] Skalka then drove both men into Arnhem to confer with Bittrich who readily agreed to the proposal, offered both some food and a drink and allowed them to fill their pockets with morphine, which had been captured from the British. They were also allowed to visit the St Elisabeth Hospital to see that British, Dutch and German medical staff were treating the wounded. The truce was soon in operation and some 500 wounded men were evacuated; more followed the next day. Among those evacuated was Hackett.[37]

Although it was Sunday, it was far from being a day of rest. Once again, the Germans had cut the road, only twenty-four hours after it had been re-opened to traffic. They had attacked early in the morning with a small force of some 200 infantry supported by five tanks striking at the paratroopers of 501 PIR defending Eerde, a village south of Veghel. A squadron of Cromwell tanks from 44th Royal Tank Regiment – from 7th Armoured Division of XII Corps – deployed to help the Americans; three Cromwells were knocked out in the savage fighting that followed. Although the situation was stabilised and the attack stopped, a further German assault began south of Koevering. A counter-attack by 502 PIR with British armour support was beaten back.

Reinforcements from 6th Fallschirmjäger Regiment, with tanks and SPGs in support, helped the Germans maintain the 'cut' during the hours of darkness. Not only could the cut isolate Allied forces to the north, it would also re-open Fifteenth Army's retreat route to Germany from the western Netherlands.

Earlier in the day, Horrocks, Sosabowski and Thomas of 43rd Division had met to plan the crossing of Sosabowski's 1st Polish Battalion and 4th Dorsetshire Regiment into the shrinking British perimeter around Oosterbeek; it had been an acrimonious meeting with Sosabowski objecting to Thomas detailing which Polish battalion would make the crossing. Also present were George Taylor, CO of 5 DCLI, and Lieutenant Colonel Edmund 'Eddie' Myers, Commander Royal Engineers (CRE) of 1st Airborne; Myers was to accompany the Dorsets. By evening, Horrocks was cut off south of Veghel, having been called to a conference with Dempsey at St Oedenrode; his visit to Sosabowski and Thomas had been to familiarise himself with the situation before meeting the Second Army commander.

The German attack had been planned as another pincer movement but Walther was even more concerned about the situation to his rear. VIII Corps was applying steady pressure in the direction of Nijmegen, which concerned him, while he had also received an inaccurate report of further Allied

A StuG of StuG Brigade 280 makes its way along a street close to the Museum. The armour side plates offered protection against man-portable anti-tank weapons while infantry keep pace with the AFV. (*Bundesarchiv 497 3531 4a PK Jacobsen*)

airborne troops dropping at Uden the previous day. O'Connor had been given responsibility for Hell's Highway north to Grave with 101st Airborne under his command, as well as 50th (Northumbrian) Division. Although 69 Brigade of the Northumbrians had been detached to Nijmegen, another brigade was assigned to the area south-east of St Oedenrode and the third was preparing to take over the area south-east of Veghel.[38]

D Day plus 7 was the day, according to Essame, when Horrocks 'faced the facts'. The corps commander appreciated that

> The position held by the airborne division had no military value. It was merely a nebulous area … . [Horrocks] therefore instructed 43 Division to carry out the evacuation … . The final decision was reached at a conference at headquarters, 43 Division, on the morning of the 24th.[39]

By this stage the strength of 1st Airborne Division in the Oosterbeek perimeter had been whittled down by death and injury to some 1,800 men dispersed in small defensive tactical groups that continued to defy the German pressure. However, the soldiers on either side of that perimeter line had been fighting for days – in many cases for a week – without adequate rest, with little sleep or food and facing death from bullet, bomb or shell. Powell notes that 'the units whose fighting was confined largely to the perimeter battle' suffered the highest proportion of deaths, not the battalions of 1 Parachute Brigade, 'as might have been expected'. Losses were highest in 1st Border, the Glider Pilot Regiment and 1 Airborne Reconnaissance Squadron while 4 Parachute Brigade had more men killed than 1 Parachute Brigade.[40]

Lieutenant Colonel W.F.K. 'Sheriff' Thompson, CO of 1st Airlanding Light Regiment, proved equally adept at commanding infantry. (*Private photograph, via Truesdale*)

The attempt to deploy more troops across the river that night to assist Urquhart's force ended in failure, the capture of 200 men, or more, and the destruction of another British battalion.[41] In this case the battalion was 4th Dorsetshire Regiment, a TA battalion of 43rd (Wessex) Division that had endured hard fighting since the summer. Middlebrook comments that 'Of the 315 Dorsets who attempted the crossing, thirteen died either on the river crossing or during the following day or night. Approximately 200 were rounded

Ubique. The detachment of No. 1 Gun, D Troop of 1st Airlanding Light Regiment in action in the Oosterbeek perimeter on 21 September, living up to the Royal Artillery motto: Quo Fas et Gloria Ducunt (Where Right and Glory Lead) (*IWM BU 1101*)

up and taken prisoner.' Powell summarises some of the problems, noting that 'All that could go wrong did': two of the lorries carrying assault boats took a wrong turning and drove into German hands, another pair slipped off the road into a ditch and the fifth delivered its nine boats but with no paddles. As a result, the crossing by the Poles was cancelled and 4th Dorsets set off at last at 0100 on Monday, coming under a storm of German fire in spite of heavy British fire intended to silence the enemy artillery and mortars. Of 350 men who set off, 315, including seventeen officers, reached the far bank, there to be faced with the Westerbouwing Heights, from which German infantry tossed grenades at them. Very few reached the Oosterbeek perimeter, most being scattered in the thick woodland. An attempt to send six DUKWs across with supplies went awry from the start as only three got into the water but then became mudbound on the north bank.[42] Among those who crossed was Lieutenant Colonel Myers, Urquhart's CRE, who carried letters to Urquhart, one of which gave him permission to evacuate the position.

Events further to the south made all the efforts by 43rd Division and Sosabowski's brigade redundant. British and American forces were engaged with German attackers all along the route of advance for Operation GARDEN.

For sixty miles desperate battles were taking place as the Germans sought to deny Hell's Highway to the Allies while also trying to open lines of escape for Fifteenth Army units and formations. Units of Guards Armoured, 7th Armoured, 43rd (Wessex) and 50th (Northumbrian) Divisions, with 506 PIR, fought to keep open the main road. The battle to open the road at Koevering raged fiercely and it took all of Monday before it was re-opened, but it was Tuesday before mines and booby-traps had been cleared and traffic could use it. An alternative route had to be opened to the east of the main road.[43]

With the authorisation from Horrocks for a withdrawal in his hands, Urquhart contacted Thomas of 43rd Division by radio and began arrangements for the evacuation of Oosterbeek that night. He was emphatic that Operation BERLIN, the withdrawal, had to be that night 'if any of his men were to survive'.[44] Montgomery had no idea of the situation at Arnhem. On Sunday evening he had signalled Brooke, the CIGS, and indicated that if heavy casualties were sustained in the attempt to cross from Driel into the Oosterbeek perimeter, he would probably 'give it up' and withdraw 1st Airborne; the decision would be taken the next morning.[45]

Although some accounts suggest that the plan for Operation BERLIN was devised at XXX Corps, it was of Urquhart's devising. When he was a young officer preparing for promotion examinations, Urquhart had studied the First World War withdrawal from Gallipoli. There the expeditionary force had been evacuated under deceptive cover, the retreat being cloaked by troops in the thinned-out front lines maintaining fire while the main body withdrew to the beaches to embark. Urquhart planned Operation BERLIN on the same lines.

> Along the perimeter small groups … would keep up a fusillade to deceive the enemy while the larger body of troops slipped away. Gradually units along the northern face of the perimeter would move down along its sides to the river to be evacuated. Then the last forces, closest to the Rhine, would follow. 'In effect,' Urquhart said later, 'I planned the withdrawal like the collapse of a paper bag. I wanted small parties stationed at strategic places to give the impression we were still there, all the while pulling downwards and along each flank.'[46]

Since the cover of darkness was critical to the success of the evacuation, the Oosterbeek garrison would have to endure another day in the perimeter. Although more wounded were evacuated throughout the day, there was no official truce and sometimes the evacuees were under fire.[47] At 1030 Urquhart held an O group with his senior officers and plans were laid for the evacuation.

In line with the Gallipoli template and his collapsing paper bag analogy, the withdrawal would begin with the units in the northern sector; the river crossing itself would begin at 2200. A detailed fire plan was agreed with the artillery; XXX Corps' guns would fire heavy concentrations just outside the gradually shrinking perimeter.[48] The gunners were to play a critical part in Operation BERLIN – the guns of XXX Corps, the field artillery of the Wessex Division and the surviving weapons of 1st Airlanding Light Regiment. There was an element of deception in the fire plan with Thomas hoping that the weight of fire 'would mislead the Germans into thinking that a further and larger attempt was being made to reinforce Oosterbeek', rather than that British 1st Airborne Division was being withdrawn. A further element of the deception plan involved a group of AFVs and other vehicles, including RE bridging lorries, apparently preparing for a river crossing close to Renkum, four miles east of Oosterbeek, where the riverbank was held by 43rd (Wessex) Reconnaissance Regiment.[49]

The Germans maintained their pressure on a cold and wet morning. From 1st Light Airlanding Regiment came information that a major attack from the east was planned, designed to cut off 1st Airborne from the river. That attack was launched during the morning and the attackers penetrated the gun lines before a counter-attack pushed them back; the remaining 75mm guns of the Light Regiment fired over open sights at close range to assist in repelling the attack while guns from across the river were also called on; close-support aircraft of 2 TAF added their firepower. A Polish 6-pounder was manhandled into position to tackle a King Tiger while 64th Medium Regiment also engaged the tanks from a range of 15,000 yards. The attack had been made by Kampfgruppe Allworden with the support of heavy tanks – a number of King Tigers of 506th Heavy Tank Battalion.[50]

All day long the pressure was unrelenting with mortar rounds and shellfire hammering into the British perimeter. Harzer later recalled that Model was still determined to destroy the British positions but, to reduce German losses, he had agreed that 'the heavy artillery should be used to provide the coup-de-grâce for what had been a crack British division, the survivors of which were still resisting so doggedly'.[51]

Elsewhere, Hell's Highway was cleared completely, the Germans abandoning their positions at nightfall while VIII Corps pushed back Kampfgruppe Walther and 180th Division. Eleventh Armoured Division advanced to the Maas at Boxmeer to link with XXX Corps. This left O'Connor with only two divisions for his north-eastern advance while 3rd Division, deployed on the Willems canal line, was holding a front of over twenty miles and would be responsible for another ten next day. Fortunately, 7th US Armored Division, returning to XIX US Corps, deployed alongside the Iron Division, thus alleviating the pressure on it.[52]

At Thomas's HQ, plans were being made for the withdrawal, although the divisional staff knew nothing of the Dorsets' situation, all communications with the battalion having broken down. On the plus side, the promised craft for the crossing had arrived. These included sixteen assault boats, manned by Royal Engineers, and twenty-three storm boats, manned by Royal Canadian Engineers, for each crossing site. Apart from some Canadian officers serving with units in 1st Airborne under the CanLoan scheme,[53] 20 and 23 Field Companies were the only Canadian soldiers to participate in MARKET GARDEN for which they were assigned to 10th Army Group Royal Engineers (10 AGRE). (Both companies had trained on storm boats at the Experimental Training Establishment in Dorset. Twenty-feet long, with a beam about one third of that, the storm boat was powered by a 50hp engine made by Evinrude of Wisconsin.) There were also some DUKWs and other craft.[54]

In accordance with Urquhart's plan, the northernmost units would withdraw first, pulling back through the more southerly groups who, in turn, would follow. Glider Pilots would organise and mark routes down to the river while XXX Corps would lay down an intense artillery bombardment. South of the Neder Rijn 43rd Division engineers and Royal Canadian Engineers oversaw the evacuation.

Information about the evacuation did not filter down until later evening,[55] although Waddy suggests that this happened during the afternoon.[56] The seriously wounded would have to be left behind with the doctors, medical orderlies and some chaplains while those non-walking wounded capable of manning a weapon would stay and continue firing, along with a rearguard. A normal routine was to be maintained by the artillery and signallers so that the Germans would have the least possible warning of 1st Airborne's evacuation.[57] Urquhart was concerned that the Germans might wreak slaughter in the embarkation areas if they knew what was happening but hoped that they might mistake the river traffic as an attempt to reinforce rather than an evacuation.[58] Those withdrawing were ordered to blacken their faces and muffle weapons and boots to assist in passing German positions or incursions into the defended area. Gunners were ordered to remove breech-blocks and gunsights, carry them to the river and cast them into the water.[59]

German shelling and mortaring continued throughout the day as preparations for evacuation continued on both sides of the river. By 2100 heavy rain was falling; for once the weather was working in favour of 1st Airborne Division. Urquhart wrote that 'The night was made for clandestine exits'.[60] Heavy rain, high winds and a pitch-black sky all combined to hide what was really happening.[61] The Royal Engineers' history notes that it began in 'pouring rain and pitch darkness only partially illuminated by distant burning buildings'.[62] The bombardment began simultaneously and units began falling back to the river. Half the engineers' boats were too far west to be used, slowing the evacuation; 43rd Division mistakenly thought that the crossing points used by the Dorsets the previous night were in British hands. The Germans shelled the withdrawal, believing it to be a re-supply attempt.[63] Meanwhile non-ambulant wounded assisted by firing their weapons or transmitting radio messages. Although the Germans heard the storm-boat engines they persisted in their belief that re-supply was underway.[64]

Operation BERLIN continued until 0500 when it was stopped due to the risks posed by the approach of daylight. The last two crossings were made by a Canadian Sapper officer, Captain R.J. Kennedy, who carried loads of lifebelts, taken from a German depot.[65]

> Each trip [Kennedy] brought back a boatload of men. In the first trip he had about five casualties. In the second hardly a man got out unhit, many were dead. It was a gallant effort but he could not be allowed to try again. Some used the life-jackets there and then, some used them next night and some escaped by ways that are stories apart and remain to be told by the men themselves.[66]

A total of 2,398 personnel were either ferried or swam across the river. Among them were 160 Poles and seventy-five Dorsets. Of 1st Airborne Division, there were 1,741 men, while 422 members of the Glider Pilot Regiment were also rescued. Some 300 men were still on the northern bank when Operation BERLIN ceased while ninety-five were killed during the evacuation.[67] The majority of those ferried across the Neder Rijn were carried by the Canadians, whose powered boats were able to make many more crossings than the oar-driven boats of the Royal Engineers.

Unaware of the withdrawal, the Germans pressed home their attacks on the morning of the 26th, cutting the bridgehead off from the river.[68] Not until after noon did they realise that the British had gone.[69] Later that day the Germans rounded up about 600 men, most of whom were the wounded in the aid stations or those left behind on the north bank. There were also some groups who, out of radio contact with divisional HQ, were unaware of the withdrawal, the largest such being D Company 1st Border.[70]

British casualties were severe: over 1,400 of the 10,000 committed to battle were dead and more than 6,000 captured, of whom about one in three were wounded. Powell notes that each parachute brigade emerged 'about a company strong' while the airlanding brigade 'numbered less than a weak battalion'.[71] Kershaw notes that official German figures indicated 3,300 casualties, of whom a third were killed but that this 'was very much an underestimate, and, in fact, more than twice as many had died'.[72] Harclerode states that the majority of German units fighting 1st Airborne Division at Arnhem and Oosterbeek 'had lost on average 50 per cent of their strengths; in one or two instances losses were as high as between 80 and 90 per cent, with one unit numbering only seven men by the end of the battle'.[73]

US Army historian Charles MacDonald lists casualty figures for what he describes as the 'airborne phase', D Day until the withdrawal across the Neder Rijn on 25 September. British losses, including glider pilots and headquarters I British Airborne Corps, lost 7,212 killed, wounded or missing. Casualties in 1 Polish Parachute Brigade totalled 378. In 82nd Airborne Division the total was 1,432, while 101st Airborne lost 2,110; 122 American glider pilots became casualties. Losses in the USAAF and RAF transport units included 596 pilots. In all, the airborne phase cost 11,850 casualties.[74]

As the survivors of 1st Airborne Division trudged south from Driel to Nijmegen they were met by their divisional seaborne 'tail' from which they were issued fresh uniforms and equipment.[75] Elsewhere, fighting continued to ensure that the road remained open and the US 506 PIR, supported by 44th Royal Tank Regiment, attacking from the north, with further British forces coming up from the south, forced the Germans back.

Over the course of Operation MARKET GARDEN, First Allied Airborne Army had deployed no fewer than 4,852 troop-carrying aircraft to the Netherlands, as well as 2,277 gliders. In addition to those gliders, 1,293 aircraft dropped paratroopers and 1,282 carried out re-supply missions. Aircraft losses were 164, plus 132 gliders. RAF Transport Command (38 and 46 Groups) suffered 294 casualties while IX Troop Carrier Command sustained 454. The airmen had transported almost 40,000 soldiers to the battle zone, including 21,074 paratroopers and 18,546 glider troops, as well as 4,595 tons of supplies. Of the supplies dropped for 1st Airborne Division, only 7.4 per cent reached it.[76]

The UK *Official History* indicates that 5,546 sorties were flown by USAAF and RAF aircraft to transport troops and supplies for the loss of 153 aircraft and 504 crew members. In addition, 152 RASC personnel were lost in those sorties and 1,242 aircraft were damaged. British and US tactical air forces, and RAF Air Defence of Great Britain (its Fighter Command title was restored in October) flew 9,794 'protection and army support' missions for the loss of 116 crew and 104 aircraft with another 176 aircraft damaged. RAF Bomber Command and US Eighth Air Force carried out 1,386 sorties against AA defences for the loss of thirty-eight crewmen and four aircraft with another twenty aircraft damaged. Finally, RAF Coastal Command flew 261 air-sea-rescue (ASR) sorties with no recorded losses.[77] The ASR sorties recovered 205 men.[78]

Badsey adds more detail to the sorties in support of MARKET GARDEN, noting that US Eighth Air Force flew more than half of the 6,172 such missions, with 2 TAF flying only 534 and US Ninth Air Force 209. He also records Browning's complaint that 2 TAF had only carried out forty-nine of ninety-five requests for close air support from HQ I Airborne Corps. The requests were generally turned down 'on grounds of poor target identification'.[79]

Chapter Twelve

Operation MARKET GARDEN had run its course. It had failed in its strategic aim, to create a bridgehead over the Rhine that would allow an Allied irruption into Germany, and the seizure of one of its principal industrial regions. It is, therefore, surprising that there were claims that it had been successful. Winston Churchill told Field Marshal Smuts that it was 'a decided victory', although the 'leading division, asking quite rightly for more, was given a chop'.[1] Although these words were included in a telegram to Smuts on 9 October 1944, Churchill included the full text in his history of the Second World War, published a decade later. Montgomery claimed that the operation had been 90 per cent successful, arguing that 90 per cent of the distance from the start line to Arnhem had been covered by the advancing troops.[2] However, in his *Memoirs*, published in 1958, that claim was not repeated and, perhaps uncharacteristically, he accepted blame for some of the errors that led to failure, while stating that he remained 'MARKET GARDEN's unrepentant advocate'.[3]

Kurt Student, commander of First Parachute Army, said that the battle had been a success for the Allies since they had gained ground and taken vital bridges while Nijmegen proved valuable as a 'jumping-off board for the offensive that contributed towards ending the war'.[4] To counter this, Powell also quotes Hackett's honest observation that 'If you did not get all the bridges, it was not worth going at all'.[5] While Student may have been demonstrating bias – he had developed and led Germany's airborne forces – that view is supported by Peter Caddick-Adams in his book *1945* (see below, p. 194).

Perhaps the most disingenuous analysis was that written by Brereton and submitted to Marshall and Arnold.

Despite the failure of the [Second] Army to get through to Arnhem and establish a permanent bridgehead over the Lower Rhine, Operation 'Market' was a brilliant success. The 101st Division took all its objectives as planned, the 82nd Division dominated the southern end of the bridge at Nijmegen until noon of D plus 1, by which time it had been planned for the Guards Armoured to be there; the 1st British Division similarly dominated the Arnhem bridge from its northern end until noon of D plus 3, 24 hours later than the time set for the arrival of the [Second] Army. Hence the airborne troops accomplished what was expected of them. It was the breakdown of the [Second] Army's timetable on the first day – their failure to reach Eindhoven in 6 to 8 hours as planned – that caused the delay in the taking of the Nijmegen bridge and the failure at Arnhem.[6]

Brereton was mixing fiction with truth, perhaps trying to convince himself that there had been success. However, the fiction is easily spotted: 101st Airborne did not seize *all* its objectives, nor did 82nd 'dominate' the southern end of Nijmegen bridge. The former failed to prevent the demolition of Son bridge, replacing which took two days, delaying XXX Corps' advance. And it was D plus 3 before 82nd, supported by Guards Armoured, dominated Nijmegen bridge. While Second Army's timetable slipped on D Day, that was not the prime factor in the delay in seizing Nijmegen bridge 'and the failure at Arnhem'. In a broader sense, Brereton's version of events was part of an evolving pattern of US generals denigrating British efforts, a pattern later taken up by some American historians.

North of the Rhine there was no failure in the sense that the soldiers of Frost Force/Gough Force had done much more than was expected of them. However, there was failure at the operational level since the Allies did not achieve their plan; it should be remembered that the division is both the highest tactical formation and the lowest operational formation. Given the task of holding Arnhem bridge for twenty-four to forty-eight hours, 1st Airborne Division held it for ninety-six. Aided by Sosabowski's 1 Polish Independent Parachute Brigade, Urquhart's division maintained its bridgehead north of the river for nine days until the situation became untenable and surviving personnel had to be evacuated across the Rhine. The withdrawal and evacuation were successful tactical actions, as was the stand of Frost's command at the bridge. However, neither that small force nor 1 Parachute Brigade achieved their tactical objectives in spite of fighting with great courage and élan over an extended period.

To what then may the strategic failure of Operation MARKET GARDEN be attributed? Blame cannot be laid at the feet of the ordinary soldiers who did as they were ordered, and often much more, but it can be laid at the feet of those who made and approved the plans. They were the senior officers of the Allied forces at the highest levels. The most senior, of course, was Eisenhower, who approved the plan. Of him, the US military historian, and former US Army infantry officer, Charles B. MacDonald, who served in Europe, wrote:

Was the decision to launch the largest airborne attack of World War II right or wrong?

It was the decision of a theatre commander to commit what was, in effect, his strategic reserve. It was a decision to reinforce one success among a number of successes that had been achieved.

The commander was General Dwight D. Eisenhower, Supreme Allied Commander … . The operation was an airborne attack deep in the enemy's rear areas to be launched in mid-September 1944 in conjunction with a ground attack by the British Second Army. …

The airborne attack was designed to lay a carpet of airborne troops along a narrow corridor extending approximately eighty miles into Holland from Eindhoven northward to Arnhem. The airborne troops were to secure bridges across several canals as well as across three major water barriers … . Through this corridor were to pass British ground troops in a push beyond Arnhem to the Ijsselmeer (Zuider Zee). The principal objective of the operation was to get Allied troops across the Rhine. Three main advantages were expected to accrue: cutting the land exit of those Germans remaining in western Holland; outflanking the enemy's frontier defences, the West Wall or Siegfried Line; and positioning British ground forces for a subsequent drive into Germany along the North German plain.[7]

Thus, MacDonald indicates that the ultimate responsibility was Eisenhower's as supreme commander. Since Eisenhower was under pressure from Marshall and Arnold to use First Allied Airborne Army we have a trinity of blameworthy individuals at the height of the US Army command chain. MacDonald also commented that MARKET GARDEN, although accomplishing 'much of what it had been designed to accomplish' had 'by the merciless logic of war' failed. It had gained bridgeheads over five major water obstacles with the one beyond the Maas proving invaluable to 21 Army Group in February 1945, while that beyond the Waal presented the Germans with the persistent threat of a northward Allied thrust. A large part of the Netherlands had been liberated, including airfields, while German formations had been redeployed from other parts of the western front and had suffered considerable losses. However, the Germans had not collapsed, as many Allied commanders had hoped would happen.

On the debit side, some might maintain that the cardinal point was the failure to precipitate a German collapse. Although the enemy's collapse was hardly a formal objective of the operation, few would deny that many

Allied commanders had nurtured the hope. In regard to more immediate and clearly defined objectives, the operation had failed to secure a bridgehead beyond the Neder Rijn, had not effectively turned the north flank of the West Wall, had not cut off the enemy's Fifteenth Army, and had not positioned the 21 Army Group for a drive around the north flank of the Ruhr. The hope of attaining these objectives had prompted the ambition and daring that went into Operation MARKET GARDEN. Not to have realised them could mean only that the operation had failed.[8]

Nonetheless, MacDonald wrote that it would show a lack of appreciation for the 'imagination and daring in military planning' that went into MARKET GARDEN to damn that plan and that anyone condemning 'the entire plan as a mistake' would be wrong. Such judgement would also ignore the contemporary climate of Allied intelligence reports. He argued that 'few criticisms have been levelled at the plan itself'.

MacDonald goes further in defence of the overall plan:

In light of Allied limitations in transport, supplies, and troops for supporting the thrust, in light of General Eisenhower's commitment to a broad-front policy, and in light of the true condition of the German army in the West, perhaps the only real fault of the plan was overambition.[9]

We have seen that Brereton attributed the delay in taking Nijmegen bridge and the 'failure' at Arnhem to Second Army not keeping to the timetable for XXX Corps' advance. That he could make such a comment suggests that Brereton was unaware of there being frictions in war and the old military aphorism that no plan survives first contact. For a senior officer and an army commander, such lacunae are almost unbelievable. Brereton also seemed unaware that all three corps of Second Army had been committed to GARDEN. While XXX Corps sustained 1,480 casualties in the eight days of MARKET GARDEN, combined losses of VIII and XII Corps came to 3,874,[10] a loss rate significantly higher than in Horrocks' command and close to that of the two US airborne divisions (3,542). The history of 15th (Scottish) Division shows that that formation, part of XII Corps, had deployed 44 Brigade and 227 Brigade in turn in the Aast bridgehead, losing over 700 men in six days.[11] Powell elaborates with the information that the division suffered 924 casualties between 13 and 21 September and a further 925 around Best over the following ten days.[12] MacDonald also notes the loss of seventy tanks by XXX Corps while VIII and XII Corps lost some eighteen tanks.[13] Those figures indicate the difficult nature of the fighting endured by VIII and XII Corps.

Other reasons are suggested for the strategic failure of MARKET GARDEN. Montgomery pointed to the adverse weather: 'We had undertaken a difficult operation, attended by considerable risks. It was justified because, had good weather obtained, there was no doubt that we should have attained full success.'[14] As already mentioned, however, the planners knew that good weather could not be guaranteed, especially at that time of year (see pp. 61–2), while diminishing daylight hours presented another problem which caused Williams, the USAAF air commander, to refuse to contemplate two lifts on D Day. (see pp. 65–6) It would seem that the air commanders failed to appreciate fully the effects of the loss of close air support should bad weather prevail around the airborne divisions' objectives.

One frequently cited reason for the failure to relieve 1st Airborne Division at Arnhem was the inadequacy of the division's radios, coupled with the fact that Urquhart had no contact with his own HQ at the most critical stage of the operation. For the first two days Urquhart was out of contact and unable to report what was happening in Arnhem. Had he been able to contact Browning, or Brereton's HQ in England, it might have been possible to fly glider-borne reinforcements from RAF airfields in England that were open and where a goodly reserve of gliders was available.[15]

For that 'problem' with communications, blame must be attributed to Urquhart who knew well that 'signal failures were no new phenomenon'. However, Powell, while stating that Urquhart 'must take his share of the blame' for the communications' problems, acknowledges that better wireless sets were needed, a matter that ought to have been addressed by Browning's HQ and the War Office, thus extending some of the blame to others in the chain of command.

> The problems which would arise when operating over extended distances in enclosed country had been foreseen, and time and time again the division's requests for more powerful radios had been rejected. When, both for COMET and for MARKET GARDEN, such conditions had to be faced, there was no way of obtaining new, more powerful sets at short notice, or of packing and loading them if they had been available. There was just not time for such changes.[16]

Powell is also critical of Urquhart on other points: failing to appreciate the potential of the Heveadorp ferry, which might have been used to approach the Arnhem bridges from the southern side and omitting to tell Hackett that Hicks would assume command should he and Lathbury be out of commission. He might be described as a bad planner but a good fighter: 'Urquhart will be remembered by all who served under him for his rock-like qualities, his cool and clear mind, and for the care he took of his men. He was an inspiring leader.'[17]

However, Powell also notes Urquhart and Lathbury's misuse of 1 Airborne Reconnaissance Squadron in that *coup de main* attempt to seize and hold Arnhem bridge.[18] Although recce *regiments* had performed such a role, it was never their intended role and Gough's squadron was a much lighter force, very different from 6th Airborne Division's reconnoitrers – a full reconnaissance regiment with a squadron of light tanks.[19]

Gough had been clear about what his squadron could achieve but Urquhart and Lathbury failed to recognise the limitations of a single squadron. This begs the question, which is beyond the scope of this book, of why 1st Airborne Division did not have a full reconnaissance regiment, unlike 6th Airborne which not only had a regiment but one with an armoured squadron. Gough had asked for the loan of a troop of Tetrarch light tanks from 6th Airborne 'but I don't think that any real effort was made to ask for them'. Even two Tetrarchs would have allowed 'for cross-country work as well as help deal with any unexpectedly difficult opposition'.[20] It has already been noted (p. 46) that two Hamilcars, unallotted for the second lift, could have been used to fly in two Tetrarchs. Had 1st Airborne Division's order of battle included a full reconnaissance regiment with a light-tank squadron, such a unit would have been able to manoeuvre and provide agile support. As it was, a single squadron ended up engaged decisively and fixed in position, preventing it from fulfilling its mission. For that crucial failure both Browning and Urquhart must share responsibility.

On Montgomery's references to the adverse effects of the weather on the airborne operation, Powell regards as a 'more accurate statement' an RAF comment that the weather had not 'unduly hampered operations'.[21] MacDonald disagrees, writing that 'Whether one can ascribe everything to weather in this manner is problematical, for other delays and difficulties not attributable to adverse weather developed'. However, MacDonald has no doubt that 'the vagaries of weather played a major role'. He provides evidence: 1st Airborne Division's second lift on D plus 1 was delayed for five hours by weather conditions. Bad weather not only prevented most re-supply north of the Neder Rijn, but also delayed by two days the arrival of 1 Polish Parachute Brigade, as well as delaying Gavin's glider regiment while a battalion of Taylor's artillery was held up for four days. Poor weather conditions, coupled with Brereton's order that no close-air-support aircraft could operate whilst airborne troops were arriving or re-supply missions taking place, 'helped deny any really substantial contribution' after D Day from tactical aircraft.[22]

Eisenhower's deputy, Air Chief Marshal Sir Arthur Tedder, de facto head of all Allied air forces and responsible for co-ordinating air operations in Europe, supported MacDonald's view, writing in his memoirs that 'The weather was most unfavourable to us'.[23] Tedder was no friend of Montgomery; antipathy between them led to Tedder calling for Montgomery to be removed from his command.[24] Eisenhower also agreed with Montgomery's assertion, writing that the operation would 'unquestionably have been successful except for the intervention of bad weather'.[25]

Harclerode emphasises that 'Bad weather was also a major factor in preventing close air support being available' and notes that Brereton's HQ had ordered all CAS operations to be suspended 'while transport aircraft were dropping troops or carrying out re-supply missions'. He adds that:

> When combined with the arrival of bad weather over airfields in England and target areas in Holland, the effect of the First Allied Airborne Army directive was such that there were many occasions when Typhoon fighter-bombers of 83 Group RAF could not take off to support the three airborne divisions.[26]

Omar Bradley recalled that, on D Day, he had flown up to Monty's command post at Brussels where he witnessed C-47s make emergency landings after dropping the airborne soldiers. He then commented that Montgomery's armour 'advanced up the [airborne] carpet' despite enemy counter-attacks and 'rammed' across the Waal at Nijmegen, after which it became bogged down in the face of increasing resistance. Noting that Montgomery 'afterward attributed his failure at Arnhem to the perversity of weather', he agreed that weather was a contributory factor:

> on the second day of attack, murky weather over the Lowlands caused Monty's re-supply and reinforcement missions to miscarry. With the exception of two days, weather restricted Allied fighter operations and enabled the enemy to form his counter-attacks without interference from [the] air. Between September 19 when the Guards Armoured reached Nijmegen and October 4 when Monty abandoned the effort, the enemy hit that long salient with 12 separate divisional attacks. Monty ruefully conceded that his 'easy' path had concealed a briar patch.[27]

As the reader will already have noted from the narrative, there is little doubt that weather conditions *did* have an adverse effect on Operation MARKET. MacDonald comments that such an effect might have been avoided had Allied air forces possessed sufficient transport aircraft to carry the entire airborne force on D Day. However, he qualifies that by stating that to have aspired to such numbers of aircraft at that time 'would have been to presume the millennium', adding that more transport aircraft were deployed on MARKET than in any other major operation thus far in the war.[28]

Powell and MacDonald disagree over the question of the intelligence provided to the airborne divisions: the former opines that too much has 'been made of the failure to provide the airborne divisions … with an accurate and up-to-date summary of the available intelligence about enemy strengths and possible intentions in eastern Holland'[29] while the latter notes that 'In the matter of intelligence, the Allies sinned markedly'.[30]

Both argue succinctly and with the experience of battlefield soldiers who fought in North-West Europe. When Powell wrote his book in 1984, the 1977 film *A Bridge Too Far* had already seeded the popular imagination with misinformation, not least the belief that intelligence had been suppressed either 'by incompetence or design'. Such, he comments, 'is excellent material for headline or filmscript'. The reality, however, can be very different, as in the case of Operation MARKET GARDEN.

Powell outlines the intelligence story. For the cancelled Operation COMET an intelligence summary (INTSUM) had been provided which indicated that a single 'broken panzer division' was north of Arnhem resting and refitting. Following the cancellation of COMET, information from the Government Code and Cypher School (GC&CS) at Bletchley Park indicated that two SS panzer divisions (II SS Panzerkorps) had moved into the Arnhem area. The information had been obtained through *Ultra* decrypts of high-level German radio and teleprinter signals traffic. Thus, the INTSUM produced for MARKET GARDEN included the possibility of there being between fifty to a hundred tanks in the Netherlands. At much the same time as that INTSUM was issued, Browning advised Urquhart that he would face no more than a brigade group that included 'a few tanks'.

As it happened, the two SS divisions of II SS Panzerkorps each equated roughly to a brigade group with very few tanks, Hohenstaufen having about twenty Panthers. Since most of Frundsberg was directed on Nijmegen from the beginning of the ground fighting, the estimate of German strength received by Urquhart 'was not too far off the mark'. Powell emphasises:

> The fact that the information about the presence of these two broken divisions in the Arnhem area was not passed to the airborne divisional commanders, and that it probably did not reach Browning either, made hardly any difference, adding … little to what those concerned already

knew about the size of the enemy forces they were about to meet. …
Whether or not Browning did suppress some of the information he had
received from his intelligence staff about the presence of German tanks
near Arnhem is hardly material to the issue.

What was not factored into the
appreciation was the effectiveness of the
SS personnel whose morale and fighting
spirit remained high.

Since *Ultra* was highly classified, the
circulation of material produced by it
was controlled strictly and its origins
were often disguised. It is most likely
that protecting *Ultra* would have meant
that the identities of the panzer divisions
in the Arnhem area were not made
known to anyone other than those in the
highest ranks; Browning and Horrocks,
as corps commanders, were not included
in those made privy to the source of the
information.[31]

Generaloberst Kurt Student, the father
of German airborne forces, was given
command of First Parachute Army,
created from a training organisation, with
orders to counter the Allied offensive.
Before long, his soldiers were attacking
British and American formations with
considerable effect. (*Bundesarchiv, Bild
146-1979-128-26 / Unknown author /
CC-BY-SA*)

MacDonald expands his comment
that the Allies had 'sinned markedly' on
intelligence by noting that they expected
the strongest opposition near Eindhoven
since it was close to the German front
line. As a result, they failed to detect,
or take account of, the presence of
II SS Panzerkorps formations in the
neighbourhood of Arnhem, or the fact
that 59th Division was on the move near Tilburg. Nor did they seem aware of
two SS divisions in the line on XXX Corps' front and that both Student and
Model had their headquarters close to the DZs and LZs. Had they appreciated
that those two headquarters were so close, they would have realised that a rapid
reaction to the landings was inevitable. Add to this the criminally irresponsible
decision of an American officer to carry a copy of the operational order on his
person and the Allies were almost doing the Germans' work for them.

Other intelligence errors included one on enemy armour in the Reichswald,
which influenced Gavin's use of his units, while an overly pessimistic estimate
of German AA defences in the Arnhem area prompted Brereton to decide

on LZs and DZs far removed from the bridges at Arnhem. This inflated assessment of AA defences was also accepted by the RAF and influenced Hollinghurst in his advice, while a mistaken belief that the ground south of the river at Arnhem was unusable by gliders contributed to Brereton's decision on LZs and DZs.[32] The failure to appreciate the ground is difficult to understand since more accurate information must have been available from Dutch sources.

Having said that, MacDonald goes on to ponder what might have happened had XXX Corps' advance been as fast as Horrocks had hoped.

> Yet all these handicaps possibly could have been overcome had the British ground column been able to advance as rapidly as General Horrocks had hoped. Perhaps the real fault was dependence upon but one road. In any event, the ground troops were delayed for varying amounts of time south of Eindhoven, at the demolished bridge over the Wilhelmina Canal at [Son], and at the Waal bridge in Nijmegen.[33]

MacDonald believed that those delays allowed the Germans to create an effective defence. Without the benefit of such delays, it is quite likely that the Germans would have been unable to delay or prevent the advance between the Waal and Neder Rijn; Horrocks' ground column would already have pushed north of the Waal by D plus 2, or even sooner. It was not until the night of D plus 3 that the Germans were able to use Arnhem bridge to move armour and other reinforcements south of the Neder Rijn, forces which then helped 'form the defensive screen that in the end constituted the greatest delay of all'.[34]

It was MacDonald's opinion that 'perhaps the most portentous conclusion' to be drawn from Operation MARKET GARDEN's collapse was that it delayed any serious thrust into the heart of Germany in the near future. Patton's Third Army was encountering strong resistance at Metz in the Moselle, and at Aachen, once Aix-la-Chapelle, just inside Germany, 1st Infantry and 3rd Armored Divisions were fighting another bitter battle that would see the historic city destroyed before it became the first German city to fall into Allied hands. Taken together, the three clashes gave the Allied command a clear message that the Germans would continue to fight fiercely to defend their homeland. Bruised and battered they may well have been, but they were still determined to fight. The war would not be over by Christmas.

Another American historian, Gerard M. Devlin, makes the point that success could have been achieved at Arnhem.

Had Operation MARKET GARDEN been pulled off only two weeks earlier than it was, chances are it would have resulted in a resounding success for the Allies. And, quite possibly, it really could have resulted in the Allies winning the war in 1944. However, the operation was not launched in early September, and because it was not, the Germans were able to significantly strengthen their positions in Holland in time to blunt the coming Allied airborne attack.[35]

Peter Harclerode, a former Army officer, writes that 'Disregard of available intelligence about enemy forces in the area of Arnhem played a major part in causing the debacle that all but annihilated 1st Airborne Division' and suggests that both Montgomery and Browning were 'dismissive of' the *Ultra* intelligence on II SS Panzerkorps, although Browning, as a corps commander, was not privy to *Ultra* intelligence. He, too, indicates that insufficient attention was paid to the German forces across the border in Germany, which provided reinforcements when the Allied offensive began.[36] However, had Brereton achieved his 'thunderclap surprise', those forces would have been too far away to have intervened effectively to prevent the Allies gaining ground and achieving success.

A summary of the intelligence picture is provided by Hinsley. Noting that Montgomery's directive for MARKET GARDEN was issued on 14 September (Badsey writes that he had issued formal orders two days earlier,[37] he summarises the plan for the advance, adding that:

> These were ambitious plans, the more so as it had become apparent while they were being drawn up that the Germans were no longer retreating in this sector, and were making efforts to stabilise a front.[38]

Bryant provides pertinent background information. Eisenhower, although in receipt of a directive from the Combined Chiefs of Staff, did not 'agree to allocate additional transport and petrol to 21 Army Group to make even this belated project [Operation MARKET GARDEN] possible' until 12 September.[39]

> It was a case of too little too late. During the five days that followed Eisenhower's decision and while the proposed aerial offensive … was being mounted, the German strength in Montgomery's path doubled. On [17 September], with only part of the Second Army supplied and in a position to fight across the sixty-four miles of enemy-held territory that separated it from the northernmost landing-zone at Arnhem, one British and two American airborne divisions were dropped beside the Rhine,

Waal and Maas crossings. Simultaneously Patton, using supplies which might have made all the difference to his northern colleagues, launched a major attack on Metz.[40]

This was typical of Eisenhower and his focus on consensus and the broad front. His decision-making was too slow but, ultimately, he failed to identify this operation as his main effort and thus did not provide adequate resources, a cardinal military sin.

Hinsley gives a timeline of developments on 'the other side of the hill' from Hitler's order creating First Parachute Army from a training organisation, placing it under command of Army Group B and making Student, its commander, responsible for defending the Albert canal between Brussels and Maastricht to MI14's assessment, on 17 September, that 70,000 men of Fifteenth Army had been ferried across the Scheldt by that morning.[41] (Details of formations included and their deployments are already noted on p. 84.)

Max Hastings, who comments that many of the causes 'of the disaster at Arnhem' were identified in the immediate aftermath, considers MARKET GARDEN 'a rotten plan, poorly executed', an assessment as inaccurate as it is unfair. This analysis ignores the nuances of the operation. While there were problems with the planning, which we shall examine, and with the execution, as we have seen, not all could have been foreseen. Nonetheless, there are pertinent questions to be asked about the Intelligence assessments. Had planners at Brereton's and Urquhart's respective HQs not identified the Germans' most likely course of action, and the most dangerous courses? Did no one, other than Freddy Gough, consider the results of his squadron not reaching the bridge in its *coup de main* dash? Did Brereton consider the possibility of 82nd Airborne being delayed?

Hastings does describe accurately the German denial of Nijmegen bridge to 82nd Airborne for three days as 'almost equally critical'. He is scathing about the communications problems in 1st Airborne Division, reflecting that in the German or Soviet armies 'some signals officers would have been shot' and makes the point that British officers ignored the local knowledge of the Dutch resistance and the availability of the local telephone network, both of which the Americans exploited 'imaginatively'.[42] He seems unaware that Gough contacted Urquhart by using the local telephone network on the morning of 20 September, surprising the latter.[43] However, Harclerode emphasises the point that Urquhart's divisional signals officer, Lieutenant Colonel Tom Stephenson, had made 'vociferous complaints' about the inadequacies of the wireless sets, had received 'assurances that suitable sets would be forthcoming' and had been let down by those to whom he addressed his appeals.[44]

Chester Wilmot sounded a very different note.

It was most unfortunate that the two major weaknesses of the Allied High Command – the British caution about casualties and the American reluctance to concentrate – should both have exerted their baneful influence on this operation, which should, and could, have been the decisive blow of the campaign in the West. This was no time to count the cost, or to consider the prestige of rival commanders. The prize at issue was no less than the chance of capturing the Ruhr and ending the war quickly, with all that meant for the future of Europe.[45]

Wilmot went on to argue that, while Eisenhower placed his strategic reserve – First Allied Airborne Army – under Montgomery's command on 4 September, thus giving the latter 'the only major force' the Allies could commit to 'clinch the victory' gained in France, he failed to provide Montgomery with adequate resources to deploy that reserve with the wherewithal to achieve its greatest potential. In 21 Army Group's advance into Belgium and on to the Meuse-Escaut canal, Montgomery had received no logistical assistance from either Eisenhower or Bradley, save for 500 tons delivered daily by air during the previous week, enough only to maintain a single division. Although that daily 500-ton supply continued, the US Army's 'Red Ball Express' was not initiated until 16 September, the eve of D Day for MARKET GARDEN. As result, 'not one ton' of supplies carried by the Red Ball Express was delivered to 21 Army Group before the offensive was launched while those transport companies carrying matériel for Gavin and Taylor's divisions did not arrive until the 20th.[46] Eisenhower was failing to reinforce success.

After the war Eisenhower emphasised his supply difficulties, advancing the argument, in *Crusade in Europe,* that a strong bridgehead representing a real threat to the Ruhr would have been possible only 'had we stopped in August all Allied movements elsewhere on the front'. He was insistent that 'at no point could decisive success have been attained' and supported his argument by claiming that no force exceeding ten or twelve divisions 'could have been supported even temporarily'.[47] Against this, Wilmot points out that the supply situation 'was not as serious as Eisenhower suggests, nor were the needs of his divisions as great as he asserts'. While Eisenhower claimed that a reinforced division in action had a daily need for 600 to 700 tons of supplies, Wilmot makes the point that this figure* was inflated and included 'all manner of

---

* Based on the official *Staff Officers' Field Manual.*

ordnance and engineer stores' that did not need replacing 'in a short swift campaign'. Instead, Allied divisions were being maintained adequately on 500 tons daily while in action *and* advancing. He emphasises this with the comment that Patton was attacking in the Moselle with eight divisions on a daily re-supply of 3,500 tons.[48]

Wilmot lists other details that counter Eisenhower's argument:

On 10 September, when Eisenhower and Montgomery met in Brussels, some 10,000 tons a day were being supplied to Patton, Hodges and Dempsey from supply dumps in Normandy and from the UK. All of it was being delivered to the fronts on the Moselle, the Meuse and the Dutch border.

Dieppe had been opened to shipping and by mid-September was unloading 3,000 tons each day for First Canadian Army. That figure increased twofold by the end of the month.

From 20 September some 14,000 tons overall was being received daily with some stores arriving by air.

A petrol pipeline from Cherbourg was 'advancing' by twenty-five miles per day and had reached Chartres by the 12th.

Rail communications from the Normandy bridgehead were open as far as Sommersous, 100 miles east of Paris, by 7 September. By the 18th Liège was connected and Eindhoven had a rail connection by the 28th.[49]

Thus, argues Wilmot, the true situation does not support Eisenhower's argument; but he goes on to show that Eisenhower's figures have been accepted generally, including by Sir Francis de Guingand, Montgomery's chief of staff in his book *Operation Victory*. De Guingand believed that Eisenhower had reduced supplies to Patton and 'held back' the latter's advance to release supplies to the north.[50] However, de Guingand was accepting figures supplied from Eisenhower's HQ staff which were not accurate. Other than in the first four days of September, Patton was receiving 'by one means or another' a daily tonnage greater than that provided for Hodges' First Army. (For those first four days, Third Army's daily allocation was 2,000 tons.)[51]

Continuing his analysis, Wilmot rehearses the fact that Montgomery did not wait to build up a large reserve of supplies but launched his offensive into Holland 'with nothing in hand at all, except what was immediately necessary to take XXX Corps to the Zuider Zee and to support limited advances by the corps on either flank'. In fact, he was unable to position VIII and XII Corps to provide maximum support to XXX Corps or I Airborne Corps. Short of transport for personnel and ammunition, XII Corps could secure but one small bridgehead beyond the Meuse-Escaut canal before D Day while VIII Corps was unable to enter the offensive until D plus 2. Furthermore, XII Corps could deploy only two divisions: 51st (Highland) Division was grounded to allow its transport to be used to supply the forward troops; it would not join the corps until after the operation.[52] Lewin notes that Montgomery had to 'use his precious transport to move up VIII Corps' as a result of promised logistical support not materialising and the failure of an operation by First US Army on his right flank.[53] Thus, during the first two days of GARDEN, only three of the nine British divisions nominally available could be deployed by Dempsey; the actual breakout was effected by two battalions along one narrow road.

> This was the direct result of Eisenhower's policy. If he had kept Patton halted on the Meuse, and had given full logistic support to Hodges and Dempsey after the capture of Brussels, the operations in Holland could have been an overwhelming triumph, for First US Army could have mounted a formidable diversion, if not a successful offensive, at Aachen, and Second British Army could have attacked sooner, on a wide front and in much greater strength.[54]

Wilmot and Bryant are largely in agreement on this point. The latter notes that Montgomery and Bradley pleaded for priority in receiving supplies, Montgomery for his strike across Holland and the Neder Rijn towards the Ruhr and the Hanover plain, and Bradley for an advance through the rolling Saar and the Palatinate to Frankfurt and Central Germany. Both were frustrated by Eisenhower, who,

> inclining first one way, then another, remained what Brooke had seen him to be, an arbiter balancing the requirements of competing allies and subordinates rather than a master of the field making the decisive choice which alone could turn the 'option of difficulties' that is war into victory.[55]

One British voice, that of Air Chief Marshal Sir Arthur Tedder, dissented.

> Montgomery has since charged, in his *Memoirs*, that the operation was not regarded at Supreme Headquarters as the spearhead of a major Allied movement in the north, designed to isolate and finally to occupy the Ruhr. This must be a matter of opinion. So far as I knew at the time, Eisenhower made every possible effort to give Montgomery the necessary supply. The weather was most unfavourable to us, the airborne forces at Arnhem itself landed too far away from the vital bridge, but above all

the operation committed the 'spearhead' to a single line of approach to a single objective, which allowed the Germans to concentrate easily against it. However, at this stage, 22 September, the outcome was not known.[56]

Remembering that relations between Montgomery and Tedder were not good, Tedder's 'This must be a matter of opinion' may be read in that light. It may also be considered in light of Bryant's comment on Eisenhower's vacillating between Bradley and Montgomery. The last named is surely correct in asserting that Eisenhower did not consider 21 Army Group's thrust as 'the spearhead of a major Allied movement in the north', since the supreme commander had written to him on 8 September that 'We must push up [to the Rhine] as soon as possible *all along the front* to cut off the retreating enemy and concentrate in preparation for the big final thrust'.[57] A week later, only two days before D Day for MARKET GARDEN, Eisenhower re-affirmed his policy in a further letter. His adherence to the policy was due for the most part to 'the consistently sanguine reports he received through Bradley from Patton'.[58]

Correlli Barnett wonders why Eisenhower gave permission for MARKET GARDEN.

> Less admirable, however, was his decision to sanction Montgomery's proposed operation to cross the three big Dutch rivers (including the lower Rhine) by a series of airborne landings to seize the bridges, followed up by ground forces. MARKET GARDEN was launched on 17 September and ended in failure on the 25th with the destruction of the British 1st Airborne Division at Arnhem. This operation has been analysed again and again in detail to establish just what went wrong. The essential point is, however, that MARKET GARDEN suffered exactly the fate which Eisenhower had foreseen for Montgomery's vastly more ambitious scheme to drive deep into Germany, with Berlin as the ultimate objective. Had that thrust run into stiff German opposition and flanking counter-strokes when far forward somewhere north of the Ruhr, the result could have been a catastrophe dooming the whole Allied campaign in the West.[59]

Once again, many of the nuances of the operation have been missed. The concept of MARKET GARDEN had been attractive to Eisenhower, especially with Marshall and Arnold figuratively looking over his shoulder. As D'Este comments (see pp. 17–18) there were coins burning holes in his pocket – the divisions of First Allied Airborne Army. By 1960, when Eisenhower and Montgomery had become completely estranged, the former could write to

General Sir Hastings Ismay* that his staff had opposed the plan for MARKET GARDEN but that 'because [Montgomery] was the commander in the field, I approved'. The comment was disingenuous: Eisenhower had wanted to use his strategic reserve in a major operation and MARKET GARDEN suited his purpose. He approved Montgomery's plan because he wanted it to work.

As Barnett comments, Operation MARKET GARDEN 'has been analysed again and again in detail to establish just what went wrong'. Blame has been attributed, most frequently to Montgomery, who, in his *Memoirs*, accepted that burden for many factors but remained the operation's 'unrepentant advocate'. However, he cannot be held responsible for all that went wrong, nor can he be held to be the principal blameworthy individual. Clausewitz referred to the fog and friction of war, a term that certainly applies not only to the conduct of MARKET GARDEN but also to the analysing of the operation and the attribution of blame. As we have seen, the main reasons advanced by a selection of writers included weather; use, or otherwise, of intelligence on enemy forces, including reserves, AA defences and intentions; poor communications, especially in the case of 1st Airborne Division; errors by commanders at various levels; and lack of 'push' by Second Army and XXX Corps.

In attributing blame, it is wise to start at the top of the chain of command. In this case, the theatre commander was Eisenhower who, therefore, headed the chain of command and with whom, in the words of Harry Truman, 'the buck' stopped. Or did it? We have seen that Eisenhower was in thrall to Marshall, Chief of Staff of the US Army, and, to a lesser extent, Arnold, commander of US Army Air Forces. Remember that, earlier in the war, Eisenhower and Lieutenant General Lesley McNair, US Army Ground Forces commander, had opposed the large-scale use of airborne forces following poor showings, for a variety of reasons. Both had been persuaded to change their minds by the outcome of the Knollwood Manoeuvre. Or had they? McNair had been killed by a USAAF bomb during Operation COBRA, the US breakout from Normandy, on 25 July 1944, and thus had no part in MARKET GARDEN. However, even in March 1944 Eisenhower had written to Marshall arguing against the wisdom of airborne operations deep in the enemy's rear – in other words, a strategic operation such as MARKET. Arnold and Marshall had both been advocating such operations in Europe. In his letter, Eisenhower made the acerbic suggestion that Marshall should advise Arnold that 'The fact is that, against a German defence, [airborne] fingers do not stab out rapidly and join

---

* Sir Hastings 'Pug' Ismay was Churchill's chief staff officer and military adviser for most of the war. He later became the first general secretary of NATO.

up in the heart of enemy-held territory unless there is present a solid tactical power and overwhelming strength'.[60]

D'Este notes that Eisenhower barely mentions MARKET GARDEN in his memoir *Crusade in Europe*, 'dismissing it with the observation' that the intervention of bad weather caused its failure. However, he cannot escape responsibility for the operation and its failure to deliver its strategic purpose. In D'Este's view that responsibility began with Eisenhower and extended to Montgomery, Brereton, Browning, Dempsey and Horrocks.[61] He does not include either Marshall or Arnold, nor does he mention Brooke, the Chief of the Imperial General Staff, who had largely been responsible for Montgomery's rise in the wartime army. (At the time of MARKET GARDEN, Brooke was attending *Octagon*, the second Quebec Conference, with Churchill.) While neither Marshall nor Arnold had any direct responsibility, their enthusiasm for, and advocacy of, airborne forces undoubtedly influenced Eisenhower to go against his own instincts. We have already noted D'Este's comment that Eisenhower was never convinced completely of the airborne concept. Although not directly blameworthy, Marshall and Arnold must share some of the blame for the strategic failure of MARKET GARDEN due to their baleful influence on Eisenhower.

Montgomery is most often regarded as being responsible for launching the operation and for its failure to achieve what was expected of it. As commander of 21 Army Group, to which First Allied Airborne Army was assigned, he had the overall operational responsibility for both MARKET and GARDEN. The concept of a deep strike into the rear of the German lines, leading to an Allied advance into, and seizure of, the Ruhr, was his, and thus he must share the responsibility. D'Este notes that although he tried 'to shift the entire blame onto Eisenhower', a disingenuous comment, Nigel Hamilton, Montgomery's biographer, made it clear that it was 'his own doing' and 'nothing less than foolhardy'.[62] But it remains a truth that Eisenhower wanted the operation:

> I not only approved MARKET GARDEN, I insisted upon it. We needed a bridgehead over the Rhine. If that could be accomplished I was quite willing to wait on all other operations. What this action proved was that the idea of 'one full-blooded thrust' to Berlin was silly.[63]

This comment was made after the publication of Cornelius Ryan's book *A Bridge Too Far* and has some echoes of Eisenhower's demand of Brereton for plans with daring and imagination.

Thus, it would appear that Eisenhower was captivated by the 'daring and imagination' embodied in the plan for MARKET GARDEN. Despite his lack of conviction about the efficacy of large-scale airborne forces, he was happy to use an airborne corps in co-operation with a ground army to force a way into Germany. However, his Hamlet-style failure to make a decisive choice 'to turn the "option of difficulties" that is war into victory' meant that he did not stop Patton's Third Army and seemed determined to continue with his broad-front strategy. Cole noted Patton's thinking:

> At the close of hostilities in Europe, however, General Patton was to express the opinion that the decision to give logistical support to the 21st Army Group and First Army instead of the Third Army 'was the momentous error of the war.' His memoirs add: 'At first I thought it was a backhanded way of slowing up the Third Army. I later found that this was not the case, but that the delay was due to a change of plan by the High Command, implemented, in my opinion by General Montgomery.'[64]

While Max Hastings may describe the overall plan as 'rotten', the US military historian Charles MacDonald would have disagreed: his comment that damning that plan would show a lack of appreciation for the 'imagination and daring in military planning' that went into MARKET GARDEN demolishes Hastings' argument. MacDonald went on to write that anyone condemning 'the entire plan as a mistake' would be wrong and was ignoring the contemporary 'climate of Allied intelligence reports'. It was his view that 'few criticisms have been levelled at the plan itself'. Acknowledging Eisenhower's determination to pursue a broad-front strategy and considering the Allied problems with transport, supplies and manpower to support the thrust as well as the true condition of the German army in the West, MacDonald was justified in suggesting that 'overambition' was the plan's only real fault. However, 'overambition' does not mean that the plan was not worthy; in the circumstances it was a viable option.

MacDonald's argument shifts a greater burden of responsibility for failure onto Montgomery, although he also points to the influence of Marshall and Arnold. Brereton's comment in his memoirs on Eisenhower's demand for 'daring and imagination' indicates that the Supreme Commander wanted the airborne army used as an *army* and believed that its mass deployment would have a devastating effect on German morale. Of course, Brereton was also keen to see his command used on 'a major operation of genuine consequence'.

While the concept of an operation using airborne and ground forces in concert for a strategic objective was Montgomery's, he had little difficulty in arguing its potential to Eisenhower, who had both Marshall and Arnold waiting for him to use the airborne army which then constituted his theatre reserve. As an army group commander, it was not Montgomery's job to plan in detail operations involving his armies, although he had the responsibility of approving such plans. The planning process was devolved: Brereton's HQ was responsible for MARKET and Dempsey's Second Army HQ planned GARDEN. Planning was further devolved to corps HQs, those of Browning, Horrocks, O'Connor and Ritchie, and to divisional HQs, including that of 1st Airborne Division.

Browning was, of course, involved at both army and corps level and it was he who flew from Brussels to confirm that the operation would take place. At First Allied Airborne Army HQ at Ascot, Browning declared that 1st Airborne Division's objective was to be 'Arnhem bridge – and hold it'. For his part, Brereton followed with the exhortation that the bridges be seized 'with thunderclap surprise'. As outlined in Chapter Six, the planning was based on that for Operation COMET. Brereton's command included the USAAF air assets, with RAF transport machines under command for the operation, and the planning had to include that for the air operation as well as the roles assigned to the airborne troops once they were on the ground. There was little doubt that the planning task was approached with enthusiasm and energy.

At divisional level, this book is concerned most with 1st Airborne Division and with Urquhart. With no experience of such operations, Urquhart accepted the DZs and LZs laid down by Brereton, with the problems thus created. As mentioned before, Richard Gale, who had commanded 6th Airborne in Normandy, would not have accepted such a plan. Urquhart's answer to the problem of the distance between DZs and LZs and the divisional objective of Arnhem bridge 'and hold it' was to use 1 Airborne Reconnaissance Squadron in a *coup de main* attack, against the advice of the squadron leader. On the ground, Urquhart's plan unravelled very quickly, compounded by his decision to remove himself from his HQ, thus losing command, control and communications in one fell swoop; the communications problem had been in his gift to resolve. Thus, in spite of his many qualities, Urquhart let his soldiers down. Although most continued to admire him, it is significant that he remained a major general in relatively unimportant posts for the rest of his service, retiring in that rank in December 1955.*[65]

Frost recalled that he had 'not been told that there was a ferry at Driel',[66] the seizure of which would have allowed ferrying operations by Royal Engineers. 'The failure of the planners at all levels to identify and make use of this useful

---

*   After the war, Urquhart held the posts of Director Territorial Army and Army Cadet Force, GOC 16th Airborne Division TA, GOC Lowland District, GOC Malaya District/17th Gurkha Division, GOC Malaya and, finally, GOC in C British Troops Austria.

asset is hard to understand.'[67] He was also very critical of Urquhart's plan to use 1 Airborne Reconnaissance Squadron to seize Arnhem bridge, an operation he believed should have been executed by airborne means: 'There were successful … precedents, in particular the capture of Pegasus Bridge in Normandy.'[68] However, he was on less certain ground when he agreed with the assertion by soldiers of Patton's Third Army that they would 'have gotten (sic) through'.[69]

Urquhart's acceptance of Brereton's overall plan meant that his spearhead brigade, commanded by Lathbury, was also misused. Deploying in three battalion columns, rather than maintaining one battalion as a brigade reserve, meant that casualties mounted as German resistance was encountered and began intensifying. Urquhart's *coup de main* plan came to naught when the leading Recce troop was ambushed at Wolfheze; its unarmoured jeeps were vulnerable to even small-arms fire, but machine guns and a flame-thrower were also used at Wolfheze. The plan as implemented had little opportunity of achieving 'thunderclap surprise'. Had Urquhart deployed both parachute brigades on D Day, one dropping to the south of the road bridge and the other 'as near as possible to the northern end', 'preceded by a glider-borne *coup de main* party, the road bridge could have been seized and held until XXX Corps arrived'.[70] In short, Urquhart failed to adhere to one of the key principles of war: he did not concentrate his force.

Corporal Ernest Mills, 181st Airlanding Field Ambulance, mourns a comrade. Trooper William McKinlay Edmond of 1 Airlanding Reconnaissance Squadron, aged 27 and a native of Midlothian, was killed on D Day. (*IWM BU 1105*)

Harclerode criticises Urquhart for his 'wholly incorrect' use of the Recce Squadron for another reason. Because the squadron was under Lathbury's command, it was not on the divisional radio net, thus depriving Urquhart of information from the 'eyes' of the division. Had he used the squadron in its correct role, 'it could well have proved invaluable in relaying information and orders where signals had failed'.[71]

Similar problems existed with 82nd Airborne at Nijmegen. The use of DZs and LZs far from the bridges over the Waal meant that men had to be deployed to defend those zones until later lifts arrived. Those setting out from the zones for their objectives also faced a long trek through country that was ideal for ambushes.[72] Frost wrote that the same voice that had told Urquhart 'Arnhem Bridge. And hold it!' also told Gavin 'The Groesbeek Heights. Nijmegen Bridge later.' Whether he was referring to Brereton or Browning, the result was still the same: 82nd Airborne was misdirected as Nijmegen bridge 'was there for the walk-over on D Day' while the Groesbeek, some miles away, did not 'constitute a noticeable tactical feature and their occupation or otherwise has little or no bearing on what happens at Nijmegen or at Nijmegen Bridge'.[73]

Powell also quotes from an RAF document in the National Archives at Kew. In a diary kept by a senior staff officer (whose name is illegible and whose appointment is not known) the writer criticised the air plan, averring that experience and common sense meant that all three divisions should have been landed 'in the minimum period of time', allowing them to form up and organise before the enemy could react. He suggests that the three divisions should have been landed in a twelve-hour time span, but that Brereton's HQ insisted on 'a plan which resulted in the second lift (with half the heavy equipment) arriving more than 24 hours after the Germans had been alerted'.[74]

Such decisions had been based on a belief that local AA defences were much stronger than they were. Afterwards the RAF admitted that the AA intelligence assessment had been wrong: it had predicted aircraft losses as high as 40 per cent, even if the defences at Eindhoven, Nijmegen, Deelen and Arnhem were avoided. Then there was the American refusal to fly a second mission on D Day. Montgomery had sent a senior officer to Ascot to try to persuade Brereton and Williams to fly such a mission, but to no avail (see p. 65). Brereton failed to appreciate the need for flexibility, or the German capacity for both quick reaction and improvisation. His decree that plans laid on 10 September could not be changed, even for Montgomery, had a fatal effect on the battle. Yet most books dealing with Arnhem make little or no mention of Brereton's role.

As for GARDEN, could XXX Corps on the centre line, or VIII Corps or XII Corps on the flanks, have performed any better? Middlebrook cites 'lack

Alan Wood, a war correspondent for the *Daily Express*, typing a despatch. He and Canadian reporter Stanley Maxted provided vivid commentary on the battle and contributed to what Cornelius Ryan described as 'some of the war's finest reporting'. (*IWM BU 1146*)

of sufficient "push" by General Dempsey at Second Army and by XXX Corps'. He states that Montgomery's order that GARDEN should be 'rapid and violent, without regard to what is happening on the flanks' was not carried out and compares XXX Corps' casualties of under 1,500 with the over 8,000 sustained by 1st Airborne Division and 1 Polish Parachute Brigade at Arnhem. He makes no mention of the flanking corps but repeats Frost's comment that Patton's men would have got through to Arnhem. As he admits, that observation (and others) was made with the benefit of hindsight, an advantage no one had on 17 September 1944.[75] Ken Ford poses questions raised over the years. Why did Guards Armoured stop on the night of D Day before Valkenswaard? Why did the Irish Guards Group not push on through Eindhoven to link with 101st Airborne that night? Why did 101st not drop on either side of the Son bridge to prevent its demolition? Why did 82nd not seize Nijmegen bridge on D Day?[76]

VIII Corps had been assigned a particularly difficult task since Dempsey had placed the corps in reserve following the Normandy campaign, had 'grounded' it and 'used its transport to increase the mobility of the rest of the Army'.[77] Not until 13 September did O'Connor learn the details of his corps' role in GARDEN when he was briefed by the army commander at Second Army's Tac HQ at Perck, where Ritchie was also briefed on XII Corps' role. During the first two weeks of September, VIII Corps came forward from France with the advance party of Corps HQ reaching Erps Querps, about eight miles east of Brussels on the 11th. Third Division was also moving from the Seine and Roberts' 11th Armoured Division came under O'Connor's command on the 16th. A day later 4 Armoured Brigade, under Brigadier Michael Carver (later Field Marshal Lord Carver), joined the corps, as did 1 Belgian Brigade. Of course, that day was D Day for MARKET GARDEN but VIII Corps was still strung out over a distance of 250 miles from the Seine to its leading formation.[78] It was far from being an ideal start. According to Baynes, on the night of the 18th another formation was assigned to O'Connor's command: 50th (Northumbrian) Division. However, this conflicts with the divisional history of the Northumbrian Division as well as Joslen's *Orders of Battle*. The former includes an outline of operations between D Day and the end of GARDEN which makes clear that the division was under Horrocks' command.[79] Joslen confirms this, showing that 50th Division was part of XXX Corps from 13 August to 26 September, passing then to VIII Corps but reverting to XXX on 1 October.[80] Of course, it is possible that O'Connor was *told* on 18 September that the Northumbrian Division would move to VIII Corps on the 26th.

In its six days involved in GARDEN, VIII Corps advanced almost fifty miles, liberating the towns of Helmond and Deurne, east of Eindhoven. It had also forced a crossing of the Zuid-Willemsvaart canal before the Germans could create a firm defensive line along it. As noted on pp. 141–2, 11th Armoured had fought a fierce battle with 107 Panzer Brigade on 21 September that ensured that Eindhoven did not fall into German hands again. The difficulties faced were summed up by Roberts, GOC of 11th Armoured, who touches on another key principle of war, the conservation of one's force:

Our military operations became quite different to anything we had met before. Now, the Germans consisted of a number of 'battle groups' bearing the name of their commanders; their divisions seemed to have broken up, but the groups still had a very high morale, particularly those of SS or Paratroops; they would often fight on without any officers. The country over which we were to fight was often 'canalised' and so, with these natural obstacles, little work was needed to convert them into a strong line of defence very quickly. In Normandy we would start off an operation with a heavy artillery bombardment and sometimes with considerable air support, against well-reconnoitred enemy positions. Now we came up against natural obstacles, sometimes fortified and sometimes not, but when held by the Germans they needed a lot of effort. …

In Normandy there was always real anxiety; if one made wrong decisions, if the front were penetrated by the Germans, if our line of communication was cut, the result could be catastrophic. Now mistakes or failures could only delay the end. Of course we wanted to finish the war as quickly as possible, but at what cost? Unless morale was high, we would not achieve our objectives; heavy casualties in a fruitless battle will not help morale. We must try to win our battles without heavy casualties; not very easy.[81]

The advance of XXX Corps was met by 'an almost fanatical defence … [as well] as frequent small counter-attacks', including one from the north-west on 22 September that, sweeping in behind the leading elements, cut the main axis and prevented traffic moving forward, leading to Dempsey placing 101st Airborne under O'Connor's command on the 23rd while 50th Division moved north to protect the US flank. With the situation stabilised, O'Connor found time to write to his wife commenting on the foul weather and describing MARKET GARDEN as 'the sort of op which is called brilliant if it comes off and bad if it does not'. He added that while he had nothing to do with planning the operation, his corps 'have had to do a lot of fighting to make it go. … We have had a lot of tough fighting with the enemy trying to cut the road'.[82]

The fighting over those six days had cost VIII Corps 663 casualties. In Ritchie's XII Corps, the armoured division, the Desert Rats, 'at first … took no part, except to offer hospitality to the crews of the odd glider or Dakota which crashed in our area' but became more actively committed on 24 September, the day before the withdrawal of 1st Airborne Division across the Rhine. The Desert Rats moved to south of Eindhoven 'in order to protect the long flank of the Guards and 43rd Divisions who so nearly succeeded in relieving the 1st Airborne Division at Arnhem'. The division was then involved in clearing the road from Eindhoven to Veghel which the Germans had cut.

The road was not a good one, narrow and embanked most of the way, and running through flat, sandy fields, interspersed by considerable stretches of birch and pine forests, which, in addition to the inevitable dykes, afforded ample cover for small parties of enemy infantry with bazookas and offered little scope for manoeuvre.[83]

With the road having been cut for twenty-four hours, movement was difficult with the congestion north of Eindhoven described as 'appalling' with Guards Armoured Division echelon vehicles waiting to move forward. On D plus eight, 5th Royal Inniskilling Dragoon Guards reached St Oedenrode, less than four miles south of Veghel, having met 'considerable opposition from enemy bazookas, who were still across the road, supported by a Panther, and in the woods to the east of it'. Patrols of 101st Airborne were contacted.[84] Enemy counter-attacks persisted but, by the 27th, armoured patrols had probed 5,000 yards to the railway line at Schijndel. Relieved of the role of protecting the centre line between Veghel and St Oedenrode by 131 (Queen's) Brigade, the armour continued enlarging the salient. Although MARKET ended with the withdrawal of 1st Airborne across the Rhine, GARDEN had not concluded and 7th Armoured Division continued its operations into October and what the divisional history describes as a 'monotonous and depressing period of routine activity'.[85]

A Cromwell of 7th Armoured Division, the Desert Rats, in Normandy in summer 1944. Although used in the reconnaissance regiments of the other armoured divisions, 7th was the sole Cromwell-equipped division; its units saw little action in the early phase of MARKET GARDEN. (*IWM B8183*)

Also involved in XII Corps' advance was 15th (Scottish) Division. As we have seen (p. 157) that formation had deployed into Operation GARDEN after a difficult battle at Gheel and created a bridgehead at Aart where it fought until relieved by 51st (Highland) Division at the end of September. Neither VIII nor XII Corps had an easy time and accusing either corps, or their commanders, of not doing enough fails to consider what each had already done and the way in which they were pitched into battle. As already noted, the combined losses of the flanking corps, at 3,874, were significantly higher than in XXX Corps and represented a loss almost as high as that of 82nd and 101st Airborne Divisions (3,542).

Where, therefore, should the blame rest? Those who point the finger at Montgomery will continue to do so. However, they might bear in mind O'Connor's words to his wife that MARKET GARDEN was 'the sort of op which is called brilliant if it comes off and bad if it does not'. Had the overall operation been successful, would Montgomery have the same numbers lauding him for his genius as now castigate him for his 'failure'? The answer to that question is almost certainly negative, since an array of generals would have paraded to receive the plaudits, chief among them Eisenhower.

Brooke, who was in Canada at the *Octagon* conference in Quebec when MARKET GARDEN was launched and for much of the operation, had returned to the UK by air and, on 5 October, attended a conference in Versailles hosted by Eisenhower. Montgomery was present, as were the other two army group commanders, Bradley and Devers, together with Tedder, Ike's deputy, Admiral Ramsay, Air Marshal Leigh-Mallory (both Ramsay and Leigh-Mallory were to die in plane crashes in the following three months), Bedell Smith and de Guingand. Writing to his wife, Brooke commented:

> During the whole discussion one fact stood out clearly, that Antwerp must be captured with the least possible delay. I feel that Monty's strategy for once is at fault, instead of carrying out the advance on Arnhem he ought to have made certain of Antwerp in the first place. Ramsay brought this out well in discussion and criticised Monty freely. Ike nobly took all blame on himself as he had approved Monty's suggestion to operate on Arnhem.[86]

Although Montgomery was Brooke's protégé, the latter was in no doubt that Monty had erred. So, too, had Eisenhower, who should have recognised the importance of opening Antwerp. Although the city had been liberated by Second Army, the port could not be used while the Germans controlled the approaches through the Scheldt estuary. While Montgomery had taken a risk,

Field Marshal Sir Alan Brooke, who was CIGS for most of the war, had been Montgomery's patron but was critical of his failure to clear the Scheldt before launching MARKET GARDEN. (*Photo by Karsh; Dutch National Archives*)

he had been backed by Eisenhower. It is worth remembering that, in his *Memoirs*, Montgomery also accepted the blame for the strategic failure of MARKET GARDEN. In his essay on MARKET GARDEN in *Command Decisions* MacDonald notes that Eisenhower referred to 'The attractive possibility of quickly turning the German north flank [that is, of getting across the Rhine] led me to approve the temporary delay in freeing the vital port of Antwerp ... .' In that same essay, he also notes that Eisenhower's expression of concern about the port situation dated only from 10 September, the day on which he authorised MARKET GARDEN.[87]

Eisenhower was under pressure from Washington to use First Allied Airborne Army, the coins 'burning holes in SHAEF's pockets'. That pressure came from Marshall and Arnold, both enthusiastic proponents of the airborne concept. Since the death of Lesley McNair on 25 July in Normandy, Eisenhower had lost the most senior voice supporting his misgivings about large-scale airborne operations. Both Marshall and Arnold must also share the blame for the strategic failure of MARKET GARDEN.

While Urquhart has become a heroic figure, he was responsible for many of 1st Airborne Division's travails. He accepted the laydown of DZs and LZs, against which a more experienced commander would have argued, and was to blame for his formation's inadequate communications. The misuse of Gough's Airborne Reconnaissance Squadron was also born of Urquhart's inexperience, while his failure to inform Hackett that he had delegated divisional command to Hicks should he be killed, wounded or otherwise out of action was inexcusable. All that occurred before he decided to join Lathbury in 1 Parachute Brigade's three-pronged advance to Arnhem bridge. Dempsey was quite certain about Urquhart's culpability:

The primary reason was inept planning by 1 Airborne Division, loss of control by Divisional HQ, and the failure of their communications. They were never in the battle as a formation. … the troops fought magnificently, and could not have done better individually … . I had 1 Airborne Div under my command in Sicily and Arnhem and 6 Airborne Div in Normandy and on the Rhine. The latter were far better at the top. There was no comparison between the two divs in that respect.[88]

Browning must also shoulder responsibility as commander of I Airborne Corps and deputy to Brereton. There was no sound tactical reason for his using some three dozen gliders to fly his HQ into the battle zone: XXX Corps was to take the airborne divisions under command as it advanced to Arnhem. The gliders used by Browning could have carried more troops or artillery which could have taken an active part in the fighting and, perhaps, made a difference.

Dempsey and his three corps commanders have all been criticised. However, Dempsey's biographer notes that Second Army's commander kept his Tactical HQ well forward and was at Nijmegen to observe 504 PIR's attack on the bridge. On 21 September he was with Horrocks and Browning and urged the former 'to keep up the pressure' although 'Horrocks needed no urging'. Next day Dempsey was at Schaft 'co-ordinating the assistance that O'Connor and Ritchie could give to the security of XXX Corps' route.' A day later he was to be found at St Oedenrode 'to confer with all three corps commanders to ensure that everything possible was being done to keep open the axis of advance, and impressed on the commander of 227 Brigade the vital role his formation would have in protecting the bridge at Son'.[89] There is little solid evidence to support the claims made against Dempsey and his corps commanders and it seems likely that the critics were unaware of the terrain over which Second Army was operating, or of the doughtiness of the opposition.

The air commanders' role in planning and executing Operation MARKET was pivotal. However, failure to countenance a second lift on D Day was that of the USAAF commander, Paul Williams. While he believed that he had valid reasons for so doing, war involves risk taking and he failed in that respect. His British subordinate, Leslie Hollinghurst, although willing to launch a second lift that day, was overruled by Williams. The air commanders had also accepted a mistaken assessment of AA defences around Arnhem which influenced planning adversely. Hollinghurst later accepted that the airmen had been wrong.

In terms of attributing blame, we have thus far not looked at one individual: he who commanded the airborne army. On 27 October 1944 Lewis Hyde Brereton wrote to Lieutenant General Barney M. Giles, Hap Arnold's chief of staff at HQ USAAF, in an apologia intended to deflect responsibility for Operation MARKET GARDEN from his HQ to that of Montgomery. He told Giles that he (Brereton) had already attempted to explain to Arnold that his Allied Airborne Army HQ had not been trusted with the planning of an operation but had been 'placed under the domination of the Army Group Planning Staff', a situation he considered that would continue to prevail.

> Until the time comes when the planning of the First Allied Airborne Army and the planning of the Ground Staff is on a purely co-equal and co-ordinating level, I see little chance of any great latitude in forcing my own ideas of properly conceived airborne operation[s].[90]

John Abbatiello also comments that not only was Brereton the first American general of the Second World War to publish his memoirs, but that 'his personnel folder is filled with correspondence enquiring about decorations and other recognition', demonstrating Brereton's determination to ensure that an accurate record of his service could be found in his official records.[91] Was he, to borrow from Hamlet's mother, protesting too much?

Brereton's claim that he was unable to 'force' his own ideas of 'properly conceived airborne operation(s)' is far from the truth. As we have seen, the planning for MARKET was carried out at Brereton's HQ at Ascot and it was Brereton who decreed that no changes could be made in the plans formulated there. Not even Montgomery's attempt to have a second drop on D Day could change Brereton's mind. That was hardly a case of Montgomery's staff dominating the planning.

Let us return to John Abbatiello's essay on Brereton, in which he draws on air power historian Colonel Phillip Meilinger's 2001 book *Airmen and Air Theory: A Review of the Sources*, and the author's reference to Brereton's memoirs as an account that is not 'enlightening':

> Because Brereton tells us in the preface that he began thinking of publishing his diaries in 1942, we get the strong suspicion that he is writing not only after the event but also with an eye to how he would look in print sometime in the future. Frankly, the memoir contains much unimportant detail but little real insight into air strategy or command problems. For example, the text barely hints at severe personality conflicts between Allied leaders at the time of D day and fails to mention the enormous struggle over targeting priorities that occurred at the same time, which nearly caused both Eisenhower and Spaatz to resign in

protest. Overall, *The Brereton Diaries* is an unsatisfactory account of little value.[92]

However, Meilinger also refers to Roger G. Miller's two-part article which refers to Brereton as 'a capable though not outstanding combat leader', a comment which the present authors describe as 'faint praise'. (see p. 29) Also providing 'faint praise' was Eisenhower in his efficiency report on Brereton for the period between 2 August and 31 December 1944, during which the latter became commander of First Allied Airborne Army and planned and executed Operation MARKET. Of thirty-two lieutenant generals 'personally known' to him, the supreme commander ranked Brereton only fourth in air or airborne commanders and tenth among field commanders. Although Eisenhower noted that his performance was 'superior' and wrote that Brereton was 'a serious, hard-working officer of considerable experience in air-ground co-operation and in airborne operations',[93] there is no suggestion that Brereton was the outstanding commander he considered himself to be. Eisenhower may not have assented 'with civil leer' but he was certainly 'willing to wound, and yet afraid to strike/Just hint a fault, and hesitate dislike'.

There is no doubt that Brereton was the organiser and planner of MARKET. In Abbatiello's words, 'he fell short and only the commanding general could bear the blame of defeat'. In this case the defeat was the failure to attain the strategic objective. Brereton had a record of failures or, at the very least, involvement in disasters. He had been commander of the Far East Air Force in the Philippines when the Japanese destroyed much of his command on the ground at Clark Field; as commander of Ninth Air Force, he had overseen the disastrous raid on the Ploesti oil refineries in Romania; he had also been in command of Ninth Air Force when, during missions to support Operation COBRA in Normandy, his aircraft had bombed American ground troops on 25 July, killing 102 and injuring 380. The dead of 25 July 1944 included Lieutenant General Lesley McNair, commander of US Army Ground Forces, who was in Normandy to observe operations; he was the highest-ranking US Army casualty of the Normandy campaign. All four tragedies occurred on Brereton's 'watch' and although he could not be held responsible personally for each of them, he was the commander on each occasion. While he may be defended by citing the fog and frictions of war, one is also prompted to consider Napoleon's reputed desire for lucky generals, a category in which Brereton certainly did not fit.[94]

While a commander leads and manages, his ultimate responsibility is for those who constitute his command. He it is who issues the orders to that command and its subordinate elements for their specific mission or missions.

Should that mission be successful, he will be remembered as the architect of victory and will accept the plaudits and rewards accruing from victory. However, should that mission be unsuccessful, it is the commander who must shoulder the burden of responsibility. In the German *Heer* or the Red Army, Brereton may well have been shot as the man responsible for a failure such as MARKET. One is tempted to think that there was poetic justice when that Luftwaffe raid on Eindhoven forced him to take cover in a ditch and ruin his dress uniform. Perhaps that was a metaphor for his leadership.

Let Dr John J. Abbatiello, Chief, Research, Integration and Research Division, Centre for Character and Leadership Development, at the United States Air Force Academy, have the last word.

> As a commander, Brereton was responsible for the units over which he had authority, the men he led and the missions assigned to him. He was responsible for the men and aircraft of the Far East Air Force in the Philippines, the 9th Air Force in North Africa and northwest Europe, and the First Allied Airborne Army, again in northwest Europe. He was responsible for important missions assigned to him by MacArthur, Arnold, Eisenhower, Montgomery and other Allied leaders. And as a commander of not just one, but four major Allied failures of the Second World War, *he is the worst military commander in history.*[95] (Authors' emphasis)

Epilogue

In his own words, Montgomery remained MARKET GARDEN's 'unrepentant advocate'. Was he justified in that view and had the operation achieved anything of value? He also claimed that the operation was 90 per cent successful, based on the fact that it had gained that percentage of the ground envisaged in the plan. That ground constituted a long, slim salient which included the Betuwe (Batavia) area, known to British troops who held it as 'The Island' and saw it as a damp and miserable low-lying posting. It is a fertile area in the delta formed by the Rhine and Meuse/Maas rivers and includes a number of islands rather than being one. Those who defended it in the aftermath of MARKET GARDEN may not have been impressed by it, but it possessed considerable value for the Allies.

In his book *1945: Victory in the West*, Peter Caddick Adams summarises the importance to the Allied advance in 1945 of that ground gained by the endeavours of British, American, Polish, Dutch, Belgian and Canadian troops in the previous autumn.

> If there was an operational benefit bequeathed by MARKET GARDEN in September 1944, it was the sixty-mile salient carved into German lines, which constantly threatened an Allied breakout. It was one which their opponents never possessed enough combat power to close by land or air. It would prove advantageous subsequently when Twenty-first Army Group launched its operations in 1945.[1]

Caddick Adams elaborates on this by pointing out that Second Army spent the remainder of 1944 'exploiting the salient in the German line … to advance on the Rhine and Meuse rivers'. The German offensive in the Ardennes in December put Bradley's armies on the back foot, leaving Montgomery's 21st Army Group to maintain the initiative and resume Allied offensive operations in January 1945.[2] That resumption of offensive operations began with Operation BLACKCOCK, in which the Roer triangle was cleared of German forces by Neil Ritchie's XII Corps between 13 and 27 January 1945. Then followed Operation VERITABLE in which Horrocks' XXX Corps, much reinforced, fought to clear the Reichswald. Horrocks later described the battle as his biggest operation, with XXX Corps some 200,000 strong, and one that he 'was very glad to have … behind me'.[3]

In the immediate aftermath of MARKET GARDEN, attention turned to clearing the Scheldt and opening Antwerp for Allied shipping. As noted on p. 188, Brooke felt that Montgomery should have ensured that Antwerp was open for shipping. However, Eisenhower was more at fault since he seemed not to appreciate the full potential of Antwerp. Against this, MacDonald wrote that:

> It should also be noted that General Eisenhower's concern about the port situation during the pursuit appears to date only from 10 September, the day he agreed to delay on Antwerp. The Supreme Commander had made little written comment about the port situation up to that time, but the failure to secure hoped-for usable ports was only then becoming marked. Little more than a week before 10 September, the possibility still existed of using the Brittany ports, in particular Brest and Quiberon Bay. Because the entire 12th Army Group was scheduled at that time to advance south of the Ardennes, these ports would still have been valuable. The Channel ports, except for Antwerp, were likely to be open to shipping in the near future. And in any event, the invasion beaches and Cherbourg were operating efficiently. A minor delay in opening Antwerp, it seemed, could well be countenanced.[4]

Long before Operation OVERLORD the planners had been aware that 'until after the development of Antwerp, the availability of port capacity will … limit the forces which can be maintained'.[5] MacDonald commented that securing Antwerp had been one of the main reasons Eisenhower had strengthened Montgomery's northern thrust. With Rotterdam out of reach at that stage, there was no alternative to Antwerp, something Eisenhower appreciated. However, he also appreciated the formidable barrier presented by the Rhine.[6] His opting to launch the airborne/ground operation to cross the Rhine before opening Antwerp may have been based on the opportunity to deploy First Allied Airborne Army and the belief that it was still possible to end the war in Europe by Christmas. MacDonald considered that:

> The operation was a daring strategic [manoeuvre] that failed. That the decision to launch it has not prompted the kind of controversy surrounding other command decisions is somewhat singular. Here was no southern France, where one ally wanted it, the other opposed. Here

was no Argentan-Falaise, where either ally could accuse the other of fault in failing to close the pocket. Even General Bradley, surely one of Field Marshal Montgomery's severest critics, has reserved his more pungent criticisms for other decisions.

Perhaps the reason for the lack of acrimony can be found in the narrow margin by which MARKET-GARDEN failed. Or, perhaps more to the point, in the licence afforded commanders under conditions of success such as existed in September 1944. As British Field Marshal Sir Douglas Haig put it on 22 August 1918, 'Risks which a month ago would have been criminal to incur ought now to be incurred as a duty'.[7]

Thus, MARKET GARDEN, and especially Arnhem, became part of history while also entering that element of folk memory that is entangled with mythology. Much of what is believed about Arnhem is not factual, such as the belief that the entire British force committed to Arnhem were paratroopers. Although the airlanding troops who arrived in gliders wore maroon berets, they were drawn from regiments of Infantry of the Line: King's Own Scottish Borderers, Border Regiment and South Staffordshire Regiment.[8] The gunners of the Royal Artillery – 1st Airlanding Light Regiment and both anti-tank batteries – as well as the Royal Engineers, Gough's Reconnoitrers, the chaplains and those men from the Royal Army Service Corps, the Royal Army Medical Corps, the Royal Army Ordnance Corps, the Pioneer Corps, the Intelligence Corps and the Corps of Military Police were all crucial to 1st Airborne Division's effort. Air despatchers of the RASC were also to be found in the aircraft that flew re-supply missions. The men who fought at Arnhem were representative of the British Army as a whole, rather than of the infant airborne arm, but that has not prevented the popular linkage of Arnhem with the Parachute Regiment.

General Dwight D. Eisenhower, Allied supreme commander, who authorised Operation MARKET GARDEN but made little mention of it in his memoirs. In the photograph, he is wearing the five stars of the newly-created General of the Army rank. (*NARA*)

Lieutenant Jack Reynolds MC, who commanded 2nd South Staffords' Mortar Platoon, was among those captured. His defiance, epitomising that of the defenders, is clear in this image. He also appears to have retained his revolver. The German soldier is pushing a captured Royal Enfield Flying Flea airborne motorbike and carrying a Sten gun. (*Bundesarchiv 497/3531A/31a*)

Airborne formations and units were new and attracted media attention. Although perceived as innovative, the only innovation was the means of transporting them to the battlefield. They were seen to be glamorous, but there is no glamour in any form of soldiering. They were seen to be supermen, but they were no more supermen than men of the Gunners, Sappers, KOSB, the Borders, South Staffords, Reconnaissance Corps or any others who fought at Arnhem. In the aftermath of war, both 1st and 6th Airborne Divisions were disbanded but the designation of 16 Parachute Brigade was intended to commemorate them. Airborne forces remain part of most armies' orders of battle although their utility is limited and they exist on a reputation gained in three short years of war. The last battalion-sized parachute assault executed by the British Army was in Operation MUSKETEER in the Suez crisis of 1956. The US Army's last such drop was in the Iraq war in 2003. More recently, a Russian parachute attack during the invasion of Ukraine was repelled.

Whatever the cap badge they wore the British soldiers who fought at Arnhem and Oosterbeek deserve respect. Bruce E. Davis, a US Army signals officer attached to Urquhart's HQ to direct CAS aircraft, wrote a report on his experience in which he recalled that he had seen men 'who were hungry, exhausted, hopelessly outnumbered, men who by all the rules of warfare should have gladly surrendered to have it all over with, who were shelled until they were helpless psychopathics; and through it all they laugh, sang, and died, and kept fighting'. He added that the finest tribute he could pay to 1st Airborne Division came from a German officer who had been captured. A soldier of the old Prussian school and a veteran of the Great War, the major admonished some of his fellow PoWs who complained that they were not getting enough food (Davis noted that they were receiving more than their captors). Calling them together, the major told them:

These men have stood up under the most terrible artillery bombardment I have ever seen. They have fought on without food or sleep for several days. Even though they are our enemies, I never saw braver men. When you complain you make me feel ashamed of being German. I suggest that you be quiet and follow their example.

… The amazing thing about the British infantry was that they carried on with the light-hearted abandon of a Sunday school class on their first spring picnic.[9]

Notes

Prologue

1. Bradley, *D-Day New Guinea*, passim. Significantly 503 PIR would carry out the last airborne assault of the war in the Pacific, the Corregidor operation.
2. Ibid., pp. 276-8.
3. Camp Mackall was named in honour of Private John T. 'Tommy' Mackall who died of wounds on 8 November 1942 during Operation TORCH. See Devlin, *Paratrooper!*, pp. 201-4.
4. Piasecki, 'The Knollwood Maneuver', passim, *Veritas*, Vol. 4 No. 1.
5. Truesdale, *Brotherhood of the Cauldron*, pp. 14-15.
6. Fairley, *Remember Arnhem*, pp. 4-5.
7. Ibid., p. 7.
8. Ibid. pp. 15-16, 27-8.
9. Ibid., pp. 26-7.
10. Barlow, *Arnhem Aftermath*, p. 1.

Chapter One

1. Tugwell, *Airborne to Battle*, Chapter 1: The Airborne Theory, pp. 17-33 provides an excellent summary of the background story of airborne forces. See also Harclerode, *Wings of War: Airborne Warfare 1918-1945*, for further information on the Italian use of airborne forces as well as the thinking of British, US and other commanders. Devlin, *Paratrooper!*, covers the US test platoon in the eponymous Chapter 3, pp. 48-77.
2. Tugwell, pp. 40-5, 52-8; Devlin, p. 80.
3. Tugwell, p. 64
4. Army Order 21 of 1942 which created the Army Air Corps as an administrative centre for both the Glider Pilot Regiment and the Parachute Regiment.
5. Powell, *The Devil's Birthday*, p. 246.
6. Ibid.
7. Devlin, op. cit., p. 162.
8. Doherty, *Only the Enemy in Front*, p. 37.
9. Doherty, *Clear The Way!*, pp. 40-1.
10. Powell, op. cit., p. 247.
11. The Douglas C-47 transport aircraft was known as the Skytrain in USAAF service and Dakota in British and Commonwealth service. The name Dakota is believed to have been an acronym of **D**ouglas **A**ircraft **Co**mpany **T**ransport **A**ircraft.
12. Flanagan, *Airborne*, p. 96.
13. Ibid.
14. Ibid., pp. 89-103 (Chapter 7: The Airborne Division Crisis). The crisis is also covered by Devlin and Harclerode while it features, as the reader shall see, in D'Este's biography of Eisenhower.
15. Flanagan, p. 98.

16. Ibid.
17. Ibid.
18. Ibid., p. 100.
19. Ibid., p. 102.
20. Vasey was killed in a plane crash in 1945; he had served in France and Flanders in the First World War, earning the DSO and two MiDs; he had earned a Bar to his DSO and two further MiDs earlier in the Second World War, as well as the Greek War Cross and the DSC (US).
21. Flanagan, p. 103.
22. Ibid.

Chapter Two
1. *The Papers of Dwight D. Eisenhower, The War Years*: IV, quoted in Graham & Bidwell, *Coalitions, Politicians and Generals: Some Aspects of Command in Two World Wars*, p. 233.
2. Graham and Bidwell, pp. 228-9.
3. The British system relied on the Royal Army Service Corps (RASC) to store and issue supplies, including food, fuel and medical supplies, as well as transporting ammunition and various other items. Each operational division had its Commander RASC, as did the higher formations. See Forty, *British Army Handbook 1939-1945*, especially Chapters 6 and 7.
4. Graham and Bidwell, p. 264.
5. Winchester, *The Men Who United the States*, pp. 305 & 308.
6. D'Este, *Eisenhower*, p. 611.
7. MacDonald, *The Siegfried Line Campaign*, p. 119.
8. Ibid., p. 3.
9. Ibid., p. 43.
10. Ibid., p. 42.
11. Ibid., p. 56.
12. Ibid., p. 57.
13. Colley, *The Folly of Generals*, p. 19.
14. Ibid.
15. MacDonald, op. cit., p. 61.
16. Ibid., p. 62.
17. Ibid., p. 48.
18. Ibid., p. 50.
19. Colley, op. cit., p. 19.

Chapter Three
1. D'Este, op. cit., p. 611.
2. Powell, op. cit., p. 234.
3. Graham & Bidwell, op. cit., p. 217n.
4. Rostron, *The Military Life &Times of General Sir Miles Dempsey GBE KCB DSO MC, Monty's Army Commander*, p. 134 (hereinafter *Dempsey*).
5. Warren, *Airborne Operations In World War II, European Theater: USAF Historical Studies* No. 97, p. 89.
6. Graham and Bidwell, op. cit., p. 241.
7. Miller, 'A Pretty Damn Able Commander', *Air Power History*, nos 47 & 48.
8. D'Este, op. cit., p. 611.
9. Smart, *Biographical Dictionary of British Generals of the Second World* War, pp. 45-6; Mead, *Churchill's Lions*, p. 85.
10. Smart, pp. 45-6.
11. Brereton, *The Brereton Diaries: The War in the Pacific, Middle East and Europe, 3 October 1941–8 May 1945*, pp. 308-9.

12. Ibid., p. 336.
13. D'Este, op. cit., p. 611.

Chapter Four
1. Montgomery, *Memoirs*, p. 288.
2. Bradley, *A Soldier's Story*, p.416.
3. Montgomery, op. cit., p. 288.
4. Ibid., p. 289.
5. Eisenhower, *Crusade in Europe*, p. 307.
6. Bradley, op. cit., p. 416.
7. Montgomery, op. cit., p. 297.
8. Ibid.

Chapter Five
1. Smart, op. cit., p. 91; Truesdale, op. cit., pp. 19-20; Devlin, op. cit., p. 474; www.BritishMilitaryHistory.co.uk, accessed 20 Jan. 2021.
2. Mitchell, *The Battle for the Peaks*, p. 320.
3. Ibid., passim.
4. www.BritishMilitaryHistory.co.uk, accessed 20 Jan. 2021
5. Lewin, *Montgomery as Military Commander,* p. 238.
6. Rostron, *The Military Life and Times of General Sir Miles Dempsey*, p. 134.
7. Ibid.
8. As related to Truesdale by the late Major Mervyn Dennison, OC A Company, 3rd Parachute Battalion.
9. The Orbat for 1 Border is courtesy of Stuart Eastwood, Border Regiment Museum, Carlisle.
10. Junier et al, *By Land, Sea and Air*, pp. 9-11 & 26-62.
11. Sigmond, *Off at Last*, pp. 9-15.
12. Major Lander was killed on 13 July 1943 during the Sicily operation. He is buried in Catania War Cemetery in grave IV.C.33.
13. Kent, *First In*, p. 94.
14. Fairley, passim.
15. Joslen, *Orders of Battle*, p. 106.
16. Fairley, pp. 26-7.
17. Powell (p. 61) believed, wrongly, that jeeps were fitted with twin Vickers Ks.
18. Fairley, op. cit., pp. 27-8.
19. Ibid., p. 16.
20. Guns in the Royal Artillery are manned by detachments, not crews or teams.
21. Truesdale, Cornelissen, & Gerritsen, *Arnhem Bridge Target Mike One*, passim.
22. Pakenham-Walsh, *History of The Corps of Royal Engineers*, Vol. IX, pp. 402-3.
23. Blair, *In Arduis Fidelis*, pp. 306-7.
24. Turnbull & Hamblett, *Pegasus Patrol*, pp. 62-3.
25. Information on squadrons and aircraft types is drawn from Halley, *The Squadrons of the Royal Air Force*.
26. Information drawn from Appendix VI of Ellis, *Victory in the West*, Vol. II.

Chapter Six
1. Ellis, *Victory in the West*, Vol. II, p. 30n.
2. Smart, op. cit., p. 308.
3. Ibid., p. 127.
4. Baynes, *The Forgotten Victor*, p. 186.

5. Ellis, op. cit., p. 30n.
6. Flanagan, op. cit., p. 243.
7. Ibid.
8. Powell, op. cit., p. 30.
9. Mead, *The Men Behind Monty* (hereinafter *The Men …*), pp. 192-3.
10. Bradley, op. cit., p. 418.
11. Mead, *The Men …* , p. 193.
12. John Keats, 1751-1821, 'Ode to Autumn'.
13. Harclerode, *Wings of War*, p. 467.
14. Ibid.; Powell, op. cit., p. 33.
15. Harclerode, op. cit., p. 467.
16. https://web.archive.org/web/20100328153100/http://www.rafweb.org/Grp04.htm Air of Authority: A History of RAF Air Organisation, accessed 28 Feb. 21.
17. Powell, op. cit., p. 34.
18. Mead, *The Men …* , p. 236. R.F.K. 'David' Belchem was largely responsible for writing Montgomery's *El Alamein to the Sangro* and *Normandy to the Baltic*, although he was not credited for either when the books were published in 1946.
19. Manston, Blakehill Farm, Broadwell, Down Ampney, Fairford, Harwell, Keevil and Tarrant Rushton.
20. Powell, op. cit., p. 36.
21. Richardson, *Send for Freddy*, p. 165.
22. Ibid., p. 166.
23. Ibid., p. 44.
24. Mead, *The Men …* , p. 195.

Chapter Seven
1. Middlebrook and Everitt, *The Bomber Command War Diaries*, p. 585.
2. Powell, op. cit., p. 51.
3. Middlebrook and Everitt, op. cit., p. 585.
4. Powell, op. cit., p. 51.
5. Middlebrook and Everitt, op. cit., pp. 585-6.
6. Air Defence of Great Britain (ADGB) was first established in 1925 but abolished in 1936 with the creation of Fighter and Bomber Commands. In 1943, with the creation of 2 TAF from Fighter Command, the remaining defensive aircraft and the Army's AA Command were renamed ADGB. However, the Fighter Command title was revived in October 1944.
7. Smith, *The History of the Glider Pilot Regiment*, p. 107.
8. Ibid.
9. Ibid., p. 108; Harclerode, *Arnhem: A Tragedy of Errors* (hereinafter *Arnhem*), p. 67.
10. Harclerode, *Arnhem*, p. 67.
11. Powell, op. cit., p. 67.
12. Rostron, op. cit., p. 139.
13. NA Kew, WO205/972, 'Operations of Second Army in North West Europe'.
14. Rostron, op. cit., p. 134.
15. Ibid., p. 143.
16. Quoted in Rostron, p. 140: from RLEW 7/7, Churchill Archive Centre.
17. Lewin, *Montgomery*, p. 237.
18. Ibid., p. 238.
19. Ellis, op. cit., p. 55.
20. Zaloga, *The American Airborne Missions*, p. 32.
21. Ibid., p. 33.
22. Ibid., p. 40.

23. Horrocks, *A Full Life*, p. 211.
24. Ibid., p. 210.
25. 2nd (Armoured) Battalion of the 'Micks', commanded by Lieutenant Colonel J.O.E. Vandeleur.
26. Horrocks, op. cit., p. 212.
27. Zaloga, op. cit., conflates the two incidents, p. 36.
28. Powell, op. cit., p. 83.

Chapter Eight

1. Tugwell, op. cit., p. 229.
2. Powell, op. cit., pp. 45-6.
3. Hills, *By Tank Into Normandy*, p. 155.
4. Ibid.
5. MacDonald, op. cit., p. 124.
6. Model was disappointed to learn that Student's army numbered no more than 20,000 at that time. See Kershaw, *It Never Snows in September*, p. 23.
7. Quoted in Rostron, op. cit., p. 133. The quotation is from Dempsey's war diary: NA Kew, WO285/10.
8. Kershaw, op. cit., p. 21.
9. Ibid.
10. Hinsley, *British Intelligence in the Second World War*, p. 542.
11. Ibid.
12. Horrocks, op. cit., pp. 213-14.
13. Powell, op. cit., p. 94.
14. Horrocks, op. cit., p. 214.
15. Student, quoted in Horrocks, op. cit., p. 214.
16. Badsey, *Arnhem* 1944, p. 41.
17. Powell, op. cit., p. 96.
18. Krafft, quoted in Powell, p. 96. Krafft's account is held in NA Kew, WO205/1124.
19. The Dutchman William Henry Nassau, Prince of Orange, was King William in Ireland, King William II in Scotland and King William III in England and Wales.
20. Hackett, *The Profession of Arms*, p. 163.

Chapter Nine

1. Rosse and Hill, *The Story of the Guards Armoured* Division, pp. 130-1.
2. Barlow, op. cit., p. 1.
3. Hibbert, *Arnhem*, p. 83.
4. Originally 371 Field Battery, a Highland TA sub-unit, it became 204 (Oban) Battery of 51st (West Highland) Anti-Tank Regiment in November 1938; the redesignation to 2 Airlanding Anti-Tank Battery occurred on 10 October 1942.
5. However, Urquhart had failed to inform Hackett of the decision.
6. From Jones, *History of the 101st Airborne Division: Screaming Eagles; The First Fifty Years.*
7. From Nofi, *The War Against Hitler Military strategy in the West.* However, this is not replicated in any official orders or after-action reports.
8. Powell, op. cit., p. 98.
9. Devlin, op. cit., p. 497
10. Ibid.
11. Ibid.
12. Ibid., pp. 498-9.
13. *London Gazette*, 25 Jan. 1945.
14. Jack Fryer, 1st Parachute Battalion, interview with Truesdale.

15. Powell, op. cit., p. 107.
16. Ibid.
17. Middlebrook, *Arnhem 1944*, p. 26.
18. Smyth died of his wounds on 26 October.
19. Powell, op. cit., p. 110.
20. Ibid.
21. Ibid.
22. Ibid., pp. 110-11.
23. Zaloga, op. cit., pp. 52-3.
24. Powell, op. cit., p. 118.
25. Orr and Truesdale, *The Rifles are There!* pp. 67-73.
26. Badsey, op. cit., p. 56; Flanagan, op. cit., p. 253.
27. Badsey, op. cit., p. 56.
28. Horrocks, op. cit., pp. 217-18.
29. Zaloga, op. cit., p. 55.
30. Flanagan, op. cit., p. 253.
31. Badsey, op. cit., p. 55.
32. Flanagan, op. cit., p. 253.
33. Ibid.; Devlin, op. cit., p. 503.
34. Powell, op. cit., pp. 135-6.
35. Ibid., p. 125.
36. *London Gazette*, 13 Nov. 1945.
37. Ibid.; Powell, op. cit., p. 125.
38. *London Gazette*, 13 Nov. 1945, op. cit.
39. Horrocks, op. cit., p. 218.
40. The armoured recce regiment of 11th Armoured Division, on loan to Taylor's command.
41. Truesdale, *Steel Wall at Arnhem*, pp. 133-4.
42. Kershaw, op. cit., p. 169.
43. Ibid.
44. Ibid., pp. 171-2.
45. *London Gazette*, 25 Jan. 1945.
46. Truesdale, *Steel Wall*, op. cit., pp. 7-8.
47. Kershaw, op. cit., pp. 102-4.
48. Ibid., pp. 104-5.
49. Ibid., p. 174.
50. Ibid.
51. Ibid., pp. 174-5.
52. *London Gazette*, 1 Feb. 1945.

Chapter Ten

1. Middlebrook, op. cit., p. 325.
2. Waddy, *A Tour of the Arnhem Battlefields*, p. 121.
3. Frost, *A Drop Too Many*, p. 229.
4. Middlebrook, op. cit., p. 311.
5. Frost, op. cit., p. 230.
6. *London Gazette*, op. cit.
7. Badsey, op. cit., p. 64.
8. Ibid., p. 68.
9. Lonsdale earned his MC on India's North West Frontier as a platoon commander in 1st Leicestershire Regiment, and the DSO as a company commander in 2nd Parachute Battalion at Primosole Bridge in Sicily.

10. Waddy, op. cit., pp. 134-5.
11. Middlebrook, op. cit., p. 339.
12. Ibid., pp. 282-6.
13. Middlebrook, op. cit., pp. 282-6.
14. Ibid., p. 282; Waddy, op. cit., p. 117.
15. Waddy, op. cit., pp. 117-18.
16. *London Gazette*, 23 Nov. 1944.
17. www.military wiki|fandom: Paul L. Williams, accessed 20 Mar. 2022.
18. Middlebrook, op. cit., p. 292.
19. Ibid., p. 392.
20. Evans, *The Battle for Arnhem*, p. 12.
21. Powell, op. cit., p. 135.
22. Delaforce, *Monty's Northern Legions*, pp. 151-3.
23. Martin, *History of the 15th Scottish Division*, pp. 150-68; Kemsley and Riesco, *Scottish Lion on Patrol*, pp. 130-2.
24. Designed by Fred Goatley, the boats, made of canvas and wood, could carry ten fully-equipped soldiers. Each weighed 330 pounds and could be assembled in two minutes by two men with a modicum of training. Some 1,000 were produced during the war.
25. Quoted in Flanagan, op. cit., p. 255.
26. John C. McManus, Operation Market Garden: 'Hail Mary' in Holland. HistoryNet Retrieved from https://www.historynet.com/operation-market-garden-hail-mary-in-holland, accessed March 2022.
27. Ibid.
28. Gorman also made the comment when interviewed by Doherty for the BBC Radio Ulster series 'One Man's War' in 1995.
29. Horrocks, op. cit., p. 220.
30. Rosse and Hill, op. cit., p. 141.
31. Flanagan, pp. 257-8.
32. Badsey, op. cit., p. 64.
33. Ibid., p. 65.
34. Powell, op. cit., p. 168.
35. *London Gazette*, 2 Nov. 1944.
36. The unit's role was to provide OP parties trained in directing the fire of XXX Corps' long-range artillery.
37. Middlebrook, op. cit., p. 403.
38. Middlebrook (p. 404) notes that 1,003 men landed.
39. Badsey, op. cit., p. 71.
40. Hunt, *Hard Fighting*, p. 274.
41. Horrocks, op. cit., pp. 220-1.
42. Baynes, op. cit., pp. 229-30.
43. Barclay, *The History of the 53rd (Welsh) Division in the Second World War*, p. 75.
44. Ellis, op. cit., p. 44.
45. Badsey, op. cit., p. 72.
46. Ibid.

Chapter Eleven
1. Waddy, p. 137.
2. Ibid., p. 147; Middlebrook, pp. 347-8.
3. Middlebrook, p. 349.
4. Ibid., p. 346.

5. www.daimler-fighting-vehicles.co.uk DFV File Part D0001a-Household Cavalry 1939-1945: On Active Service, Household Cavalry 1939-1945: The Daimler Fighting Vehicles Project, Part d1a. Accessed Mar. 2022.
6. Truesdale, *Brotherhood*, p. 142. Jack Fryer, former T Company, 1st Parachute Battalion, interview with Truesdale, May 1990.
7. Badsey, p. 72.
8. Ibid., pp. 72-3; Horrocks, p. 226, defines the road closure as lasting twenty-five hours.
9. Horrocks, p. 229.
10. Middlebrook., p. 410.
11. Waddy, p. 173.
12. Powell, p. 192.
13. Beevor, *Arnhem: The Battle for The Bridges 1944*, p. 314.
14. Badsey, p. 73.
15. Middlebrook and Everitt, op. cit., p. 587.
16. Badsey, p. 72.
17. Kershaw, op. cit., pp. 266-7.
18. Ryan, *A Bridge Too Far*, p. 409.
19. Quoted in ibid.
20. Ryan, p. 409.
21. Powell, p. 204.
22. Ibid., p. 205.
23. Ryan, p. 409, quoting Urquhart: 'Resupply by air; very small quantity picked up.'; Powell, pp. 201-2.
24. Powell, pp. 206-7; Blake, *Mountain and Flood*, p. 63; Shilleto, *The Fighting Fifty-Second*, p. 31.
25. Powell, p. 207; Brereton, *The Brereton* Diaries, p. 355.
26. Powell, p. 136.
27. Ryan, p. 407.
28. Ibid., p. 409; Powell, pp. 201-2.
29. Powell, pp. 200-1.
30. Sims, *Arnhem Spearhead*, p. 127.
31. Gill & Groves, *Club Route in Europe*, pp. 80-1.
32. Ibid., p. 81.
33. Waddy, p. 174.
34. Middlebrook, p. 411.
35. Badsey, p. 76; Powell, p. 208.
36. His official title was ADMS, Assistant Director Medical Services.
37. Powell, pp. 210-11; Middlebrook, p. 383.
38. Powell, p. 212.
39. Essame, *The 43rd Wessex Division at War*, p. 132.
40. Powell, p. 205.
41. Ibid., pp. 214-15; Middlebrook, p. 422.
42. Middlebrook, p. 422.
43. Powell, pp. 214-15.
44. Ibid., pp. 215-16.
45. Ryan, p. 436.
46. Powell, p. 218.
47. Ryan, p. 436.
48. Waddy, p. 156.
49. Middlebrook, pp. 423-4; Powell, pp. 219-20.
50. Powell, p. 220.

51. Badsey, p. 81; Waddy, pp. 140-1.
52. Powell, p. 220.
53. Badsey, p. 83.
54. Canada had officers to spare and some went on loan to the British Army, serving in Italy and North-West Europe, being described as CanLoan officers.
55. Ryan, p. 437.
56. Ibid., p. 438.
57. Waddy, p. 161.
58. Ryan, pp. 436-7.
59. Ibid., p. 437.
60. Middlebrook, p. 428.
61. Urquhart, *Arnhem*, p. 173.
62. Powell, p. 221.
63. Pakenham-Walsh, op. cit., p. 409.
64. Middlebrook, p. 431.
65. Powell, p. 221.
66. Ibid.; Middlebrooks, p. 433.
67. Quoted in Pakenham-Walsh., pp. 409-10.
68. Middlebrook, p. 434; Waddy, p. 166; Harclerode, *Tragedy*, p. 153, puts the number of glider pilots at 420.
69. Kershaw, p. 301.
70. Middlebrook, p. 432.
71. Powell, p. 222.
72. Kershaw, p. 301.
73. Harclerode, *Tragedy*, p. 153.
74. MacDonald, *Siegfried Line*, p. 199.
75. Badsey, p. 84.
76. Ibid.
77. Ellis, op. cit., p. 54.
78. Badsey, p. 84.
79. Ibid.

Chapter Twelve

1. Churchill, *The Second World War, Book XI: Triumph and Tragedy: The Tide of Victory, June–December 1944*, p. 175. The telegram to Smuts was dated 9 Oct. 1944.
2. Powell, p. 232.
3. Montgomery, op. cit., pp. 295-8.
4. Quoted in Powell, p. 232.
5. Powell, p. 233.
6. Brereton, p. 360.
7. MacDonald, *American Endeavor*, pp. 429-30, US Army Center for Military History, accessed Jan. 2022.
8. MacDonald, *Siegfried Line*, p. 198.
9. Ibid.
10. Powell, p. 240.
11. Martin, op. cit., p. 147.
12. Powell, p. 240.
13. MacDonald, *Siegfried Line*., p. 199. He attributes the British ground forces figures to the Cabinet Office Historical Section.
14. Montgomery. *Normandy to the Baltic*, p. 242.
15. Wilmot, *The Struggle for Europe*, pp. 587-8.

16. Powell, p. 241.
17. Ibid., pp. 241-2.
18. See p. 45.
19. Joslen, op. cit., p. 106.
20. Fairley, op. cit., p. 28.
21. Powell, p. 242.
22. MacDonald, *Siegfried Line*, pp. 199-200.
23. Tedder, *With Prejudice*, p. 595.
24. Probert, *High Commanders of The Royal Air Force*, p. 38.
25. Eisenhower, *Crusade in Europe*, p. 349.
26. Harclerode, *Wings of War*, p. 537.
27. Bradley, *A Soldier's Story*, pp. 418-19.
28. MacDonald, op. cit., p. 200.
29. Powell, p. 237.
30. MacDonald, p. 199.
31. Powell, pp. 237-8.
32. MacDonald, p. 200.
33. Ibid.
34. Ibid.
35. Devlin, op. cit., p. 478.
36. Harclerode, *Wings of War*, p. 536.
37. Badsey. op. cit., p. 25.
38. Hinsley, op. cit., p. 542.
39. Bryant, *Triumph in the West*, pp. 284-5.
40. Ibid., p. 285.
41. Hinsley, p. 5542.
42. Hastings, *Armageddon*, p. 66.
43. Powell, pp. 147-8.
44. Harclerode, *Wings of War*, p. 537.
45. Wilmot, p. 589.
46. Ibid., pp. 589-90.
47. Eisenhower, op. cit., p. 336.
48. Wilmot, pp. 590-1.
49. Ibid., pp. 591-2.
50. De Guingand, *Operation Victory*, p. 413.
51. Wilmot, p. 592.
52. Ibid., pp. 591-2; Joslen, p. 84.
53. Lewin, *Montgomery*, p. 237.
54. Wilmot, p. 593.
55. Bryant, p. 284.
56. Tedder, p. 595.
57. Cole, *The Lorraine Campaign*, p. 56.
58. Wilmot, p. 590.
59. Barnett, *Lords of War*, p. 231.
60. D'Este, *Eisenhower*, pp. 617-18.
61. Ibid., p. 618.
62. Hamilton, *Monty the Field Marshal 1944-1976*, pp. 89-90.
63. Quoted in D'Este, p. 617.
64. Cole, pp. 55-6.
65. Smart, op. cit., p. 314.
66. Frost, op. cit., p. 256.

67. Ibid., pp. 256-7.
68. Ibid.
69. Ibid., p. 241.
70. Powell, p. 235.
71. Harclerode, *Tragedy*, p. 165.
72. Powell, p. 235.
73. Frost, p. 242.
74. Powell, pp. 235-6.
75. Middlebrook, op. cit., p. 444.
76. Ford, *The British XXX Corps Missions*, p. 92.
77. Rostron, op. cit., p. 126.
78. Baynes, op. cit., pp. 228-9.
79. Clay, *The Path of the 50th*, pp. 298-301.
80. Joslen, p. 82.
81. Roberts, *From the Desert to the* Baltic, p. 214.
82. Baynes, p. 232.
83. Lindsay and Johnston, *History of 7th Armoured Division, June 1943-July19 45*, p. 91
84. Ibid.
85. Ibid., pp. 91-2.
86. Danchev and Todman, *War Diaries 1939-1945; Field Marshal Lord Alanbrooke*, p. 600.
87. MacDonald, *Command Decisions*, p. 440.
88. Dempsey, quoted in Rostron, p. 143.
89. Rostron, p. 142; 227 Brigade, commanded by Brigadier E.C. Colville, was part of 15th (Scottish) Division in VIII Corps.
90. Quoted in Abbatiello 'Lewis Brereton' in Jennings and Steele, *The Worst Military Leaders in History*, p. 164. The original letter is held in Brereton's personnel file in NARA.
91. Ibid., pp. 164-5.
92. Meilinger, *Airmen and Air Theory*, p. 47.
93. Abbatiello, op. cit., p. 164.
94. Ibid., p. 165.
95. Ibid.

Epilogue

1. Caddick-Adams, *1945: Victory in the West*, p. 18.
2. Ibid., p. 87.
3. Horrocks, op. cit., pp. 249 & 255.
4. MacDonald, *Command Decisions*, p. 440.
5. Quoted in ibid., p. 439.
6. Ibid., p. 442.
7. Ibid.
8. The King's Own Scottish Borderers amalgamated with The Royal Scots as The Royal Scots Borderers on formation of the Royal Regiment of Scotland in 2006; in 2021 it was redesignated as a battalion of the Ranger Regiment and lost all its history. Today the Border Regiment is part of the Duke of Lancaster's Regiment and the South Staffordshire Regiment part of the Mercian Regiment.
9. Quoted by Hackett in Chandler (ed.) *Great Battles of the British Army as Commemorated in the Sandhurst Companies*, pp. 219-20.

Bibliography

Andrews, E.N. & Morgan E.B., *Vickers Aircraft Since 1908* (Putnam, 1988)

Anon, *Taurus Pursuant: A History of 11th Armoured Division* (np, nd)

Badsey, Stephen, *Arnhem 1944: Operation Market Garden* (Osprey Publishing, Oxford, 1993)

Bankhead, Harry, *Salute to the Steadfast* (Ramsay Press, 2002)

Barclay, C.N., *The History of the 53rd (Welsh) Division in the Second World War* (William Clowes & Sons, London, 1956)

Barlow, Arthur, *Arnhem Aftermath* (np, nd)

Barnett, Correlli, *The Lords of War: Supreme Leadership from Lincoln to Churchill* (Praetorian Press/Pen & Sword Books, Barnsley, 2012)

Baynes, John, *The Forgotten Victor: General Sir Richard O'Connor Kt GCB DSO MC* (Brassey's UK, London, 1989)

Beevor, Antony, *Arnhem: The Battle for the Bridges, 1944* (Penguin, London, 2018)

Blair, J.S.G., *In Arduis Fidelis: Centenary History of the Royal Army Medical Corps* (Scottish Academic Press, Edinburgh, 1998)

Blake, George, *Mountain and Flood: The History of the 52nd (Lowland) Division 1939-1946* (Jackson, Son & Co., Glasgow, 1950)

Blandford, Edmund L., *Green Devils – Red Devils: Untold Tales of the Airborne in World War II* (Leo Cooper, London, 1992)

Blumenson, Martin et al, *Command Decisions* (Center of Military History, Dept of the Army, Washington DC, 2000)

Bradley, Omar N., and Carr, Caleb, *A Soldier's Story* (The Modern Library, New York, 1999)

Bradley, Phillip, *D-Day New Guinea: The Extraordinary Story of the Battle for Lae and the greatest combined airborne and amphibious operation of the Pacific War* (Allen & Unwin, Crow's Nest, NSW, Australia, 2019)

Brereton, Lewis H., *The Brereton Diaries: The War in the Pacific, Middle East and Europe, 3 October 1941-8 May 1945* (William Morrow & Co., New York, 1946)

Bryant, Arthur, *Triumph in the West: Completing the War Diaries of Field Marshal Viscount Alexander* (Collins, London, 1959)

Buzzell, Nora (Ed.), *The Register of the Victoria Cross* (This England Books, Cheltenham, 1988)

Caddick-Adams, Peter, *1945: Victory in the West* (Hutchinson Heinemann, London, 2022)

Carver, Michael, *Out of Step: The Memoirs of Field Marshal Lord Carver* (Hutchinson, London, 1989)

Chandler, David G. (ed. in chief), *Great Battles of the British Army As Commemorated in the Sandhurst Companies* (Arms and Armour Press, London, 1991)

Cherry, Niall, *Red Berets and Red Crosses* (R.N. Sigmond Publishing, Renkum, 2014)

Cholewczynski, George, *Poles Apart: The Polish Airborne at the Battle of Arnhem* (Sarpedon, Conshohocken, PA., 1993)

Churchill, Winston S., *The Second World War, Book XI: Triumph and Tragedy: The Tide of Victory, June–December 1944* (Cassell & Co., London, 1954)

Clay, E.W., *The Path of the 50th: The Story of the 50th (Northumbrian) Division in the Second World War* (Gale and Polden, Aldershot, 1950)

Cole, [Colonel] Hugh M., *The Lorraine Campaign* (*United States Army in World War II in The European Theater of Operations*) (Center of Military History United States Army Washington, DC, 1993)

Colley, David P., *The Folly of Generals: How Eisenhower's Broad Front Strategy Lengthened World War II* (Casemate, Philadelphia, and Oxford, 2021)

Danchev, Alex, and Todman, Daniel (eds), *War Diaries 1939-1945: Field Marshal Lord Alanbrooke* (Weidenfeld & Nicolson, London, 2001)

Darby, Hugh, and Cunliffe, Marcus, *A Short History of 21 Army Group* (Gale & Polden, Aldershot, 1949)

Deeley, Graham, *Worst Fears Confirmed* (Barny Books, Peterborough, 2005)

Delaforce, Patrick, *Monty's Ironsides: From the Normandy Beaches to Bremen with the 3rd Division* (Sutton Publishing, Stroud, 1995)

——, *Monty's Northern Legions: 50th Northumbrian and 15th Scottish Divisions at War 1939–1945* (Sutton Publishing, Stroud, 2004)

D'Este, Carlo, *Eisenhower: Allied Supreme Commander* (Weidenfeld & Nicolson, London, 2002)

Devlin, Gerard M., *Paratrooper: The Saga of US Army and Marine Parachute and Glider Combat Troops* (St Martin's Press, New York, 1979)

Doherty, Richard, *Clear The Way! A History of 38 (Irish) Brigade, 1941–47* Irish Academic Press, Dublin, 1993)

——, *Only the Enemy in Front (Every other beggar behind …): The Recce Corps at War 1940-1946* (Tom Donovan Publishing, London, 1994)

——, *The British Reconnaissance Corps*, (Osprey Publishing, Botley, 2007)

Duncan, W.E. (Ed), *The Royal Artillery Commemoration Book 1939-1945* (Bell & Sons, London, 1950)

Duyts, W.J.M & Groeneweg, A. (edited), *De Oogst Tien Jaar/The Harvest of Ten Years* (published by the Airborne Museum, Hartenstein, 1988)

Dyer, Gwynne, *War: The Lethal Custom* (Carroll & Graf, New York, 2004)

Eastwood, Stuart; Gray, Charles & Green, Alan, *When Dragons Flew* (Silver Link Publishing, Horncastle, 1994)

Eisenhower, Dwight D., *Crusade in Europe* (Doubleday and Co., New York, 1948)

Ellis, Chris & Chamberlain, Peter, *Handbook on the British Army* (Arms & Armour Press, London, 1976)

Ellis, John, *Brute Force: Allied Strategy and Tactics in the Second World War* (Andre Deutsch, London, 1990)

Ellis, Major L.F. and Warhurst, Lt Col A.E., *Victory in the West*, Volume II: *The Defeat of Germany* (HMSO, London, 1968; reprint by the Imperial War Museum/Battery Press, Nashville, Tenn., 1994)

Essame, Major General Hubert, *The 43rd Wessex Division at War: 1944-1945* (William Clowes, London, 1952)

Evans, Martin Marix, *The Battle for Arnhem* (Pitkin, London, 1998)

Fairley, John, *Remember Arnhem: The Story of the 1st Airborne Squadron at Arnhem* (Peaton Press, Bearsden, 1978)

Flanagan, F.M., *Airborne: A Combat History of American Airborne Forces* (Ballantine Books, New York, 2002)

Ford, Ken, *Operation Market Garden 1944 (3) The British XXX Corps Missions* (Osprey Publishing, Oxford, 2018)

Forty, George, *British Army Handbook 1939-1945* (Sutton Publishing, Stroud, 1998)

Frost, Major General John, *A Drop Too Many* (Cassell, London, Barnsley, 1980)

Fullick, Roy, *Shan Hackett: The Pursuit of Exactitude* (Pen & Sword, Barnsley, 2003)

Gallagher, Mike, *With Recce at Arnhem: The Recollections of Trooper Des Evans, A 1st Airborne Division Veteran* (Pen & Sword Books, Barnsley, 2015)

Gerritsen, Bob & Revell, Scott, *Retake Arnhem Bridge* (R.N. Sigmond Publishing, Renkum, 2010)

Gijbels, Peter, and Truesdale, David, *Leading the Way to Arnhem: An Illustrated History of the 21st Independent Parachute Company, 1942 to 1946* (R.N. Sigmond Publishing, Renkum, 2008)

Gill, Ronald, and Groves, John, *Club Route in Europe: The Story of XXX Corps in the European Campaign* (np, Hannover, 1946)

Gorman, Sir John, *The Times of My Life: An Autobiography* (Leo Cooper, Barnsley, 2002)

Graham, Dominick, and Bidwell, Shelford, *Coalitions, Politicians and Generals: Some Aspects of Command in Two World Wars* (Brassey's, London, 1993)

Guingand, Major General Sir Francis de, *Operation Victory* (Hodder & Stoughton, London, 1947)

Hackett, Sir John, *I Was A Stranger* (Chatto & Windus, London, 1977)

——, *The Profession of Arms* (Sidgwick & Jackson, London, 1983)

Hagen, Louis, *Arnhem Lift: A Fighting Glider Pilot Remembers* (Leo Cooper, London, 1993)

Halley, James J., *The Squadrons of the Royal Air Force* (Air-Britain (Historians) Ltd, Tonbridge, 1985)

Hamilton, Nigel, *Monty: The Field Marshal 1944-1976* (Hamish Hamilton, London, 1986)

Harclerode, Peter, *Arnhem: A Tragedy of Errors* (Caxton, London, 1994)

——, *Wings of War: Airborne Warfare 1918-1945* (Weidenfeld & Nicolson, London, 2005)

Hart, Stephen A., *Colossal Cracks: Montgomery's 21st Army Group in Northwest Europe, 1944-45* (Stackpole Mechanicsburg, PA, 2007)

Hastings, Max, *Armageddon: The Battle for Germany, 1944-45* (Macmillan, London, 2004)

Hibbert, Christopher, *Arnhem* (B.T. Batsford, London, 1962; Weidenfeld & Nicolson, London, 1998)

Hills, Stuart, *By Tank into Normandy* (Cassell, London, 2002)

Hinsley, F.H., (HMSO, London, 1993)

Holland, James, *Brothers in Arms: One Legendary Tank Regiment's Bloody War from D-Day to VE-Day* (Transworld, London, 2021)

Holmes, Richard, *Soldiers: Army Lives and Loyalties from Redcoats to Dusty Warriors* (Harperpress, London, 2011)

Howard, Michael, *British Intelligence in the Second World War: Vol. V, Strategic Deception* (HMSO, London, 1990)

Hunt, Jonathan, *Hard Fighting: A History of The Sherwood Rangers Yeomanry 1900-1946* (Pen & Sword Books, Barnsley, 2016)

Jennings, John M., and Steele, Chuck, *The Worst Military Leaders in History* (Reaktion Books, London, 2022)

Jones, John Philip, *Battles of a Gunner Officer: Tunisia, Sicily, Normandy and the Long Road to Germany* (Pen & Sword Books, Barnsley, 2014)

Jones, Robert E., *History of the 101st Airborne Division: Screaming Eagles; The First Fifty Years* (Turner Publishing, Nashville, 2010)

Joslen, Lieut Col H.F., *Orders of Battle Second World War 1939-1945* (HMSO, London, 1960; London Stamp Exchange, London, 1990)

Junier, Alexander, and Bart Saunders with Jaap Korsloot, *By Land, Sea and Sea: An Illustrated History of the 2nd Battalion The South Staffordshire Regiment 1940-1945* (R.N. Sigmond Publishing, Renkum, NL, 2003)

Kemsley, W., and Riesco, M.R., *The Scottish Lion on Patrol: Being the Story of the 15th Scottish Reconnaissance Regiment, 1943-1946* (White Swan Press, Bristol, 1950; updated version by Tim Chamberlin published by Pen & Sword Books, Barnsley, 2010).

Kent, Ron, *First In! Parachute Pathfinder Company: A history of the 21st Independent Parachute Company, the original pathfinders of the British Airborne Forces, 1942-1946* (B.T. Batsford, London, 1979)

Kershaw, Robert, *It Never Snows in September: The German View of Market Garden and the Battle of Arnhem, September 1944* (Ian Allan Ltd, London, 1994)

Leonard, Roger Ashley (Ed.), *A Short Guide to Clausewitz on War* Weidenfeld & Nicolson, London, 1967)

Lewin, Ronald, *Military Commanders: Montgomery* (B.T. Batsford, London, 1971)

——, *Ultra Goes to War* (Grafton, London, 1998)

Lindsay, Capt. Martin and Capt. M.E. Johnston, *History of 7th Armoured Division: June 1943-July 1945* (HQ 7th Armoured Division, Germany, *1945*)

Lindsay, Oliver (ed), *A Guards General: The Memoirs of Major General Sir Allan Adair* (Hamish Hamilton, London, 1986)

Litchfield, Norman H., *The Territorial Artillery: 1908-1988* (The Sherwood Press, Nottingham, 1992)

Lowe, James Philip, 'Nadzab (1943): the first successful airborne operation' (2004). LSU Master's Theses. 3068. https://digitalcommons.lsu.edu/gradschool_theses/3068

MacDonald, Charles B., *The Siegfried Line Campaign* (*United States Army in World War II in The European Theater of Operations*) (Center of Military History United States Army Washington, DC, 1993)

Mallinson, Allan, *The Shape of Battle: Six Campaigns from Hastings to Helmand* (Bantam Press, London, 2021)

Martin, Lieutenant General H.G., *The History of the Fifteenth Scottish Division 1939-1945* (William Blackwood, London, 1948)

McLaughlin, Redmond, *The Royal Army Medical Corps* (Leo Cooper, London, 1972)

Mead, Richard, *Churchill's Lions: A Biographical Guide to the Key British Generals of World War II* (Spellmount, Stroud, 2007)

——, *The Men Behind Monty: The Staff and HQs of Eighth Army and 21st Army Group* (Pen & Sword Books, Barnsley, 2015)

Meilinger, Phillip S., *Airmen and Air Theory: A Review of the Sources* (Air University Press, Maxwell Air Force Base, Alabama, 2001)

Middlebrook, Martin, *Arnhem 1944: The Airborne Battle* (Viking, London, 1994)

——, and Everitt, Chris, *The Bomber Command War Diaries: An Operational Reference Book, 1939-1945* (Viking, London 1987)

Miller, Roger G., 'A Pretty Damn Able Commander', *Air Power History*, Nos 47 & 48.

Mitchell, Ian, *The Battle of the Peaks and Longstop Hill: Tunisia, April-May 1943* (Helion & Co., Warwick, 2019)

Montgomery, Field Marshal the Viscount of Alamein, *Normandy to the Baltic* (Hutchinson, London, 1946)

——, *Memoirs* (Collins, London, 1958)

Munro, Ronald Lyell, *Above the Battle: An Air Observation Post Pilot at War* (Pen & Sword Books, Barnsley, 2016)

Nofi, Albert A., *The War Against Hitler: Military Strategy in the West* (Da Capo Press, New York, 1982)

O'Reilly, John, *From Delhi to Arnhem: 156 Parachute Battalion* (Thoroton Publishing, Nottingham, 2009)

Orr, David, and Truesdale, David, *'The Rifles Are There' 1st & 2nd Battalions The Royal Ulster Rifles in the Second World War* (Pen & Sword Books, Barnsley, 2005)

Pakenham-Walsh, Major General R.P., *The History of the Corps of Royal Engineers,* Vol. IX (The Institution of Royal Engineers, Chatham, 1958)

Piasecki, Eugene G., 'The Knollwood Maneuver: The Ultimate Airborne Test', *Veritas* (The Office of the Command Historian, US Army Special Operations History), Vol. No. 1, pp. 54-63.

Pijpers, Gerrit & Truesdale, David, *Arnhem: Their Final Battle* (R.N. Sigmond Publishing, Renkum, 2012)

Powell, Geoffrey, *The Devil's Birthday: The Bridges to Arnhem 1944* (Leo Cooper, London, 1984 & 1992)

Probert, Henry, *High Commanders of the Royal Air Force* (HMSO, London, 1991)

Revell, Scott; Cherry, Niall and Gerritsen, Bob, *Arnhem: A Few Vital Hours* (R.N. Sigmond Publishing, Renkum, 2013)

Richardson, General Sir Charles, *Send for Freddie: The Story of Montgomery's Chief of Staff: Major General Sir Francis de Guingand KBE CB DSO* (William Kimber, London, 1987)

Roberts, Major General G.P.B., *From the Desert to the Baltic* (William Kimber, London, 1987)

Rosse, Captain The Earl of, and Hill, Col E.R., DSO, *The Story of The Guards Armoured Division* (Geoffrey Bles, London, 1956; Pen & Sword, Barnsley, 2017)

Rostron, Peter, *The Military Life & Times of General Sir Miles Dempsey GBE KCB DSO MC, Monty's Army Commander* (Pen & Sword Books, Barnsley, 2010)

Ryan, Cornelius, *A Bridge Too Far* (Hamish Hamilton, London, 1973)

Shilleto, Carl, *The Fighting Fifty-Second Recce: The 52nd (Lowland) Divisional Reconnaissance Regiment RAC in north-west Europe, September 1944-March 1945* (Eskdale Publishing, York, 2000)

Sigmond, Robert, *Off At Last: An Illustrated History of the 7th (Galloway) Battalion The King's Own Scottish Borderers* (R.N. Sigmond, Renkum, NL, 1993)

Sims, James, *Arnhem Spearhead: A Private Soldier's Story* (Arrow Books, London, 1989)

Smart, Nick, *Biographical Dictionary of British Generals of the Second World War* (Pen & Sword Books, Barnsley, 2005)

Smith, Claude, *The History of The Glider Pilot Regiment* (Leo Cooper, London, 1992)

Steer, Frank, *To The Warrior His Arms: The Story of the Royal Army Ordnance Corps, 1918-1993* (Pen & Sword, Barnsley, 2005)

Sutton, John (ed), *Wait for the Waggon: The Story of the Royal Corps of Transport and its Predecessors, 1794-1993* (Leo Cooper, Barnsley, 1998)

Tedder, Lord, *With Prejudice: The War Memoirs of Marshal of the Royal Air Force Lord Tedder GCB* (Cassell & Co., London, 1966)

Thompson, Julian, *The Imperial War Museum Book of Victory in Europe: The North-West European Campaign 1944-1945* (Sidgwick & Jackson Ltd, London, 1994)

Tieke, Wilhelm, *In The Firestorm of the Last Years of the War* (J.J. Fedorowicz Publishing, Winnipeg, 1999)

Truesdale, David, *Brotherhood of the Cauldron: Irishmen in the 1st Airborne Division from North Africa to Arnhem* (Redcoat Publishing, Newtownards, 2002)

——, *Steel Wall at Arnhem: The Destruction of 4 Parachute Brigade, 19 September 1944* (Helion & Co., Solihull, 2016)

——, Cornelissen, Martijn and Gerritsen, Bob, *Arnhem Bridge Target Mike One: An Illustrated History of the 1st Airlanding Light Regiment RA 1942-1945: North Africa, Italy, Arnhem, Norway* (R.N. Sigmund, 2015)

Tugwell, Maurice, *Airborne to Battle: A History of Airborne Warfare 1918-1971* (William Kimber, London, 1971)

Turnbull, John, and John Hamblett, *The Pegasus Patrol* (privately published, 2009)

Urquhart, Major General R.E., *Arnhem* (Collins, London, 1958)

Verney, Major General G.L., DSO MVO, *The Desert Rats: The 7th Armoured Division in World War II* (Hutchinson, London 1954)

Waddy, John, *A Tour of the Arnhem Battlefields* (Pen & Sword Books, Barnsley, 1999)

Warren, Dr John W., *Airborne Operations In World War II, European Theater: USAF Historical Studies No. 97* (USAF Historical Division, Air University, 1956).

Wilkinson, Peter, *The Gunners at Arnhem* (Spurwing Publishing, 1999)

Willmott, H.P., *The Great Crusade: A New Complete History of the Second World War* (Maxwell Macmillan International, New York, 1989)

Winchester, Simon, *The Men Who United The States: The Amazing Stories of the Explorers, Inventors and Mavericks Who Made America* (William Collins, London, 2013)

Woollacott, Robert, *Winged Gunners* (Quote Publishers, Zimbabwe, 1994)

Zaloga, Steven J., *Operation Market Garden, 1944 (1): The American Airborne Missions* (Osprey Publishing, Oxford, 2014)

Websites

https://www.nationalww2museum.org/medal-honor-recipients

https://www.BritishMilitaryHistory.co.uk

https://web.archive.org/web/20100328153100/http://www.rafweb.org/Grp04.htm   Air   of   Authority: A History of RAF Air Organisation.

https://www.military wiki|fandom

https://www.historynet.com/operation-market-garden-hail-mary-in-holland

https://www.daimler-fighting-vehicles.co.uk

https://www.82ndairbornedivisionmuseum.com

https://www.history.army.mil/museums/fieldMuseums/fortCampbell/index.html   (for   101st   Airborne Division Museum)

National Archives, Kew

AIR24/43: reports of Allied Expeditionary Air Force (AEAF) on Operation MARKET GARDEN.

AIR37/615: AEAF and 2 TAF – Operation MARKET.

AIR37/1214: AEAF and 2 TAF – Operations (sic) MARKET and GARDEN.

AIR37/418: 2 TAF reports from Nos 38 and 46 Groups RAF on Operation MARKET.

AIR37/981: No. 38 Group Operation GARDEN.

AIR37/1249: AEAF, 2 TAF and 21 Army Group: Operation MARKET GARDEN.

CAB44/252: Official histories, draft chapters: Advance from the Seine to the Siegfried Line and the battle for Arnhem, 29 August to 30 September; HQ 21 Army Group directives and intelligence summaries.

WO171/287: war diary VIII Corps.

WO171/310: war diary XII Corps.

WO171/341: war diary XXX Corps.

WO205/313: HQ 21 Army Group – outline plan Operation GARDEN.

WO205/314: HQ 21 Army Group – outline plan Operation GARDEN.

WO205/693: HQ 21 Army Group – plans for Operation MARKET GARDEN.

WO205/850: HQ 21 Army Group – report on Operation COMET.

WO205/1124: HQ 21 Army Group - Report, in war diary form, with maps of the Arnhem battle by Sturmbannführer Sepp Krafft, SS Panzer Grenadier Depot and Reserve Bn 16.

WO285/10-15: General Sir Miles Dempsey personal war diaries.

Other war diaries from the series WO171 were consulted, as were documents from the series AIR16 relating to US forces in Operation MARKET GARDEN.

Veterans who were interviewed by either author are mentioned in the text.

Index

Individuals

General